THE LANGUAGE MYTH

THE
LANGUAGE MYTH

ROY HARRIS

Professor of General Linguistics
in the University of Oxford

DUCKWORTH

First published in 1981 by
Gerald Duckworth & Company Ltd.
43 Gloucester Crescent, London NW1

ISBN 0 7156 1528 9

British Library Cataloguing in Publication Data

Harris, Roy, b. 1931
    The language myth.
    1. Language and languages
    I. Title
    401   P121

    ISBN 0-7156-1528-9

30755

S'
(Rub)

Printed in Great Britain by
Ebenezer Baylis and Son Limited
The Trinity Press, Worcester, and London

Experience does not err: it is only your judgment that errs in expecting from her what is not in her power.

Leonardo

Until some great artist comes along and tells us what to do, we shall not know how the muddled words of the tribe and the too precise words of the textbooks should be poetically purified, so as to make them capable of harmonising our private and unsharable experiences with the scientific hypotheses in terms of which they are explained.

Aldous Huxley

Contents

Preface

One reason why theories of language are important today is that, in an age only too conscious of the formative role played by processes of communication, they have come to be central to what Habermas calls 'the self-understanding of modern societies'.

That is also one reason why it is important for people to understand that a great deal of impressively authoritative modern theorising about language is founded upon a myth.

The myth in question is the subject of this book.

Like many other modern myths, it has ancient origins in the Western tradition. Like all important myths, it flatters and reflects the type of culture which sponsors it. It has many contemporary ramifications. But nowhere has it become better established, or commanded more unquestioning credence, than through the development of modern linguistics. There its rapid metamorphosis into 'science', by fiat of the dominant academic figures in the subject, constitutes one of the most revealing and disturbing episodes in the intellectual history of the twentieth century.

Chapter One

Idols of the Market

Anyone looking for cautionary mottoes to carve over the allegorical gateways of Inquiry into Language need look no further than the famous passage in the *Novum Organum* where Bacon warns us against the misunderstandings engendered by words themselves. These errors Bacon called in a celebrated phrase *idola fori*, or 'idols of the market':

> idols formed by the reciprocal intercourse and society of man with man ..., from the commerce and association of men with each other; for men converse by means of language, but words are formed at the will of the generality, and there arises from bad and unapt formation of words a wonderful obstruction to the mind. Nor can the definitions and explanations with which learned men are wont to guard and protect themselves in some instances afford a complete remedy,—words still manifestly force the understanding, throw everything into confusion, and lead mankind into vain and innumerable controversies and fallacies.[1]

There is no reason to think that Bacon had inquiry into language specifically in mind, but his observations are remarkably apt. Our attempts to understand language seem to be at the mercy of words, but words are designed primarily for purposes other than that. Here straight away, it might seem, we see lucidly identified for us one of the main sources of the difficulties which threaten to thwart whatever attempts man may make to reflect analytically upon this process of creative renewal which is language. Words, the product of that process, obscure the process itself.

This may be true in many ways: perhaps in respects other than those Bacon envisaged, and not necessarily for the reasons he would

[1] *Novum Organum*, tr. J. Devey (*The Physical and Metaphysical Works of Lord Bacon*), London, 1853, I, xliii.

have given. What Bacon says, none the less, raises an issue sufficiently close to the heart of the problem to demand attention. It may even be a first step towards understanding the creativity of the linguistic process to realise that some idols of the market may be bogeymen, conjured up by a distorted view of how language functions.

Language is, for most of us, part of the familiar, talked-about world of everyday experience. Inquiry into language is not. We do not in the course of our daily affairs have occasion to ask ourselves what language is. We do not inquire how it is that language is available to us. We are content simply to take advantage of its availability. But if one's purpose is inquiry into language, the question of the reliability of words presses for consideration at the very outset. Inquiry must proceed by way of words, for it cannot proceed otherwise. If our aim is to construct a science of language, such a science will itself rely on language for the description of its investigations, the formulation of its hypotheses and the statement of its conclusions. But we have no prior guarantee that language used in the service of such a science will itself be free from the risks to which Bacon alludes. If that is right, then inquiry into language must be doubly hazardous. Not only will the object of inquiry be plentifully supplied with sources of potential misunderstanding, but the instrument of inquiry as well.

The warning is one which the inquirer initially cannot afford to ignore, even if he comes eventually to regard Baconian pessimism about language as unfounded. 'Pessimism' is hardly too strong a term. For these remarks in the *Novum Organum* present a gloomier view than Bacon gives in *The Advancement of Learning*, where it would seem that idols of the market can be avoided by taking due care over the matter of defining our terms.[1] Whereas here, on the contrary—and this is what bodes ill for an inquiry into language— we are told explicitly that definitions and explanations themselves offer no safeguard, for 'words still manifestly force the understanding'. It is an observation which invites comparison with Frege's equally gloomy remark, 'one fights against language'.[2] But the philosophical 'fight against language' was being fought centuries

---

[1] *The Advancement of Learning* (ed. G. W. Kitchen, repr. London, 1973), II, xiv, 11.
[2] 'Der Gedanke', 1918 (*Logical Investigations*, ed. P. T. Geach, Oxford, 1977, p. 13, fn. 4).

before Frege, and before Bacon too. It goes back at least to Plato's teacher Cratylus, whose distrust of language was so profound, we are told, that he renounced the use of words altogether, and 'contented himself with moving his finger only'.[1]

Whatever else moving the finger only may be good for, it will not get anyone very far with describing language. At some point, description must take the plunge into words. But that is no excuse for failing to exercise due caution; and the first occasion for exercising caution will be presented by the word *language* itself.

The word *language* is a layman's word. It is a word formed, as Bacon puts it, 'at the will of the generality'. Anyone who takes it as mapping out a certain field of inquiry, or at least as providing a starting point, would do well to ask himself what exactly that commits him to.

*　　*　　*

It is widely accepted that in English the word *language* has at least two uses, which are sufficiently distinct to give rise to ambiguity. In one of these uses, the noun has a plural (namely, *languages*), and may be accompanied by the definite or indefinite article. Whereas in the other use, it has no plural and is not accompanied by an article. This morphological and syntactic distinction in English has its semantic counterpart. To speak of 'a language' is to speak, in the clearest cases, of a specific system of verbal communication long established in daily use throughout a more or less extensive community; such as English, or French, or Latin. These are 'languages', in the layman's typical application of the term.

To speak of 'language', on the other hand, is evidently to speak of something more general. In what sense 'more general'? Apparently, it might be replied, in the same sense as that in which to say 'Sport is very popular' is to make a more general statement than 'This sport is very popular', when referring, for example, to cricket. Sport in general may be very popular even if a particular sport is not. Similarly, what may be true of language in general may not be true of a particular language. But the parallel is not entirely a convincing one. It leaves us with an uneasy feeling that somehow cricket, hockey, tennis, etc., do not stand to sport in general in the same kind of relationship as individual languages stand to language.

[1] K. Freeman, *The Pre-Socratic Philosophers*, 2nd ed., Oxford, 1949, p. 284.

Language is, undeniably, a type of activity; but it is not just a type of activity in the same way as sport. Language also exists in the individual as a form of neurophysiological programming, associated with the control of certain specific motor activities and with certain centres in the brain. Human beings engage in language as a type of activity just as they engage in sport as a type of activity. But sport is in no sense a human faculty, as language is.

The importance of the distinction may be pointed out by observing that the opposite of linguistic knowledge in the sense of 'knowledge of a language or languages' is linguistic ignorance. When we ask of someone 'How many languages does he know?', what is at issue is his knowledge of English, or of French, or of Latin, as opposed to his ignorance of those languages. When we ask 'How good is his knowledge of English?' we are usually asking about a degree of practical expertise in speaking or writing or reading or comprehending; or perhaps less usually, about the amount and quality of factual or historical information he knows about the English language. In all these cases, the opposite of linguistic knowledge is linguistic ignorance. But when language is considered as a general capacity or type of activity, the corresponding opposite is not linguistic ignorance but deficiency of language.

This points to at least one respect in which it would be inadequate to regard the word *language* just as a kind of vague generic term for the collectivity of languages. The notion 'deficiency of language' has its clearest application in the cases of those individuals in whom, for whatever reason, normal linguistic development fails to take place. This may happen if a child suffers prolonged deprivation of linguistic contact with others at an early age. That is not, however, to imply that deficiency of language is a clinically well defined condition.

The first seriously documented case history of early language deprivation on record in modern times is that of Victor of Aveyron,[1] who was captured when living wild at about the age of twelve, and put on public display in 1798 in the village of Lacaune in Southern France. He could neither speak, nor understand what was said to him. The great scientific interest shown in him by French scholars of the day was due to his importance as a rare piece

[1] H. Lane, *The Wild Boy of Aveyron*, London, 1977.

of empirical evidence in current debates over such issues as the definition of *homo sapiens*, the existence of innate ideas, and the relation between society and human nature. Victor was taken to the National Institute for Deaf Mutes in Paris, and given a special course of training by Jean-Marc Itard, a disciple of Condillac, and one of the great pioneers of education for the severely handicapped. As a result, the boy eventually learned the alphabet, and also to write down and understand single written words and elementary combinations of words. But he never learned to speak, although there seemed to be nothing physiologically wrong with his organs of speech. Virtually the only vocal word he ever mastered was the French monosyllable *lait*, meaning 'milk'; and after a period of five years his educational programme was abandoned.

The most recent case is that of Genie, an American girl admitted to hospital in Los Angeles in 1970, at the age of 13, who had been isolated by her parents since the age of 20 months in a small room, and punished if she made any sound.[1] At the time of her admission to institutional care she was, like Victor, entirely mute. However, after a few months she began spontaneously to produce single words she had picked up from the speech addressed to her. After eight months she could produce two-word utterances, like *more soup* and *Genie purse*. She also soon became familiar with the letters of the alphabet, and learned to assemble printed words into grammatically correct sequences. She went on to acquire in her spoken repertoire the use of grammatical devices such as negative particles, plural suffixes and possessives. Dichotic listening tests revealed an interesting fact. In Genie, who was right-handed, the work of belatedly acquiring these language skills was apparently being undertaken by the right brain hemisphere. This is in contrast with what happens with normal right-handed children, who have left hemisphere lateralisation for language. Thus the case suggests that although it is not impossible to acquire spoken language after puberty, as was at one time maintained, success may depend on whether and to what extent one hemisphere is able to take over functions which the other hemisphere would normally have

---

[1] V. Fromkin et al., 'The development of language in Genie: a case of language acquisition beyond the "critical period" ', *Brain and Language*, vol. I, 1974, pp. 81–107: S. R. Curtiss, *Genie: a Linguistic Study of a Modern Day 'Wild-Child'*, Los Angeles, 1976.

acquired. How complete such a belated recovery may be remains to be seen.

A comparison of these two cases suggests a number of conclusions, of which doubtless the most obvious is that our understanding of the biology of language is still in its infancy. A second conclusion, none the less, is that the cases of Victor and Genie are very different. Even allowing for the fact that Genie had the benefit of considerably more accumulated medical expertise than was available in Victor's case, the failure of attempts to teach Victor to speak contrasts strikingly with the relative ease with which this was accomplished in the case of Genie. During her earliest examinations by doctors, Genie would spontaneously imitate random words in the speech addressed to her, and it was the lack of any such facility for vocal imitation that emerges so conspicuously from the records of Victor's case. Evidently, then, there are different types of language deficiency, which have yet to be accurately identified from a medical point of view. But what is clear enough in both cases is that the doctors were dealing with language deficiency and not linguistic ignorance. No one supposed for a moment that if only the medical men had tried out Chinese or some other language on these children, then it might have emerged that they could speak perfectly well all the time. An individual in the state in which Victor was when first captured is not someone who happens to be extremely ignorant of his native language. He is languageless. Being languageless is not a zero degree of mastery of one's native language, any more than being a bachelor is a zero degree of being married.

The point is worth making inasmuch as one of the pitfalls for the unwary that may be associated with the term *language* is that its dual usage sponsors the confused notion that language is knowable. This is because the adjective *linguistic* is neutral as between the two uses of the noun *language*, and thus an expression like *linguistic knowledge* appears to have two possible interpretations. It is reasonably clear how to make sense of the notion of 'linguistic knowledge' when interpreted as 'knowledge of a language or languages'. But it is by no means so clear how to make sense of the alternative interpretation 'knowledge of language'. We understand what is meant when someone asks 'Does he know French?' or 'How many languages does he know?', whereas 'Does he know language?', or

'How much language does he know?' are questions which, to say the least, sound very odd indeed. And yet the expression *linguistic knowledge* may tempt us to treat language itself as an object of knowledge, on a par with individual languages. The temptation is the more insidious in that the two uses of the word *language* run very close together in English. For example, if we say as Bacon does, that 'men converse by means of language', it is perhaps not immediately obvious that we have said anything different from 'men converse by means of languages'.

Confirmation that the dual usage may give rise to a tendency to speak of language as knowable, just as languages are said to be knowable, is provided by the occasional appearance of the phrase *knowledge of language* in discussions of linguistic theory. Significantly, this phrase does not appear to be used as if it were syntactically and semantically parallel to, say, *knowledge of biology* or *knowledge of geography*. In other words, it does not refer to knowledge about—that is to say, on the subject of—language. Instead, it seems to be used in a way to which there is no counterpart for a phrase like *knowledge of biology*. One is obliged either to guess at some metaphorical or mystical sense in which language might be known as languages are, or else to suppose that the writer is deliberately or unwittingly blurring the difference between the two uses. Cases like Victor and Genie here serve to remind the inquirer to be on his guard lest expressions like *linguistic knowledge* harbour a category mistake.[1]

A second respect in which the use of the term *language* may mislead is even more important. Idols of the market, in Bacon's view, are of two kinds.[2] The less pernicious sort arise when words function as 'names of things which have no existence'. These idols are relatively easy to unmask, once it can convincingly be shown that there is nothing existing to which the word could correspond.

---

[1] The risk of confusion may be increased by tendentious suggestions for terminological reform, such as Chomsky's proposal to distinguish between *knowing* and *cognizing a language* (N. Chomsky, *Reflections on Language*, New York, 1975, p. 164 et seq.). Cognizing English would then apparently include a grasp of 'the principles of universal grammar', whereas merely knowing English would not. This obscure distinction appears to puzzle even some of Chomsky's followers. (Cf. J. Ambrose-Grillet, *Glossary of Transformational Grammar*, Rowley, Mass., 1978, p. 29, where it is assimilated to the difference between having learned a language as a native speaker and having learned it as a foreigner.)

[2] *Novum Organum*, I, lix–lx.

But the more pernicious idols are 'intricately and deeply rooted'. This class includes the cases of words which do indeed correspond to actualities and not to fictions; but they are names 'confused, badly defined, and hastily and irregularly abstracted from things'. They mislead because they conflate under a single designation things which are distinct in reality. The harm which may thus be caused to the understanding is clearly this: that we may be led to believe, by reason of the single designation, in an underlying unity present in what in fact is a collection of merely associated but disparate things.

At first sight, it might appear that on this score no intelligent person is likely to be deceived by the word *language*. Even to the layman's casual observation, language takes many forms. An individual is not automatically cut off from linguistic contact with others simply because one form of language is denied to him. Loss of speech does not deprive the dumb of language, nor loss of sight the blind. Language is too diverse to be thought of as any single set of accomplishments. Equally, it seems evident that language fulfils a multiplicity of functions. It provides a means of exercising control over one's environment, of exchanging information, of influencing the behaviour of others, of adopting certain public roles, of establishing interpersonal contacts, of expressing one's own individuality, of exercising the imagination, of reasoning, and of maintaining social cohesion. No one seriously disputes the multifarious nature of mankind's linguistic activities.

Unfortunately, lip-service paid to the diversity of language does not detract from the lure of looking beyond this diversity in the hope of finding an underlying unity that the single term *language* can plausibly be held to stand for. Here the influence of the idols begins to take on subtler forms. Scholars who openly proclaim the variety of human linguistic activities are quite capable of speaking in the same breath of the capacity of human beings for language acquisition, as if nature had provided mankind with a single piece of biological equipment from which there somehow flowed the whole range of diverse behaviour acknowledged as 'linguistic'. Others find no inconsistency in pointing out how various are the uses to which men put the words at their command, and then proceeding forthwith as if nothing else mattered in the analysis of language apart from constructing an account of truth-telling, or an

account of syntax. In these and similar ways, academically respectable forms are found to accommodate the urge to find some core of
unity which justifies one comprehensive term, *language*.

*   *   *

There is one particular complex of interconnected errors of this
second Baconian type which has come to occupy a key position in
modern thinking. It may be called 'the language myth'. For
although it appears in various academic guises, the story it tells is
one which embodies popular beliefs concerning natural and historical phenomena. Furthermore, it is pre-eminently endowed with
that elusive fictional quality, which both protects it against literal-
minded scepticism and simultaneously makes it credible as the
expression of a fundamental truth.

The language myth in its modern form is a cultural product of
post-Renaissance Europe. It reflects the political psychology of
nationalism, and an educational system devoted to standardising
the linguistic behaviour of pupils. But its roots go much further
back in the Western tradition.

The language myth is the product of two interconnected
fallacies: the telementational fallacy and the determinacy fallacy.
The telementational fallacy is a thesis about the function of language, while the determinacy fallacy is a thesis about the mechanism
of language. Although logically independent, the two fallacies complement each other. Historically, too, they are closely associated.

According to the telementational fallacy, linguistic knowledge is
essentially a matter of knowing which words stand for which ideas.
For words, according to this view, are symbols devised by man for
transferring thoughts from one mind to another. Speech is a form
of telementation. This theory can be traced back through the
medieval modistic grammarians to Aristotle. Words, says Aristotle
at the beginning of *De Interpretatione*, are 'symbols or signs of
affections or impressions of the soul'. 'As writing,' he continues, 'so
also is speech not the same for all races of men. But the mental
affections themselves, of which these words are primarily signs, are
the same for the whole of mankind, as are also the objects of which
those affections are representations or likenesses, images, copies.'[1]

---

[1] *On Interpretation*, tr. H. P. Cook (Loeb Classical Library ed.), London, 1938, 1.

The determinacy fallacy, or 'fixed code' fallacy (as it might alternatively be called) provides the explanation of how the telementation process works, and indeed of how telementation is possible. This fallacy too has Aristotelian roots. If we agree with Aristotle that all men are provided by Nature with the same ideas, then all it needs is for men to agree upon some fixed set of correlations between ideas and verbal symbols, in order to provide themselves with a viable system for exchanging thoughts. Languages are, precisely, systems of this kind. A language community is a group of individuals who have come to use the 'same words' to express the 'same ideas' supplied by Nature, and to combine those words in the same ways into sentences for purposes of connected discourse.

In brief, the model of linguistic communication offered is as follows. Individuals are able to exchange their thoughts by means of words because—and insofar as—they have come to understand and to adhere to a fixed public plan for doing so. The plan is based on recurrent instantiation of invariant items belonging to a set known to all members of the community. These items are the 'sentences' of the community's language. They are invariant items in two respects: form and meaning. Knowing the forms of sentences enables those who know the language to express appropriately the thoughts they intend to convey. Knowing the meanings of sentences enables those who know the language to identify the thoughts thus expressed. Being invariant, sentences are context-free, and so proof against the vagaries of changing speakers, hearers and circumstances, rather as coin of the realm is valid irrespective of the honesty or dishonesty of individual transactions.

Thus the basic account of how human beings communicate goes like this. Suppose *A* has a thought that he wishes to communicate to *B*, for example, that gold is valuable. His task is to search among the sentences of a language known both to himself and to *B*, and select that sentence which has a meaning appropriate to the thought to be conveyed; for example, in English, the sentence *Gold is valuable*. He then encodes this sentence in its appropriate oral or written form, from which *B* is able to decode it, and in virtue of knowing what it means, grasp the thought which *A* intended to convey to him, namely that gold is valuable. Stated in this simple way, it sounds suspiciously like an analysis dictated by common

sense; and sounding like common sense is one of the powerful
sources of appeal of the language myth.

Stated in a slightly more abstract way, the language myth
assumes that a language is a finite set of rules generating an infinite
set of pairs, of which one member is a sound-sequence or a sequence
of written characters, and the other is its meaning; and that it is
knowledge of such rules which unites individuals into linguistic
communities able to exchange thoughts with one another in
accordance with a prearranged plan determined by those rules.
There may be room for argument about what it is to know the
meaning of a sentence, or about what it is to know the form of a
sentence, or about how much of human communication this system
of rules covers. But none the less that remains the basic model in
terms of which the arguments are formulated. Such a model is said
to be 'bi-planar'; that is to say, it envisages language as separable
into the two planes of form and meaning, which are interconnected
but distinct. This bi-planarity conforms to the popular view that
there are two basically different kinds of information to be known
about the expressions we use. We can ask questions about the form
of a sentence; for example, about how it is spelt, or how it is
pronounced, or how its elements are arranged. Or we can ask
questions about what it means, or what the words or constructions
in it mean. And when we know these things, we know as much as
needs to be known to use it for purposes of communication.

In the manner to which Bacon alludes, the language myth draws
its strength from being embodied in the very words we use to talk
about linguistic communication. In a recent paper,[1] Reddy lists for
present-day English alone more than a hundred expressions which
are based on what he calls 'the conduit metaphor', and argues that
it is almost impossible for an English speaker to discuss verbal
communication at all without committing himself in some degree
or other to that metaphor. Reddy calls it 'the conduit metaphor'
because it assumes that 'language functions like a conduit'; through
this 'conduit' thoughts are transferred from one person to another.
Associated with this assumption are three others. One is that in
speaking and writing people somehow 'insert' or encapsulate their
thoughts and feelings in the words they use. Another is that the

[1] 'The conduit metaphor—a case of frame conflict in our language about language',
Metaphor and Thought, ed. A. Ortony, Cambridge, 1979.

words used have the property of 'containing' the thoughts or feelings, and can thus 'convey' them to others. Thirdly, in listening or reading, people 'extract' the thoughts or feelings from the words in which they are 'conveyed'. In this way, the English language itself supplies what Reddy describes as 'a preferred framework for conceptualising communication'.

This 'preferred framework' is not unique to English. From the expressions Reddy lists, it would in many cases be possible to find strikingly close parallels in other European languages. Nor is this surprising. For a second and no less influential source of metalinguistic support for the language myth comes from those two great instruments of European education, the grammar book and the dictionary.[1] An educational system based upon grammar books and dictionaries has already succeeded in institutionalising the fixed code fallacy. The authority of the grammarian and the lexicographer would simply have no basis if it were not assumed that rules and meanings are in principle determinate. That authority is not just a superficial byproduct of the semantic structure either of English or of any other European language.

The ramifications of the language myth are many and various. The first that should be mentioned is that it promotes a certain view about the relationship between the different uses of the word *language*. This view assigns priority to that use of the word *language* in which it is pluralisable in English. It holds that our talk about 'language' in any more general sense is parasitic upon our talk about languages, and that any useful concept of 'language' has to be based upon our concept of 'a language'. This is a thesis associated in particular with the teachings of the founder of modern synchronic linguistics, Ferdinand de Saussure. It was Saussure who was responsible for institutionalising this as a basic theoretical distinction, and introducing accordingly the terminological opposition between *langue* ('a language') and *langage* ('language'). For Saussure, 'What is language?' was a question not answerable except insofar as it could be reduced to or replaced by the question 'What is a language?'. This has remained the view characteristic of modern linguistic orthodoxy ever since.

It is not, however, a view confined to linguists. Philosophers have sometimes been inclined to regard the dual usage of the word

[1] R. Harris, *The Language-Makers*, London, 1980, ch. 6.

language in English with even graver suspicion. It has been described as 'a mistake'[1] (presumably a mistake of just the kind against which Bacon's remarks in the *Novum Organum* are directed). Specifically, it has been claimed that 'the word "language" has a clear and correct use only as an individuative term'[2] (that is to say, in the sense in which it is pluralisable). Hence the question 'What is language?' is rejected as a pseudo-question, which borrows its plausibility from genuine questions concerning substances (e.g. 'What is vinylite?').

In general, the language myth, because it has a telementational basis, sponsors the serious pursuit of Baconian doubts about whether the usages of our language are always appropriate to convey the thoughts presumably intended.

Idols of the market would be troublesome enough, even if they could be isolated and dealt with one by one, as might perhaps be thought possible in respect of certain key terms like *language*. But the question of the reliability of words, once raised, has wider implications. There seems no reason to suppose that the only misapprehensions we need be on guard against are those of a kind which may have found their way into dictionaries. It is not merely men's vocabularies, but their entire apparatus of procedures for verbalisation which may conceal traps for the unwary.

Long before Bacon, grammarians had been at pains to point out to their pupils instances in which two quite different thoughts were expressed in identical verbal form. For example, the Latin phrase *amor Dei* is, like its English translation, *the love of God*, open to two interpretations, in one of which we understand that God loves, and in the other of which we understand that God is loved. Such cases are the basis of the distinction in traditional grammar between a 'subjective genitive' and an 'objective genitive'. Long after Bacon, grammarians continued to call attention to such examples, although they might describe them differently; for instance, as single surface forms transformationally derived from two underlying structures.[3] In such cases, language may in an obvious sense be misleading. That is to say, although it will be clear to the speaker or writer which of the two interpretations was intended, it may not always be

---

[1] N. L. Wilson, *The Concept of Language*, Toronto, 1959, p. 4.
[2] ibid.
[3] J. Lyons, *Introduction to Theoretical Linguistics*, Cambridge, 1968, p. 249.

clear to the hearer or reader; and when it is, that is only because the hearer or reader has been able to pick up other clues which solve the problem. The word forms themselves do not help.

It might seem that such a case does not offer an exact grammatical parallel to the second class of Bacon's idols, simply because the two thoughts subsumed under the same form of expression are so manifestly distinct that no one is likely to be deceived into confusing them. No one, that is, is going to suppose that loving God is the same as being loved by God (except perhaps for some reason to do with theology rather than with grammar). But in grammar as in vocabulary, the distinction between homonymy and polysemy is not always so easily drawn. Nor is it clear what general criteria, if any, are available which would allow it to be drawn consistently and systematically.

There are in any case, according to at least some modern theorists of grammar, many instances in which the surface forms of grammar do in fact mislead both speaker and hearer; in that language-users may fail to realise that the expressions they are using conflate more than one distinct idea. For example, it has been suggested that few people may be aware that the single surface sentence form *I had a book stolen* conflates three distinct statements that might be made about the stealing of a book.[1] Furthermore, it is conceded that grammarians themselves may be deceived about such matters by superficial similarities of grammatical form, thus treating as analogous constructions which are fundamentally different (for example, *I persuaded John to leave* and *I expected John to leave*).[2] If this is so, grammar obviously conceals as many pitfalls for the unsuspecting as does vocabulary. Indeed, we would seem to be driven to the conclusion that, in one sense, ordinary people most of the time just do not understand what they are saying.

Perhaps this would not matter very much if nothing of any importance depended on it. However, according to various schools of thought, a great deal may in certain circumstances depend on it—matters of life and death, war and peace, enlightenment and confusion. The fallibility of mankind's linguistic equipment has at one time or another been blamed for just about everything, from belief in a Divinity to the perpetuation of sex discrimination. Reformers

[1] N. Chomsky, *Aspects of the Theory of Syntax*, Cambridge, Mass., 1965, pp. 21-2.
[2] ibid., p. 22.

and crusaders of various persuasions have promoted campaigns to improve matters. On the one hand, there have been proposals to improve already existing languages (for example, by providing English with unisex pronouns).[1] On the other hand, there have been schemes for entire rival systems which would eliminate the shortcomings of existing languages; for example, Wilkins's 'real character'[2] and Leibniz's *calculus universalis*.[3] Movements have also been launched to combat misguided attitudes and convictions allegedly inculcated by language. In the 1930s, General Semantics set out to protect the public at large from 'the tyranny of words';[4] while Ordinary Language Philosophy set out to protect philosophers in particular from what Ryle called 'recurrent misconceptions and absurd theories' having their source in 'linguistic idiom'.[5]

The record does not exactly bear witness to overwhelming confidence in language. However, it will be relevant for present purposes to distinguish between two very different types or levels of linguistic unreliability.

One of these can usefully be summed up in the phrase Ryle used, 'systematically misleading expressions'; provided we are willing to allow a little more generous use of it than Ryle had in mind.[6] Under this head, Ryle included what he called 'quasi-ontological statements', such as 'Carnivorous cows do not exist'. A second class of systematically misleading expressions included 'quasi-Platonic statements', such as 'Virtue is its own reward'. A third class included 'quasi-descriptions', as in 'Poincaré is not the king of France'. In all these cases, Ryle held, the grammar of the expression was, for various reasons, improper to the nature of the facts expressed. 'Carnivorous cows do not exist' is not a statement about a certain class of cows, although it appears to be so from its grammatical form. 'Virtue is its own reward' is not a statement about some

---

[1] As in the correspondence columns of *The Times*, 24 October 1978 and following days.

[2] J. Wilkins, *Essay towards a Real Character and a Philosophical Language*, London, 1668.

[3] G. W. Leibniz, *Specimen calculi universalis* (*Die philosophischen Schriften von Gottfried Wilhelm Leibniz*, ed. C. J. Gerhardt, Berlin, 1890, vol. 7, 200, pp. 218–27).

[4] A. Korzybski, *Science and Sanity. An Introduction to Non-Aristotelian Systems and General Semantics*, 3rd ed., Lakeville, Conn., 1948; S. Chase, *The Tyranny of Words*, London, 1938.

[5] A. G. N. Flew (ed.), *Essays on Logic and Language*, Oxford, 1951, p. 6.

[6] ibid., pp. 11–36.

invisible recipient of rewards. 'Poincaré is not the king of France' does not deny the identity of two individuals. Yet in all these and other cases, we may easily be misled because the expressions used are grammatically analogous to other expressions which do indeed express statements of the kinds which these examples are not.

The systematically misleading expressions which Ryle subjected to philosophical analysis were, not unnaturally, those he considered likely to mislead philosophers. He denied that 'the naive users of such expressions are in any doubt or confusion about what their expressions mean or in any way need the results of the philosophical analysis for them to continue to use intelligently their ordinary modes of expression or to use them so that they are intelligible to others'.[1] None the less, he also pointed out that one does not need to be a professional philosopher in order to be misled in these cases. The expressions are potentially misleading, as he put it, 'to any man who embarks on abstraction'.[2] This appears to beg the question of the extent to which any of us can be a fluent speaker of his own native language without 'embarking on abstraction'. But that is not an issue which needs to be pursued at this point. What is relevant is that these systematically misleading expressions exemplify a type under which we can subsume not only many philosophically interesting but also many more philosophically banal cases.

It may be that ultimately nothing in language is philosophically banal, but one can invoke here a currently established division of academic labour. Philosophically banal cases one would expect to be the concern of the grammarian rather than the philosopher. But regardless of who deals with it professionally, there would be no essential difference in the grounds for holding the expression to be misleading. An example of a philosophically banal case is one mentioned by the authors of the most influential grammar book of post-Renaissance times, the Port Royal grammar of 1660, who point out that in certain languages, such as Italian, the definite article is misleadingly used with proper names.[3] This usage is regarded as improper in much the same kind of way as Ryle takes the grammar of his systematically misleading expressions to be improper. What the Port Royal grammarians say is that the definite article cannot correctly be used with proper names because proper names already

---

[1] ibid., p. 13.   [2] ibid., p. 17.
[3] *Grammaire générale et raisonnée*, Paris, 1660, pp. 56–7.

uniquely identify individuals. There can be no question of supplying some further determination by means of the article. In other words, just as in Ryle's examples, anyone who took the grammar of the expression at its face value could be misled into concluding that somehow the proper name in these cases was doing a different job from the one it was in fact doing; for example, functioning as a common noun, because the grammar of the definite article is appropriate to the determination of common nouns. So the banal counterpart of the kind of philosophical error with which Ryle is concerned would be supposing, when one heard an author referred to as *il Boccaccio*, that that was some kind of description of him, and not his name.

A different but equally banal type of case, much discussed by modern theorists of case grammar, concerns expressions like *The door opened*. Here, although *the door* is the grammatical subject of the verb *opened*, it is held to be, at least by some, in the objective case. That is to say, the sentence *The door opened* is not, although it might appear to be, grammatically parallel to *The man sat down*. So we would be misled if we supposed that the sentence *The door opened* tells us about an action the door performed, in the same way that *The man sat down* tells us about an action the man performed. The door performed no action of opening. Even in those cases where, as common usage has it, 'the door opened by itself', it is not that the door somehow caused itself to open. It is merely the grammar of the sentence which might make it look as if it did. In that sense, expressions like *The door opened* are improper to what they express, because they assume the typical form of 'agent-action' sentences; whereas what they are saying would be more clearly said by some such construction as, for example, *There occurred an opening of the door*.

An even more banal example, which is also the subject of comment by the Port Royal grammarians, concerns grammatical gender. It is improper, in the sense here under consideration, that the word for 'tree' should be feminine in Latin but masculine in French, or that the word for 'tooth' should be masculine in Latin but feminine in French.[1] But this is because properly the notion of sex differentiation applies to neither trees nor teeth, but only to animate beings. In the unlikely event that a Frenchman were to

[1] ibid., p. 40.

suppose that trees were male because of the grammatical gender of the word *arbre*, then he would be being misled by his native language. It is not inconceivable that French children are sometimes misled in some such way.

The gender example, although more banal than the others, is also more important in two respects. In the first place, it is fairly obvious even to a layman that not everyone would agree with the Port Royal analysis of gender. Once it is conceded that the function of gender is to express sex, then it becomes misleading to make the word for 'tree' masculine. But only then. If we do not concede that the proper role of gender is tied to sex, it makes not the slightest difference that the word for 'tree' should behave grammatically in certain respects like words for male human beings. And *mutatis mutandis* the same applies to all systematically misleading expressions, from the most banal to the most philosophically interesting. Invariably, a criterion is presupposed by which the linguistic formulation under criticism can be held to be in some way 'wrong'. But what kind of criterion is this?

The question leads directly to the second important point illustrated by the gender example. In Ryle's cases, there is always some alternative formulation which would better capture the facts to be expressed. 'Carnivorous cows do not exist' would be less misleadingly put as 'Nothing is both a cow and carnivorous'. 'Virtue is its own reward' would be more clearly expressed as 'Anyone who is virtuous is benefited thereby'. 'Poincaré is not the king of France' would be better replaced by 'Poincaré does not reign over France'. It would be even simpler to put right the misleading Italian usage of the definite article with proper names, simply by dropping it. *The door opened* could be replaced, as occasion required, by *Someone opened the door, The door was blown open by the wind*, and so on. But in this company, gender stands out as a marginal case, precisely because it is not clear what Frenchmen are supposed to do if they are not allowed to treat the word for 'tree' as masculine, nor as feminine either. The Frenchman's language, as it were, forces that mistake upon him, leaving him no alternative. There is simply no less misleading form of expression which the French language makes available.

None the less, in the present context it will not be a mistake to continue to include cases like gender under the head of systematically misleading expressions (granted that we accept the analysis which warrants their inclusion). For it is not complete nonsense to suggest that Frenchmen could have evolved a less misleading gender system (not as individuals, of course, but as a linguistic community). They could, for example, have had a system of three genders—masculine, feminine and neuter—and have assigned the neuter gender to words like the word for 'tree'. This involves a sense of 'could have' which doubtless demands a great deal of none too straightforward explanation—the sense in which a language could have been other than what it is. But in this particular instance, it does not seem utterly nonsensical: certainly not as nonsensical as suggesting, for example, that French could have developed a Past Imperative. Furthermore, this assumption about gender parallels the assumption implicit in Bacon's examples of idols of the market. We have to assume, if Bacon's warning is to have any point, that a language community need not impose upon itself the use of fallacious terms. People did speak of 'unicorns' and 'phlogiston', and they did believe in the existence of such things. But they could have done otherwise. It is that 'could have' which holds the key to seeing in what sense they were wrong.

However, the main reason for wishing to be allowed to treat the example of gender in this perhaps question-begging fashion (granted, once again, the analysis we have to accept in order to count it as misleading at all) is that it is more important to distinguish between that whole range of cases which are 'systematically misleading'—even if putting some of them right is going to require one or two minor systematic adjustments to the structure of the language in question—and the range of cases where language is fallible in a fundamentally different way altogether. It is only on the yonder side of that distinction, where we are no longer concerned with idols of the market and their like, that we begin to deal with the question of how the renewal of language may be obscured by the very products of that creative process itself, namely the linguistic units and structures which appear to emerge from it.

* * *

One way of broaching the issues of linguistic reliability which belong to this further level of consideration is to ask what are the requirements for establishing a science of language. That must depend, one will be told, on the view that is taken of science: and at least some views of science themselves involve theses concerning language.

The view of science, for example, taken by Mach culminated in the linguistic doctrines of the logical positivists and the radical scepticism concerning the reliability of language professed by those who adopted the 'strong' version of the verification principle. If science deals in the last resort with human sensations, and if the meaning of a proposition is its method of verification, one is obliged to conclude that a great deal of what is said in most linguistic communities cannot mean what the members of those communities suppose that it means. Thus 'Caesar crossed the Rubicon' would not be, as it might seem, a statement about Caesar, nor about his crossing the Rubicon. It would actually mean, according to Ayer,[1] something like 'If I look up such-and-such a history book I will see such-and-such words written', or 'If I dig in a certain place I will find such-and-such relics'. In this and similar ways, ordinary language could be regarded as deceiving its users on a gigantic scale. For it disguised as simple statements of fact what were at best complex conditionals and at worst pieces of utter nonsense. The position which the logical positivists arrived at was doubtless an extreme one. But it at least had the merit of presenting in an intellectually challenging form such questions as how the statements of science relate to those of ordinary language, and what it is that ultimately determines the meaning of a statement.

Dissatisfaction with words as ordinarily used is not just a bee in philosophical bonnets. Some kind of 'fight against language', a search for some more soundly based descriptive system, can be traced in many different branches of science. Indeed, according to a commonly invoked view of science, championed in its most intransigent form by scientific empiricists, it is typical of the development of scientific inquiry to proceed from an initial stage, in which questions and answers are formulated in the layman's language of everyday discourse, to more advanced stages which require the elaboration of technical concepts and a corresponding technical terminology which goes beyond the linguistic resources available to the non-specialist. In all advanced cultures, it is claimed, the languages of science are languages which the layman cannot

---

[1] B. Magee (ed.), *Men of Ideas*, London, 1978, p. 123.

understand. Dictionaries of scientific terms contain thousands of wordsmeaningless to the majority of the educated population, who are not even in a position to comprehend the definitions which such dictionaries provide. Scientific textbooks employ notations which are totally unfamiliar to most of those whose reading is confined to the columns of a daily newspaper. Thus scientific enlightenment for the few appears to go hand in hand with increased obscurity for the many. One of these is the price a community pays for the other.

The justification the scientific empiricist gives for developing terminologies with a high degree of communicational opacity is that the layman's language is not sufficiently precise for scientific purposes. According to Hempel,[1] analytic definitions of the kind required by empirical science are not available in everyday language, since such definitions presuppose languages whose expressions have precisely fixed meanings. By this is meant that it should at least be possible to determine whether any two expressions are or are not synonymous. But this condition, it is held, is not generally satisfiable for the English or the French or the Russian that the layman uses. Thus the need to develop a language with precisely determined meanings is presented as the reason for rejecting the language of everyday discourse, and so sacrificing ready accessibility to the non-specialist.

The premiss that the expressions used in everyday language lack the requisite semantic precision is often based simply on the assertion that observably this is so. For example, Hempel argues that in order to determine the meaning of an expression in a given language as used by a specified linguistic community—for example, the word *hat* in contemporary English as spoken in the United States of America—it is necessary to ascertain the conditions under which the members of the community use and are disposed to use that expression. This would involve ascertaining, for example, what kinds of objects, whether actually occurring or not, the word *hat* would be applied to in contemporary American usage. But such an investigation will show, in Hempel's view, that a word like *hat* lacks both (i) determinacy of usage, and (ii) uniformity of usage. It will lack determinacy of usage in the sense that its conditions of application are not well determined for every user; that is to say, it

[1] C. G. Hempel, *Fundamentals of Concept Formation in Empirical Science*, Chicago, 1952, pp. 9–10.

is possible to find or describe objects such that the user is undecided whether to apply the term *hat* to them. Secondly, it will lack uniformity of usage in the sense that inconsistencies can be found either between different users, or in the same user on different occasions, in respect of whether or not to apply the word in given instances. Such objections hold for both analysandum and analysans of an analytic definition, and thus Hempel concludes that where everyday language is concerned 'the idea of a true analytic definition, i.e. one in which the meaning of the analysans is the same as that of the analysandum, rests on an untenable assumption'.[1] This follows because in a language which fails to meet both the determinacy condition and the uniformity condition there are no uniquely identifiable referents for the expressions of the language. Thus we cannot say whether an analytic definition which equates, say, the expression *hat* with the expression *head covering* is true, since it is impossible to identify in the first place exactly what it is in the real world that the English expression *hat* stands for.

If the scientific empiricist is right, then, there is a more fundamental and pervasive fallibility which affects everyday language, which has nothing to do with the presence of systematically misleading expressions. For it affects every expression. It is not the result of grammatical or lexical structures of particular languages. Rather, it is an inescapable concomitant of the conditions under which words are used in daily life.

A different fallibility, but of the same general order, is pointed out by the ethnomethodologist. Unlike the scientific empiricist, he is not particularly concerned with the problem of the truth of statements formulated in ordinary language. But he is very much concerned with the problem of what people mean by what they say. For the ethnomethodologist, the salient characteristic of everyday language is its irremediable 'indexicality'. In his view, it is an unavoidable condition of using language that speakers 'mean something different from what they can say in just so many words'.[2] Accordingly, 'however extensive or explicit what a speaker says may be, it does not by its extensiveness or explicitness pose a task of deciding the correspondence between what he says and what he

[1] ibid., p. 10.
[2] H. Garfinkel & H. Sacks, 'On formal structures of practical actions'. In J. C. McKinney & E. A. Tiryakian (eds), *Theoretical Sociology*, New York, 1970, p. 342.

means that is resolved by citing his talk verbatim.'[1] Mastery of ordinary language is accordingly construed as including the mastery of procedures for the recovery of meaning by glossing what was said. The expressions we ordinarily use are held to be 'expressions whose meaning relies on the context in which they are used in such a way that attempts to delineate the meanings of words in some more general way are both misleading and incomplete'.[2] Thus for the ethnomethodologist, as for the scientific empiricist, it is just an observable fact that the expressions used by the layman in the business of everyday discourse do not themselves have precise meanings. For if they did, their use would hardly give rise to the problems of interpretation which are manifestly posed for their users.

Somewhere in between the scientific empiricist and the ethnomethodologist comes the theorist of contextualised speech acts. He complains that words may mislead us insofar as ordinary usage fails to make clear in very many cases exactly what force a remark is intended to have. Consequently we must be on our guard against taking the superficial grammar of an utterance to be a reliable guide. The speech act theorist does not necessarily deny that the words the layman uses have precise meanings. But he insists that there is in any case more to mastery of language than an ability to assess what is said in terms of its truth or falsity. Even for those occasions on which assessment of the truth or falsity of what is said makes sense, that must depend, so he claims, 'not merely on the meanings of words but on what act you were performing in what circumstances'.[3] But many assertions presented in normal declarative form may, in spite of appearances, be neither true nor false. This is the case, according to Austin, for a claim like 'Lord Raglan won the battle of Alma', which is a kind of exaggeration. An exaggeration will be suitable to some contexts but not to others: 'it would be pointless to insist on its truth or falsity.'[4] Thus understanding the statement 'Lord Raglan won the battle of Alma' will be a matter of seeing and assessing its relevance to a particular context of discussion, rather than a mechanical decoding of the words used and

[1] ibid., p. 344.
[2] A. Wootton, *Dilemmas of Discourse*, London, 1975, p. 19.
[3] J. L. Austin, *How to Do Things with Words*, Oxford, 1962, p. 144.
[4] ibid., p. 143.

consideration of whatever fixed meanings they are deemed to have. Truth and falsity, for Austin, are not in any case guaranteed by a simple invariant relationship between the meanings of expressions and the state of the world. 'It is essential to realise that "true" and "false", like "free" and "unfree", do not stand for anything simple at all: but only for a general dimension of being a right and proper thing to say as opposed to a wrong thing, in these circumstances, to this audience, for these purposes and with these intentions.'[1] By this insistence on the ways in which particular occasions alter what may be said and how it may be interpreted, the speech act theorist endorses the scepticism of the scientific empiricist and the ethnomethodologist concerning the validity of treating the expressions we ordinarily use as invariants, unaffected by the specifics of actual communication situations in which they occur. Inasmuch, furthermore, as it is unclear how in principle a language could, even by the use of explicit performative verbs or other devices, make systematic provision for specifying the exact illocutionary force of every conceivable utterance, the speech act theorist is pointing to a problem of the same order of generality as the ethnomethodologist.

It would be comforting to be able to write such questions off as pseudo-problems engendered by the scientific empiricist's erroneous view of science, or the ethnomethodologist's naive approach to the description of verbal exchanges, or the speech act theorist's illusion of illocutionary force.[2] Unfortunately, suspiciously similar general issues are raised if we pursue the analysis of systematically misleading expressions beyond the point at which it is often left by philosophers and grammarians. To speak of systematically misleading expressions implies that there are at least some expressions which are not systematically misleading. A comparison is involved, and it is therefore a legitimate question to ask what the basis of this comparison is. In what, in other words, does the unmisleadingness of systematically unmisleading expressions consist?

The general answer which needs to be given is clear enough. Unmisleading expressions must be unmisleading because in some sense they say what they mean. But exactly in what sense is less clear. It seems to call for some general account of how the expressions

---

[1] ibid., p. 144.
[2] L. J. Cohen, 'Do illocutionary forces exist?', *Symposium on J. L. Austin*, ed. K. T. Fann, London, 1969.

we use reveal in their structure what it is intended they should convey. An attempt to give a detailed answer along these lines is provided by the authors of the Port Royal grammar, although it is an answer which goes back at least to the modistic grammarians of the Middle Ages. It is presented as an explanation of how words signify by expressing thoughts, and it stands as one of the classic statements in the historical documentation of the language myth.

The analysis which the Port Royal grammar gives of the signification of words is based on the recognition of three operations of the mind: conception, judgment and reasoning:

Conception is nothing more than a simple contemplation of things by the mind, either in a purely intellectual way, as when I am aware of being, of duration, of thinking, of God; or by means of corporeal images, as when I imagine a square, a circle, a dog, a horse.

Judgment is an affirmation that a thing we conceive is or is not thus. As when, having conceived what the earth is, and what roundness is, I affirm of the earth that it is round.

Reasoning is using two judgments in order to make a third. As when, having judged that all virtue is praiseworthy, and that patience is a virtue, I conclude that patience is praiseworthy.

From which one sees that this third operation of the mind is but an extension of the second. Thus it will suffice for our purpose to consider the first two, or what is included of the first in the second. For men hardly speak simply to express what they conceive; rather it is almost invariably to express their judgments concerning the things which they conceive.

The judgment we make concerning things, as when I say 'The earth is round' is called a proposition; and so every proposition necessarily embraces two terms: one called the subject, which is that concerning which the affirmation is made, for instance the 'earth'; and the other called the attribute, which is what one affirms, for instance 'round': and in addition the link between these two terms, 'is'.

Now it is easy to see that the two terms properly belong to the first operation of the mind, because this is what we conceive, and this is the object of our thought: and that the link belongs to the second operation, which can properly be considered the action of our mind, and the manner in which we think.

And so the most important distinction relating to what goes on in our mind is that between what may be considered the object of our thought; and the form or manner of our thought, of which judgment is the chief one. But one should not omit conjunction, disjunction and other similar operations of the mind; and all the other movements of the soul, such as desires, command, interrogation, etc.

Whence it follows that, mankind having need of signs to indicate all that goes on in the mind, there is need also for the most general distinction among words, some signifying objects of thought, and others the form and manner of thought, although often they do not signify that alone, but with the object, as we shall show.

The words of the first sort are those which have been called nouns, articles, pronouns, participles, prepositions and adverbs. Those of the second are verbs, conjunctions and interjections. Which are all derived by a necessary progression from the natural manner in which we express our thoughts, as will now be shown.[1]

In short, the propriety or unmisleadingness of an expression will consist in its conformity to those elements and operations of thought which it expresses. Words, their various types and possible arrangements are held to mirror the organisation of an inner mental world, by reference to which what is said may be judged.

A more complex type of answer might involve a matching not simply of verbal structures with mental structures but with corresponding structures in the world. Thus the unmisleadingness of an expression will consist, or ideally would consist, in its reflecting without distortion the actuality it purports to represent. This is the answer proposed in its most uncompromising form in Wittgenstein's *Tractatus*, where it is held that, at least in the ideal case, 'the configuration of objects in a situation corresponds to the configuration of simple signs in the propositional sign'.[2] It is an answer which claims, as Ryle puts it, that 'what makes an expression formally proper to a fact is some real and non-conventional one-one picturing relation between the composition of the expression and that of the fact'.[3]

Both types of answer, however, raise more problems than they solve. If we are to look for correspondences simply between verbal structures and mental structures, in some such manner as that suggested by the Port Royal grammarians, it is unclear how we can be sure when these correspondences have been found, and when

[1] *Grammaire générale et raisonnée*, pp. 27–30.
[2] L. Wittgenstein, *Tractatus Logico-Philosophicus*, tr. D. F. Pears & B. F. McGuinness, London, 2nd ed., 1971, §3.21.
[3] Ryle, op. cit., p. 34.

not. For it is unclear how we know what is in the mind as potentially expressible, except through the forms in which it eventually
comes to be linguistically expressed. The nature of the difficulty is
shown up clearly by some of the more contentious explanations
which the Port Royal grammar offers for grammatical distinctions.
For example, as regards gender, it is unclear how we know that
gender distinctions express a mental classification of beings into
male and female, which is therefore improperly applied to inanimate
objects. At least two other hypotheses are available. Perhaps
gender distinctions express no mental classification at all, any more
than the division of verbs into conjugations reflects a mental
classification of the relevant actions. Or perhaps both genders and
conjugations express mental classifications of which the exact nature
escapes our conscious reflection. In general, it is difficult to see what
the mental structures postulated by the Port Royal grammarians
are, other than psychological extrapolations from traditional grammatical and logical doctrines concerning the parts of speech and the
sentence. Thus the kind of explanation offered is simply a reversal
of the process by which the analysis itself was produced. What are
hypothetically projected back into the mind as unobservable mental
realities are abstractions derived from analysis of the observable
verbal structures themselves. This is a procedure very characteristic
of the language myth in all its forms.

If we are to look for correspondences between verbal structures
and structures of reality, the task is equally mysterious. Again it is
quite unclear exactly what we are looking for, or how we shall know
when it has been found. For it is difficult to see, as Ryle argues,
'how, save in a small class of specially-chosen cases, a fact or state of
affairs can be deemed like or even unlike in structure a sentence,
gesture or diagram'.[1] In, for example, Socrates being angry, there
is simply 'no concatenation of bits such that a concatenation of parts
of speech could be held to be of the same general architectural
plan'.[2] Ryle's point is equally apposite, whether we consider the
surface structures of sentences or their hypothetical deep structures:
the level of analysis or abstraction is immaterial. In short, it is
entirely obscure how we are to make sense of the notion that reality
has structures which are comparable to structures of the kind
relevant to verbal analysis. Even if, for example, we provisionally

[1] ibid.   [2] ibid.

agree to count Socrates as one bit of reality and the emotion anger as another bit of reality, it is puzzling to know what counts as evidence for answering the question whether these bits of reality would, if in fact Socrates were angry, be structurally related in exactly the way reflected in anything that might count as the structure of the sentence *Socrates is angry*. Or if we consider two sentences like *The dog bit the postman* and *The postman was bitten by the dog*, and compare these with some actual event of the kind either might reasonably be used to describe, it is difficult to see how an analysis of the structure of reality (in this case the biting of the unfortunate postman) would allow us to determine in principle which sentence would be the more appropriate report. And this is because it is quite unclear how to make sense of the tasks of analysing a particular segment of reality and analysing a sentence so as to be able to discover in any non-question-begging way structures which did or did not match.

Thus neither the postulation of mental structures nor the postulation of structures of reality seems to provide any uncontroversial descriptive basis from which to compare verbal structures one with another and assess their relative appropriateness.

Ryle's own answer to the question of how we can discover in particular cases whether an expression is systematically misleading or not is a lame one. The evidence he recommends us to look for is that provided by paralogisms and antinomies. Thus if we believe that expressions like *Mr Pickwick is a fictitious person* or *The Equator encircles the globe* 'are saying what they seem to be saying', we can disabuse ourselves of those misconceptions by discovering that certain propositions which ought consequentially to be true are in fact false. We can, for example, discover that it is not true that Mr Pickwick was born in such and such a year, and that it is not true that the Equator is of such and such a thickness. These discoveries, in Ryle's view, should lead us to see 'that being a fictitious person is not to be a person of a certain sort, and that the sense in which the Equator girdles the earth is not that of being any sort of a ring or ribbon enveloping the earth. And this is to see that the original propositions were not saying what they seemed on first analysis to be saying.'[1]

The strategy Ryle recommends, however, has its drawbacks.

[1] ibid., p. 35.

There seems in general to be no reason for classifying an expression as systematically misleading just because some Simple Simon has failed to grasp what it means (even if the Simple Simon in question has succeeded in persuading many of his philosophical colleagues into the same error). Thus one would be inclined to say of someone who inferred from 'Mr Pickwick is a fictitious person' that somewhere there should be a birth certificate recording Pickwick's birth that he evidently did not understand the meaning of the word *fictitious*. But this may not be anything to do with the fact that *fictitious* is an adjective: for it would be a Simple Simon indeed who supposed that all adjectives functioned in the same way. What is more probably the case is that he does not grasp the difference between the fictional and the non-fictional: which is nothing mere grammar (in the grammarian's sense) can be held accountable for. Analogously, anyone who inquires how thick the Equator is has not understood what is meant by *the Equator*. Of such cases there is no more to be said, until or unless such 'misunderstandings' turn out to be so prevalent that we might ask whether they are properly classified as misunderstandings, or whether the words in question no longer mean what they once did.

Even if the Simple Simon has in fact been misled by grammar, Ryle's strategy affords no way of demonstrating to him the nature of his mistake. If he was simple enough to suppose originally that Mr Pickwick had a birth certificate, there is no reason why his failure to discover one should lead him to revise the belief that Mr Pickwick is a person of a certain sort. He might just as well conclude that not all persons have birth certificates, or are born, or have parents, and so on. In other words, he amends his definition of *person*, but not his assumption that fictitious persons are a proper subset of persons. Analogously, in the case of the Equator, he might decide to revise the belief that rings or ribbons are always of a certain thickness, or visible to the naked eye. Nothing can force him to agree that after all Mr Pickwick is not a person, and the Equator is not a kind of ring or ribbon.

Perhaps this is why Ryle acknowledged there was no way of proving conclusively that an expression is not systematically misleading. All he claimed was that, given two expressions which record the same fact, we can know that one is less misleading than the other. What is difficult to see is how we can know even this, if we have no test by which to reassure ourselves that the apparently less misleading expression is not itself misleading us grossly in some quite unsuspected way. For if we do not have that reassurance we have no guarantee that the comparison which singles out one expression as more misleading is itself soundly based. In short, we cannot even rely upon language to mislead us systematically.

More generally, it may be questioned whether there is any one standpoint from which the misleadingness or otherwise of an expression may be judged absolutely. Common sense suggests that a remark which is quite unmisleading in certain circumstances could be very misleading in other circumstances. If Smith junior has to write an essay on 'The evolution of the cow' for his schoolteacher, and asks his father to tell him a few useful facts for that purpose, it would doubtless be highly misleading for Smith senior to start off by saying 'Carnivorous cows don't exist', which might well be understood by Smith junior as meaning that, like the dodo, the carnivorous cow had died out. But if Smith junior already has the misguided notion that certain cows are carnivorous (perhaps because man-eating cows feature in some television science-fiction serial he watches), and proposes to have a paragraph on carnivorous cows in his essay, then Smith senior will be doing him a service by saying 'Carnivorous cows don't exist'. That formulation says just what we would wish to get across to anyone who mistakenly believes, for whatever reason, that carnivorous cows do exist. Likewise, 'Mr Pickwick is a fictitious person' would be an unobjectionable formulation for correcting someone who mistakenly thought that Mr Pickwick was a fictitious racehorse. Once we see this, we may be led to wonder whether the reason why philosophers have apparently been so prone to be misled by the verbal structures of ordinary language may not be their own insistence on decontextualising them, in the way legitimised and encouraged by belief in the language myth.

So it is not merely from one theoretical standpoint alone that problems of a very general kind may be raised about whether language does or can do all that we might unreflectingly suppose that it can be relied upon to do. The difficulties in the way of answering questions of this order centre upon the infinite variability of the circumstances in which our verbal equipment in practice has to be used. Even this way of putting the matter risks oversimplification, for it seems to take for granted that at least the verbal equipment is uncontroversially identifiable. Whereas the variability which confronts the inquirer appears to be such as to make it questionable to what extent any elements of linguistic behaviour are consistent enough or delimitable enough to be describable. An alternative way of putting the problem initially might be this. On what basis is it possible to disengage from the incessant variability of language any clearly defined object of analysis at all? This is the basic problem for a science of language.

Chapter Two

A Science of Language

An uncompromising but controversial solution to the basic problem for a science of language is that represented by the version of the language myth enshrined in the orthodox tradition of modern linguistic theory. Those working within this tradition, while not denying in principle that the specific contexts in which utterances occur affect their interpretation, have usually taken the view that it is not the business of the linguist to account for such matters. A language in their view is to be treated as a system of decontextualised verbal signs, organised into complexes called 'sentences', and mastery of a language is interpreted as mastery of the decontextualised system. Some such idealisation, it is claimed, is theoretically essential if there is to be a science of language.

Language, in short, is described by modern linguistic orthodoxy from a certain point of view, which generativists have usually referred to as that of the 'ideal speaker-hearer'.[1] This 'ideal speaker-hearer' does not appear to have to bother with many of the practical problems of communication which beset the ordinary language-user. In fact, the term 'ideal speaker-hearer', rather like the term 'free enterprise', is loaded in a way which begs a number of questions. Just as the term 'free enterprise' invites us to prejudge certain rather important issues concerning freedom, so the term 'ideal speaker-hearer' invites us to prejudge equally important issues concerning speaking and hearing. The linguist's 'ideal speaker-hearer' is said to be a member of a 'completely homogenous speech–community, who knows its language perfectly and is unaffected by such grammatically irrelevant considerations as

[1] Sometimes, less frequently, the term 'ideal speaker-listener' is used, but no substantive difference appears to hinge on this, and the vacillation of terminology will be ignored in the following discussion.

memory limitations, distractions, shifts of attention and interest, and errors (random or characteristic) in applying his knowledge of the language in actual performance'.[1]

The designation 'speaker-hearer' evidently recognises both an active and a passive role of the individual in linguistic interchange. But these roles appear to be construed in a much more restricted way than is commonly implied by the layman's use of such terms as *speaking* and *hearing*. For the layman, speaking is usually understood to involve a whole gamut of skills and activities, varying according to the demands of the occasion. It is certainly not something which is confined to vibrations of the vocal cords and configurations of the vocal tract, but involves such features as appropriate facial expression, gaze, body posture and gesture. It also involves choice and relevance of what is said. 'He spoke convincingly' is not usually a comment on someone's skill in articulation. Hearing likewise is taken to involve much more than the mere aural reception of sound waves. 'I did not hear what you said' does not necessarily imply any failure to register stimulation of the tympanum. Nor is 'Did you hear him insult me?' an inquiry about anyone's threshold of auditory discrimination.

The competence of the 'ideal speaker-hearer' thus turns out to be noticeably restricted within the range of abilities which go to make up speaking and hearing as understood by the layman for purposes of ordinary communicational exchange. The 'ideal speaker-hearer', it might appear, is in fact a communicational cripple. For he can apparently utter and hear only as much of what is said as is represented by certain rather limited sets of phonetic symbols. Thus his hearing is, for example, vastly inferior to the sensitivity of even the cheapest tape-recorder. Moreover, he can mean and comprehend no more than is captured by the semantic representations corresponding to the sound-sequences these phonetic symbols designate. Whatever else may be involved in verbal communication lies outside his linguistic competence. Yet, by definition, he speaks 'the language' perfectly.

In other words, 'the language' he has mastered is an abstraction from the totality of verbal communication. It is an abstraction structured so as to be representable by a system of correspondences between the two planes of 'meaning' and phonological 'form'. (For

---

[1] N. Chomsky, *Aspects of the Theory of Syntax*, Cambridge, Mass., 1965, p. 3.

writing is an activity which gets short shrift from modern linguistics: the 'priority of the spoken language' over the written is elevated to the status of a theoretical principle.)[1] A 'sentence' of the language accordingly appears as a pairing of one string of symbols representing a certain phonological form, and another string of symbols representing the alleged meaning of that form. Sentences are complexly interrelated by a set of procedures for generating them, and this constitutes the 'grammar' of the language.

But there is also a second and even more striking respect in which it might appear that the 'ideal speaker-hearer' of modern linguistic theory is communicationally handicapped. For his linguistic competence, as represented by the system of bi-planar pairings, contains no guarantee whatsoever that he can actually use any form of words appropriately in a given type of communicational setting. In short, the entire situational and interpersonal context of language is omitted from consideration. It is rather as if the 'ideal cabinet-maker' were represented theoretically as someone who knew how to plane wood, hammer in nails, make joints of certain kinds, and do various other separate operations; but there was no theoretical representation at all of any ability to combine these skills relevantly in constructing a piece of furniture when commissioned by a client to do so. One might well be surprised to find a hypothetical craftsman who lacked any such ability designated an 'ideal cabinet-maker'. It is as if the theorist who designed the 'ideal cabinet-maker' had somehow, by concentrating too narrowly on specifying certain technical details, quite forgotten what society in the end wants cabinet-makers for.

It should be noted that this is quite a different objection from the complaint that knowing how to do something in theory does not imply an ability to put that knowledge effectively into practice. The point is worth making inasmuch as the notion of 'linguistic competence' invoked by generative theorists often involves a confusion of the latter distinction with that between knowledge and its relevant application. There is an important difference between a cabinet-maker who is just a shoddy craftsman, and one who produces superbly crafted constructions quite unsuited to the design situation.

However that may be, it remains the case that the linguist is

---

[1] J. Lyons. *Introduction to Theoretical Linguistics*, Cambridge, 1968, p. 38 et seq.

disposed to take a sanguine view of the feasibility of scientific inquiry into language, and of constructing an adequate scientific language for that purpose. His caveat is that one must not be too ambitious. Success depends on deliberately restricting the inquiry to certain levels of abstraction, which will make it possible to organise one's findings into a coherent descriptive whole. How to conduct such an inquiry, the linguist claims, is shown in practice by the successive achievements of linguists. Those achievements may in certain respects be limited, but at least they are solid, and provide a basis for further inquiry. They give the lie to the sceptic who doubts whether a science of language is possible. Likewise, that it is possible to formulate a language adequate for the purposes of such a science is demonstrated by citing the highly technical and recondite analyses published by contemporary linguistic theorists. Indeed, the claim that what orthodox modern linguistics has to offer *is* the science of language is repeated endlessly in introductory textbooks, and even in the nomenclature of academic posts and university departments.

The inquirer who is mindful of Bacon's idols will doubtless not be slow to point out that the mere fact that a certain discipline appropriates the title *linguistics*, thereby staking some kind of proprietary claim to the investigation of language, does not in itself guarantee very much. Certainly, before any prerogative is granted to such a discipline, some more searching scrutiny of its credentials seems to be required. No one is nowadays naive enough to suppose that language must be no more and no less than it is pronounced to be by linguists (no one, that is, except possibly a linguist).

The version of the language myth propounded by modern linguistics has it that there is only one descriptive standpoint which allows us to proceed to a systematic analysis of linguistic phenomena. Describing language must start by describing languages. And describing languages is not envisaged as describing anything that people do, but as describing what they are assumed to know. It involves describing what a person is assumed to know in order to qualify as a fully competent member of a particular linguistic community. Specifically, there is no assumption that in practice a person always acts linguistically in accordance with that knowledge. This is constantly emphasised by modern linguistic theorists. 'In no sense is a linguistic description an account of actual "verbal behavior".'[1] The distinction between linguistic knowledge and linguistic behaviour is often explained by analogies drawn from other areas of science. One is told, for example, that 'just as the physicist distinguishes between the nature of matter and its observable behavior, so the transformationalist distinguishes between the speaker's *linguistic competence* (the internalised rules that he knows) and his *linguistic performance* (what he does on the basis of knowing such rules)'.[2] Linguistic theory, it is claimed, 'is concerned with discovering a mental reality underlying actual behavior'.[3]

It is worth while for anyone embarking on an inquiry into language to stop to consider why the language myth takes this particular academic form; how it has come about that the preferred mode for raising linguistic questions should be one which asks about what is known, rather than about what is done, or how it is done; and what exactly are the implications of this preference for the epistemic mode of formulation.

It would be naive to suppose that there is no more to it than that the verb *to know* commonly takes names of languages as direct object, as in questions like 'Does he know French?' Manifestly, in some sense or other language must involve knowledge. By common consent, one does not understand what a person is saying unless one knows what the words he utters mean. Nor can one express one's hopes, fears, needs or desires in a language unless one knows the appropriate sounds to utter or marks to inscribe. But this takes us no further than the sense of the verb in questions like 'Does he know French?' And it is difficult to believe that the verb *to know* here presents such a 'wonderful obstruction to the mind' as to prevent anyone from seeing that it is merely a stand-in, called upon to do duty because there is no specific superordinate verb which subsumes the common verbs *to speak*, *to read*, *to write* and *to understand*. If there were a verb *to language* which fulfilled this role, then we could reformulate our question as 'Does he language French?', and release the verb *to know* for more serious duties. As it is, the verb *to know* in such contexts is often replaced by the verb

[1] P. M. Postal, 'Underlying and superficial linguistic structure', *Language*, ed. R. C. Oldfield & J. C. Marshall, Harmondsworth, 1968, p. 195.
[2] J. J. Katz, *Linguistic Philosophy*, London, 1972, pp. 51–2.
[3] Chomsky, op. cit., p. 4.

to speak, or, in older usage, by the verb *to have*. Shakespeare, according to Ben Jonson's well-known line, 'had small Latin and less Greek'; and perhaps this role of the verb *to have* could well be revived. It would remove any possible temptation to read too much significance into common usages like *knowing French*. When we ask 'Does he know French?' there is usually nothing of importance that turns on this choice of the epistemic mode for the question.

When expressions like *linguistic knowledge* are used by linguistic theorists, on the contrary, the epistemic mode is often intended to carry much more theoretical weight than its ordinary usage will bear. One major reason for this can be traced back to the formative circumstances in which the modern discipline which appropriated the title *linguistics* originally established itself. The switch to emphasis on the epistemic mode of description, the 'internalisation' of the object of study, was principally due to the work of Saussure. But its significance can hardly be appreciated without reference to earlier attempts in the course of the nineteenth century to secure the position of the linguist in the academic world of that era.

A study of the development of modern linguistics makes it clear that the entrenchment of the language myth as a basic theoretical assumption arose from the need to establish for linguistic studies respectable academic status as a 'science'. Negatively, this took the form of an effort to dissociate linguistic studies from the educational role played by the grammarian as a pedagogue, concerned merely with the establishment of normative rules of correct linguistic usage. On the positive side, it was part of a more general movement throughout the nineteenth century to bring serious studies of human behaviour into a new framework of empirical investigation, for which the natural sciences provided the exemplars.

Linguistics was at that time not the only candidate seeking admission to status as a 'science'. Socio-political theorising, for example, was in a similar position. Marx and Engels envisaged the theory of historical materialism as playing a scientific role comparable to that of Darwinism in biology. Marx wanted to dedicate the second volume of *Das Kapital* to Darwin, but Darwin declined. In the case of language studies, important groundwork had already been done in the first quarter of the nineteenth century. Considerable progress had been made towards working out the relationships between the various Indo-European languages, in the wake of the discovery of Sanskrit and the realisation of its connexion with Latin and Greek. Bopp's *Conjugationssystem*, which compared the grammars of Sanskrit, Greek, Latin, Persian and Germanic, had appeared in 1816; Rask's essay on Old Norse in 1818; and the influential revised version of the first volume of Grimm's *Deutsche Grammatik*, with its formulation of the 'sound shift' which later became known as 'Grimm's law', in 1822. The work of these comparativists did not in itself establish the claim of linguistics to be considered a science, although it doubtless contributed considerably to promoting a view of grammatical studies as being a scientific type of pursuit rather than a merely pedagogical one.

It is part of the romantic *amour-propre* of science to present itself, wherever possible, as providing long-awaited solutions to problems which mankind has forever been trying to solve without success. Often, in sober fact, just the opposite may be the case. The problem allegedly solved may be one which science itself only recently discovered. Previous ages had not been waiting with bated breath for its solution; for previous ages had been quite unaware of its existence. Sometimes it may even happen that we do not hear mention of a 'science' at all, until fortuitous discovery makes available the key to an investigation which no one had ever seriously proposed. Science is, in this respect, a form of intellectual endeavour in which questions may well be preceded by their answers.[1]

So it was in the case of linguistics. Saussure himself implicitly conceded the principle that answers may precede questions when he pointed out that, in order for the comparative method developed by scholars such as Bopp and Grimm to become a scientific method, it was necessary to find a domain of inquiry in which that method could be seen to provide plausible solutions to plausible problems. But the appropriate domain was found only subsequently to the development of the method. It was the domain of linguistic evolution.[2]

Saussure was not particularly concerned to situate this fact in any broader perspective of the history of ideas in European culture. But

---

[1] Both this and Say's law in economics ('Supply creates its own demand') may be regarded as special cases of the more general principle now known as Sevareid's law ('The chief cause of problems is solutions'). For further examples of the application of Sevareid's law in modern linguistics, see pp. 55, 93 and 110.

[2] *Cours de linguistique générale*, 2nd ed., pp. 14–19.

it is necessary to do so if we wish to understand how subsequent developments in linguistic theory relate to an underlying philosophy of science.

This aspect of the origins of modern linguistics is perhaps most clearly illuminated by the more or less fortuitous, independent and hence untainted testimony of a nineteenth-century writer who was neither a historiographer nor a linguistic theorist, but a poet.

Included in the volume of verse which Robert Browning published in 1855 under the title *Men and Women* is a poem called 'A Grammarian's Funeral'. It is cast in the form of an eulogistic monologue delivered at the burial of a Renaissance grammarian by one of his pupils. The theme of the monologue is devotion to learning. It paints a vivid picture of an unworldly scholar, who ruined his eyesight and his health through the single-minded study of the details of Greek syntax.

> So, with the throttling hands of Death at strife,
> Ground he at grammar;
> Still, thro' the rattle, parts of speech were rife.
> While he could stammer
> He settled *Hoti*'s business—let it be!—
> Properly based *Oun*—
> Gave us the doctrine of the enclitic *De*,
> Dead from the waist down.[1]

There has been some debate among literary critics as to whether Browning's reader is intended to admire the grammarian. According to one view, the grammarian exemplifies a cardinal principle of Browning's philosophy, that the individual's first and highest duty is self-fulfilment. A 'lifetime of devotion to settling "*Hoti*'s business", properly basing *Oun*, and providing "us the doctrine of the enclitic *De*" entitles the grammarian to a final resting-place on the heights'.[2] However, it may be pointed out by those who do not share this view that the eulogy of the grammarian does not come from the poet, but is put into the mouth of someone who might be expected to share the grammarian's interests, namely his pupil; and it is, moreover, delivered as a kind of funeral oration; that is to say, in circumstances where criticism of the dead man would indeed be out of

[1] 'A Grammarian's Funeral', ll. 125–32.
[2] E. D. H. Johnson, in *Browning: 'Men and Women' and Other Poems: a Case Book*, ed. J. R. Watson, London, 1974, p. 99.

place. The poet himself never comments directly at any point in the poem.

The correct interpretation of Browning's message is of more relevance to the history of European linguistics than may at first sight appear. It is worthy of note, in the first place, that Browning is careful to place his grammarian in a very precise historical context. He died, so the rubric of the poem tells us, 'shortly after the revival of learning in Europe'. ('What's in the scroll,' quoth he, 'thou keepest furled?')[1] In other words, he was one of the generation for whom the arrival of new classical manuscripts in the West provided a hitherto unknown fund of evidence about ancient Greek. Thus his situation is basically analogous to that of the early Indo-European comparativists, for whom the discovery of Sanskrit brought to light a hitherto unknown fund of evidence about the structure of the original mother tongue of the Indo-European peoples. It was the comparative method which provided them with the tools to work what Max Müller was later to call 'this newly opened mine of scientific inquiry'.[2]

Secondly, in Browning's poem it is clearly not for the grammarian's qualities as a teacher or educator that his pupils venerate him, but for his research and his passion for it. Indeed, it would seem that he did not seek pupils: rather, they sought him.

'Learned, we found him.'[3]

Thirdly, although the grammarian's capacity for sheer acquisition of knowledge might make him appear a fundamentally passive, even negative figure, none the less he does not leave the academic world as he found it. His legacy, the crowning results of a life-long devotion to learning, are the definitive formulation of certain rules of Greek syntax.

Fourthly, the poem was written at almost exactly the same time as there first appears in English—if the lexicographers of the *New English Dictionary* are right—a new use of the word *grammar*. Hitherto, *grammar* had been a term designating a particular branch of study: specifically, 'that department of the study of a language which deals with its inflexional forms or other means of indicating

---

[1] 'A Grammarian's Funeral', l.47.
[2] *Lectures on the Science of Language*, vol. I, London, 1861, p. I.
[3] 'A Grammarian's Funeral', l.52.

the relation of words in the sentence, and with the rules for employing these in accordance with established usage: usually including
also the department which deals with the phonetic system of the
language and the principles of its representation in writing'.[1] The
new use of the term *grammar*, first attested in 1846 according to the
NED, is as a designation not of that branch of study, but of the
linguistic phenomena studied. The term *grammar* thus joins company with a group of other English words which share the same
type of ambiguity (for example, *music*, *politics*), being not only (i)
what the subject is called, but also (ii) what the subject-matter itself
is called.

It is tempting to see in the appearance of this new use of the term
grammar some reflexion of a change in the public image of the
grammarian. The old notion of the grammarian *qua* pedagogue is
challenged by a new notion of the grammarian *qua* scientist. The
older view remains epitomised in one line of another well-known
nineteenth-century poem, 'The Jackdaw of Rheims':

> Heedless of grammar, they all cried 'That's him'.

But it is the new concept of the grammarian which motivates
Browning's poem. The historical background to the change was the
new impetus to grammatical studies provided by such scholars as
Bopp, Rask and Grimm. It is the work of the comparativists of the
first half of the nineteenth century which may be seen as validating
the poet's choice of a grammarian to represent a certain form of
intellectual endeavour.

For Browning's point is one about the value of human knowledge.
What later generations come to regard as a trivial or obvious fact
may originally have taken a lifetime of research to discover.
Browning's grammarian, then, is not a master who corrects the
linguistic mistakes of his pupils and directs their efforts at
improvement; but an investigator who, by his own intellectual
energy and tenacity, pushes back the frontiers of uncertainty and
ignorance. The grammarian is thus chosen by Browning as the
paradigm figure of the pure scientist. His discoveries have no
practical consequences; at least, not as Victorian materialism judges
practicality. No improvement in trade or prosperity will follow from
them. They cannot be put to any use. For they are discoveries about

[1] *New English Dictionary*, vol. IV, pt. ii, p. 344.

the past. Their value is simply the value they have in virtue of being
a contribution to the sum total of human knowledge, achieved by
utterly committed intellectual endeavour. And that is a valuation
which cannot, for Browning, be rendered in strictly human terms:

> God surely will contrive
> Use for our earning.[1]

It hardly needs to be emphasised how utterly inappropriate for
Browning's purposes would have been the old concept of the
grammarian *qua* pedagogue. Take away the objective and adventure
of intellectual discovery, and even God would be hard put to it to
find a use for pedantry. What in Browning's grammarian is a
relentless drive towards a goal would be reduced to a pointless
automatism.

Nor does it need to be stressed how different is the formulation
of a grammatical rule in the hands of the grammarian-scientist as
compared with his pedagogue counterpart. The justification of a
rule for the pedagogue is practical efficiency; that is to say, conformity to it produces results which are judged superior, by whatever criteria are appropriate, to the results produced by infringing
it; whereas the justification of a rule for the grammarian-scientist
is its validity; that is to say, its capacity to account for the available
evidence. Hence the assimilation of formulating grammatical rules
to discovering laws of nature. It is within this intellectual framework
that grammar comes to be regarded naturally as a range of
objectively existent facts related in ways and according to principles
which the grammarian, by investigation, may discover. For the
grammarian-scientist, grammar is reality, not recommendation.

Grammar remained, none the less, in an important sense 'outside'
the speaker. Although now regarded as 'in the language' and not
merely in the eye of the grammarian, grammar was treated as an
essentially public, observable range of phenomena. It is important
to see that this 'externality' of grammar was not coincidental. It was
in fact an essential condition if linguistics was to acquire the kind of
scientific status which it sought at that time.

By the early 1860s, Max Müller felt able to assure the general
public, somewhat cautiously, that 'there *is* a Science of Language',[2]

[1] 'A Grammarian's Funeral', ll. 79–80.
[2] *Lectures on the Science of Language*, vol. II, London, 1864, p. 1.

even though it was 'a science of very modern date', and one 'scarcely received as yet on a footing of equality by the elder branches of learning'.[1] None the less, Müller claimed, 'without the Science of Language, the circle of the physical sciences ... would be incomplete'.[2] The kind of science which Müller had in mind was one amenable to methods akin to those of the geology, the astronomy and the botany of his day, as the following explicit comparison makes very clear:

> ... the language which we speak, and the languages that are and that have been spoken in every part of our globe since the first dawn of human life and human thought, supply materials capable of scientific treatment. We can collect them, we can classify them, we can reduce them to their constituent elements, and deduce from them some of the laws that determine their origin, govern their growth, necessitate their decay; we can treat them, in fact, in exactly the same spirit in which the geologist treats his stones and petrifications,—nay, in some respects, in the same spirit in which the astronomer treats the stars of heaven, or the botanist the flowers of the field.[3]

Two things above all, in Müller's view, confirmed the status and place of the new Science of Language. One was that its results were obtained by methods of comparison, classification and analysis of specimens, exactly analogous to the procedures of the natural sciences. But the other was that this new science served no other intellectual interests than its own. It studied language for its own sake, and for no ulterior purpose. Linguistic scholarship had at last gained emancipation from subservience to the ends of philology. The philologist, argued Müller, whether he be a classicist or an orientalist, was interested in linguistic facts merely 'as a key to an understanding of the literary monuments which by-gone ages have bequeathed to us, as a spell to raise from the tomb the thoughts of great men in different ages and different countries, and as a means ultimately to trace the social, moral, intellectual and religious progress of the human race'.[4] That was both why philology ranked among the historical sciences, and why the new Science of Language did not. Thus from the beginning laying the foundations of a science of language was bound up with taking a certain view of the

---

[1] ibid., vol. I, p. 3.   [2] ibid., vol. II, p. 7.
[3] ibid., vol. II, p. 1.   [4] ibid., vol. I, p. 23.

philosophy of science, and finding an academic niche not already occupied by some other discipline.

Nor could the teaching of living languages, in Müller's view, normally be regarded as other than a means to an end: namely, to provide the learner with 'letters of introduction to the best society or to the best literature of the leading nations of Europe'.[1] Whereas, on the contrary, with the new Science of Language 'language itself becomes the sole object of scientific inquiry . . . We do not want to know languages, we want to know language.'[2]

*   *   *

Müller's words 'We do not want to know languages, we want to know language' may stand as a statement of the acknowledged goal of a science of language down to the present day. But it is one of the more interesting features of modern intellectual history that how to establish the empirical bases for such a science should still be a matter of fundamental and unresolved controversy. The fact that we can trace no analogous and equally divisive controversy in other sections of what Müller called 'the circle of the physical sciences' is itself one reason which might justify scepticism as to whether linguistic science properly belongs in this circle. A more radical scepticism might perhaps claim that a hundred years of failure to resolve such fundamental issues is long enough to demonstrate that Müller and other linguistic theorists were more basically mistaken: that is, one must conclude that modern linguistics has proved to be no science at all.

The programmatic slogan 'We do not want to know languages, we want to know language' itself points to the ultimate crux of the problem. The abstract object of knowledge, 'language', is at double remove from direct observation. It is once removed in that we cannot hope to see the workings of language except insofar as they are manifested through particular languages. But it is twice removed in that particular languages, as such, are not directly available to observation either. All that we can observe directly (in the sense in which 'direct observation' is conducted in the natural sciences generally) are specific speech events, utterances, inscriptions, and reactions to them by members of a linguistic community.

What cannot be doubted is that the search for a satisfactory way

[1] ibid., vol. I, p. 23.   [2] ibid., vol. I, p. 23.

of relating what is directly observable to pursuit of the objective 'to know language' has predominantly motivated the development of linguistic theory from Müller's day onwards. It was because Saussure felt that the nineteenth century had not established the necessary basis for a science which aimed 'to know language' that he proposed the radically different approach of structuralist analysis.

Saussure's criticism of the limitations of nineteenth-century linguistics was well founded, at least in the following respect. The facts amenable to systematic treatment within the framework proposed by Indo-European historical grammar, and the laws which could be formulated to subsume those facts, bore little if any relation to language as experienced by the individual. The regularities of sound change, and the other gradual processes by which languages developed, involved a time scale and a perspective too broad to analyse the realities of language as they existed for any given speaker or generation of speakers. Language as 'known' to the historical grammarian could only be something knowable with the benefit of laborious comparative analysis and centuries of hindsight. But this was not language as 'known' to those who constantly relied on the availability of language in the present to deal with the communication situations of everyday life. As Saussure saw it, a linguistic science which failed to provide an intuitively satisfactory theoretical framework within which to explicate the linguistic knowledge of the ordinary speaker would have failed to come to grips with its subject matter.

The step Saussure took was in one crucial respect a retrograde step. In effect, he reversed the aims implied in Müller's distinction between knowing languages and knowing language. In Saussure's view, linguistic knowledge was, for the individual, equatable with knowing a language. By distinguishing between *le langage* and *la langue*, and insisting that the latter was the proper object of study for a science of language, whereas the former could not possibly constitute such an object, Saussure anchored the development of the discipline firmly to the antecedent Western grammatical tradition. For the concept of *la langue* which he proceeded to expound as a basis for linguistics was in certain essential respects by no means new. It was an updated version of the old concept of a national language, as established under the aegis of the orthological dogma promoted by Renaissance nationalism, and enshrined in the practice of many subsequent generations of European grammarians and lexicographers.[1] The central fiction of this view was that one nation spoke one language. Any individual whose speech differed from the hypothesised national standard was simply not speaking the language correctly.

In this crucial respect, the linguistics introduced by Saussure placed theoretical constraints upon the freedom of the individual speaker no less rigid than the authoritarian recommendations of the old-fashioned grammarian-pedagogue. But instead of the rules being imposed by educational pedants, they were envisaged as being imposed from within the language itself.

This concept of a language was in certain respects very different from that required by the historical grammarian, for whom innovations condemned by one generation might be forerunners or continuations of important and widespread developments, all systematically related within the language. Saussure saw no way of reconciling the idea of a language as a continuously changing set of usages with that of a language as a coherent system; and he clearly believed that the latter accorded better with psychological reality for the ordinary language-user.

To free language studies from the tyranny of the historian, however, it did not suffice merely to distinguish synchronic from diachronic perspectives. It was necessary to argue that the material falling within the scope of a synchronic study demanded an analysis *sui generis*, an analysis which the historian could not supply. Furthermore, if linguistics was to be a science in its own right, the analysis had to be one which could not be supplied by any other discipline, even though other disciplines, such as physiology, sociology and psychology, might include aspects of linguistic behaviour within their purview. The answers to these problems were supplied jointly by the Saussurean doctrine of the linguistic sign and the Saussurean separation of *la langue* from *la parole*. The combined effect of these strategies was to remove *la langue* not merely from the clutches of the historian, but from the province of observable behaviour altogether. Languages were declared to be systems of cognitive structures, actualised in the form of associations between acoustic images and concepts inside the heads of individual members of the language community.

[1] R. Harris, *The Language-Makers*, London, 1980, ch. 6.

By this 'internalisation' of the object of study, Saussure turned linguistics from being a somewhat marginal appendage to social history into a rather central branch of cognitive psychology, a status which was later loudly acclaimed by Saussure's generativist successors (mainly in order to discomfit their behaviourist rivals). But it was not Saussure's intention, any more than it was the generativists', to allow mere psychologists to tell linguists how to run linguistics. Quite the reverse. It would be the linguistic theorist who told the psychologist how to study language scientifically.

The foundation for this claim is laid in the Saussurean doctrine of the linguistic sign, which simultaneously explains the sense in which the rules which constrain the language-user come from within the language itself. The linguistic sign, according to Saussure, unites a signifier (*signifiant*) and a signified (*signifié*). But neither signifier nor signified are independently given. Not only does the one not exist without the other, but neither signifier, signified, nor the association between them exist except in the context of the particular system of such associations which constitutes the language. They are created by the language, not external to it. Consequently, the psychologist is simply mistaken if he thinks that he has available his own methods of analysis which allow him independent access to the study of words as mental objects, or of the ideas they supposedly stand for. The only methods available will be the methods of structural linguistics, since these alone are immune from the fallacy of assuming that a language is merely a nomenclature, a complex set of verbal labels which happen to be attached to things. Thus although linguistics may, on this view, be a branch of psychology, none the less in order to study language the psychologist is obliged himself to adopt the methods of the linguist if he wishes to come to terms with the nature of the mental realities he is dealing with. Otherwise he will merely be studying various psychological facets of *la parole*, and without a proper understanding even of these when he divorces them from *la langue*.

By 'internalising' the object of analysis for linguistics in this way, Saussure achieved a remarkable feat of academic politics. He rescued his subject from the historians by finding a place for it within psychology; but at the same time safeguarded it from the

possible encroachments of psychologists. He established a programme which psychology had no ready-made ways of dealing
with. He thus simultaneously provided his subject with a new
academic location and its own distinctive methods appropriate to
that location. Anyone who can achieve such a feat has as good a
claim as any to be regarded as the founder of a new discipline: and
in this instance it was achieved not through the adventitious discovery of a fresh range of facts to be explained, but by an original
approach to an already quite familiar range of facts.

The new map which Saussure drew for the future study of
language none the less incorporated certain features carried over
from the former style of cartography which it immediately super-
seded. There is a sense in which Saussurean structuralism was still
historical grammar, but minus the history. The concept of *la langue*,
like the more recent concept of linguistic competence, was a palimp-
sest with traces of an earlier and unsuccessfully obliterated text
showing through.

Although the Saussurean structuralist was obliged to describe
language from the point of view of the language-user, or at least
more nearly so than the historical grammarian ever attempted to
do, he was none the less in certain important respects not allowed to
go as far as looking at language through the eyes of the language-
user. Between the individual and his speech act, Saussurean
structuralism interposed an abstract social object, *la langue*, a
totality which the individual never sees at all as he goes about his
everyday linguistic business, any more than he sees the totality of
the society of which his own life is part. But according to the
Saussurean structuralist, it was only through *la langue* that the
individual was able to act, in the sense of 'acting linguistically'.
Hence the hypothesis that the individual, without being aware of
it, must somehow carry around a representation of *la langue* inside
his head. For otherwise, by the somewhat naive psychologising
which Saussurean structuralism involves, it would not be clear in
what sense one could claim that the individual was actually using
'the language', nor that he was using 'the same language' as other
individuals in his linguistic community. It was thus inevitable that
the linguistic community should come to be seen simply as a collection of individuals united by the fact that they are all internally
programmed with identical linguistic knowledge. If this were not

so, or assumed theoretically to be so, then the statements of linguistics could never be scientific statements in the sense in which Saussure was trying to establish linguistics as a science. There would be strictly nothing to be said, scientifically, about English, or about French; because 'English' and 'French' would be just names of fortuitous aggregates of the behaviour of individuals. Phrases like 'the English language' would be tantamount to systematically misleading expressions in Ryle's use of the term.

La langue, furthermore, was an abstract social object of the same order of abstraction as the historical grammarian's languages. The English used by the English-speaking community at one given period was the English whose evolution had been traced through earlier periods by means of surviving records and reconstructions. All the structuralist did in describing *la langue* was to 'freeze' some historically evolving system at an arbitrarily chosen point, and ignore the inconsistencies which might show up at that point from competition between older and newer usages. This correspondence between the levels of abstraction involved in diachronic and synchronic study is a point often passed over in silence by Saussure's commentators, but it is one of central importance to the present discussion. Its validity is confirmed both by the terminology Saussure used and by the comparisons which illustrated his explanation of how a synchronic account of any given language stands in relation to an account of its historical development. The study of development would be 'evolutionary linguistics' (*linguistique évolutive*), as opposed to synchronic study, which would be 'static linguistics' (*linguistique statique*). The difference between the two would be analogous to the difference between examining a perpendicular section of the stem of a plant cut lengthwise from top to bottom, and examining a cross-section of the stem as revealed by a horizontal cut at any chosen point.[1] What the cross-section reveals, said Saussure, is nothing other than the same longitudinal fibres in the stem of the plant, but forming a coherent horizontal pattern which no perpendicular section of the fibres can possibly reveal. In other words, as the linguist shifts from the evolutionary perspective of growth to the static perspective of the cross-section, there is no alteration in scale of abstraction or relative grossness of the features examined. The one is not an inspection with the

[1] *Cours de linguistique générale*, 2nd ed., p. 125.

naked eye, as opposed to the microscopic examination of the other. Nor does one investigation take in more than the other. The object under examination remains the same.

   This in part explains why Saussurean structuralism takes no more account of variations between particular communication situations than historical grammar did. It is in this respect that Saussure envisaged a language as being what the historical grammarian described, but minus the history. However, the historical grammarian had three justifications, which the structuralist lacked, for refusing to take into consideration the particular circumstances of language use. In the first place, circumstances are in an obvious sense not comparable across wide generation gaps. Literally, few individuals ever live in the same world as their great-grandparents. In the second place, such differences were seemingly irrelevant to the features which the historical grammarian was concerned to record. Sometimes there was stability for generation after generation. Sometimes there was rapid and decisive change within a relatively short span. But it was entirely unclear that there was any systematic correlation between linguistic changes and non-linguistic changes in society, except in the case of major upheavals such as foreign invasions. For these could result in giving the language a new population of speakers. Otherwise, the development or importation of new words to designate new artifacts or new social institutions seemed to be rather marginal phenomena, which usually left the phonology and grammar of the language unchanged. It was mere conjecture, for example, to seek an explanation of the systematic changes undergone by the Latin consonant system in the course of its development into Early Old French by reference to precise factors in the social circumstances of language use in Gaul. Nor could such factors explain satisfactorily why Old French grammar partially retained the Latin case system for nouns and adjectives, while at the same time Old Italian, also inheriting the Latin system, had abandoned case distinctions. Vocabulary apart, languages seemed to the historical grammarian to lead lives of their own, more or less unrelated to the lives their speakers led. The events he recorded in the life of a language made sense when related one to the next in a historical sequence, but not when considered as direct consequences of events in the life of the community, still less in the lives of individuals. Finally, the historical grammarian in any case had virtually no access to detailed information about the circumstances of language use in periods of the remote past. So he was effectively precluded, by sheer lack of evidence, from making any serious attempt to analyse languages and their development at a level which took such evidence into consideration. Since he would never have the opportunity of hearing primitive Indo-European spoken by its native speakers, or asking them questions about it, or observing its use in the transactions of daily life, whatever information such observations might have given him would find no place, theoretically or practically, in his schema of linguistic studies.

What the historical grammarian, not unreasonably, excluded from his purview could not likewise be excluded on the same grounds from the purview of the structuralist. None the less, it was excluded. One of the major criticisms that may be levelled against Saussurean structuralism bears on just this point. By accepting the same limitations as the historical grammarian had been forced to accept, Saussure turned what had been a reasonable point of view into a simple article of faith. He thereby failed to carry through the logic of switching from a historical to a synchronic perspective on language.

The *Cours de linguistique générale* rightly insists that the linguist cannot enter into the consciousness of the language-user except by suppressing history.[1] For the language-user is unaware of the historian's chronological sequence of linguistic facts. But while, negatively, this is true, what the *Cours de linguistique générale* fails to ask is what positive steps must be taken if the linguist does indeed wish to 'enter into the consciousness' of the ordinary speaker. Suppressing history, in itself, is not enough. For it is possible to suppress history without suppressing the framework which history imposes. This failure can be seen in the very terms in which the *Cours de linguistique générale* characterises the viewpoint of the language-user. The crucial passage reads: 'The first thing that strikes us when we study linguistic facts (*faits de langue*) is that for the speaker their succession in time does not exist: he is confronted with a state.'[2] But there is a concealed *non sequitur* here. The alternative to a chronological succession is not automatically a state, unless a state is defined stipulatively as being whatever a chronological

---

[1] *Cours de linguistique générale*, 2nd ed., p. 117.   [2] ibid.

succession is not. In other words, it is gratuitous to suppose that the viewpoint of the speaker coincides with that of the historian, but for the circumstance that the speaker is deprived of the historian's historical perspective. Language-users are not would-be historians who simply lack hindsight. The historical perspective creates its own facts, whether we are studying languages, lemmings or ladies' fashions. Once the historical basis for comparison is removed, all the historian's facts vanish with it. They do not automatically regroup themselves into a-historical states-of-facts, which are manifest as current realities to successive generations of contemporaries. We do not know, for example, what the record attendance was at the Colosseum on any day between its inauguration in A.D. 80 and the end of the fifth century. But if this were known, the fact would be a historian's fact. It would be nonsense to suggest that it was in some sense also a fact for those who were present at the Colosseum on that day. Unless by that we mean that some of the participants subsequently learned about it from Roman statisticians. Only in rare cases do the viewpoints of the participant and the historian coincide. (This is rare, although not impossible. When Roger Bannister in 1954 became the first athlete to run a mile in less than four minutes, he doubtless fully appreciated the historical significance of what he was doing, as did Neil Armstrong on 21 July 1969, when he became the first man to set foot on the moon.) But it can only be a historian's fact that the last part of the French word *aujourd'hui* is etymologically derived from Latin *hodie*. That is not in some mysterious way a compound of two synchronic facts, one known to the present-day Parisian, and the other to Caesar's legionaries.

The Saussurean 'state' of linguistic facts was as much an artifact of the historian's perspective as the notion of a chronological 'succession' of linguistic facts. Looking at languages as states, far from freeing linguistics from the dominance of the historian, meant a perpetuation of the historian's dominance in a less obvious guise. What Saussure would have needed to do in order to carry through the logic of looking at language through the eyes of the language-user would have been to realise that substituting the concept of a 'state' for the concept of a 'succession' was simply to replace one historian's concept by another. Instead, he should have first asked himself what role succession in time plays in the layman's experience of language, as distinct from the role it plays in the historian's records.

Perhaps Saussure did ask himself this question, but did not like the answer. In any case, it very much suited his book, as the strategist of synchronic linguistics, to ignore it: just as it suited him to accept as an article of faith the historian's exclusion of circumstantial variations in language use. A linguistics which endeavoured to come seriously to terms with the layman's perspective on such matters could hardly have claimed to be an independent science. It would have owed too much and too obviously to forms of investigation shared with other disciplines concerned with the study of human behaviour. In short, it would have found itself in precisely the awkward position Saussure described as forced upon the investigation of *langage*, 'straddling several domains simultaneously, physical, physiological and psychological, belonging both to the individual and to society'.[1]

---

[1] ibid., p. 25.

Chapter Three

The Grammarians' Legacy

The two scholars who supplied the modern academic version of the language myth with most of its descriptive terminology died before synchronic linguistics was conceived. They were Priscian and Donatus, the two great grammarians of late antiquity, whose works taught Europe Latin for a thousand years.[1] Their contribution to the language myth is all the more remarkable in that their descriptive framework was developed for quite different ends from any that Saussure had in mind. It none the less provided something which Saussure never lived—or never bothered—to provide, but which modern sciences need.

The situation in which an established descriptive format devised for one particular purpose is taken over and adapted to serve some new and quite different purpose is a situation fraught with potential errors and inconsistencies of all kinds. It is a situation over which Bacon's idols of the market are predestined to reign as patron deities. When modern linguistics took over for purposes of synchronic analysis the old descriptive framework handed down by the Western grammatical tradition, just such a situation was brought about. Its brood of disastrous consequences have plagued linguistic theory ever since. Anyone seeking to understand why modern linguistics has failed to come to terms with the creativity of language must first look here for the source of that failure.

The irony which pervades this chapter of modern intellectual history is that whereas linguistics urgently needed a comprehensive descriptive apparatus in order to pass muster as a science, borrowing

---

[1] Donatus, the tutor of St. Jerome, bequeathed to the Western world the schoolboy's *Ars Minor*, which deals with the parts of speech, and an *Ars Major*, which deals with grammar generally. Priscian's more extensive *Institutiones Grammaticae* (*c.* A.D. 500) survived in a thousand manuscripts before its first printed edition in 1470.

this particular apparatus effectively put the possibility of formulating scientific statements about language beyond immediate reach
altogether. Instead, it created straight away the problem of explaining what exactly the descriptive statements capable of being formulated were descriptions of.[1] The answer had to be that they were
descriptions of some kind of 'linguistic knowledge', once the
Saussurean 'internalisation' of the object of analysis was accepted.
The difficulty, given this internalisation, was that it was quite
unclear what, objectively, linguistic knowledge was and hence
how the linguistic scientist could ever be sure whether he had
succeeded in describing it. Thus he found himself not in the investigatory stance of an empirical scientist at all, but setting out
on the path of anti-science. For he had to find—or invent—something describable, to fit the descriptions at his disposal. New
descriptive work had to be found for the old terminology of *noun,
verb, sentence, subject, predicate,* and the rest of Priscian's and
Donatus' legacy.

Inevitably, the linguistic scientist was driven to claim, in effect,
that by great good fortune the terminology developed by his grammarian ancestors to teach their pupils Latin did actually correspond
to the realities of linguistic knowledge as lately revealed by the
application of structuralist theory. No happier coincidence could be
imagined in the whole history of science. If anyone experienced a
slight sensation of *déjà vu* at this point, that was hardly an accident
either. For it had been a precisely analogous coincidence which
enabled the grammarians of Port Royal in the seventeenth century
to use the traditional terminology of the parts of speech in order to
disclose the workings of the human mind.

The descriptive impedimenta of the Western grammatical tradition had to be adapted to synchronic analysis in accordance with
the requirements of the language myth. Preoccupation with the
problems involved had a variety of unfortunate consequences. It
effectively prevented linguists from realising, first, that the contextualisation provided by circumstances is what establishes the
kind of determinacy required in language, and it is fruitless to
expect or look for determinacy beyond that point; secondly, that a
certain level of indeterminacy is necessary in order to provide the
flexibility which communication demands.

[1] Sevareid's law again.

Having inherited an analytic apparatus for grammatical description, it was predictable that modern linguistics would not seriously question the validity of grammar as an identifiable component of linguistic knowledge. Thus it never embarked on any reappraisal of the communicational relevance of different types of formal patterning in language, or examined how they related to the integrational tasks facing language-users in different situations. The assumption was that grammar existed in a communicational vacuum. Language-users had to obey the rules of grammar, come what may, and therefore it was pointless to ask further questions. Individuals must meet grammar's requirements, not grammar theirs. None the less, there was some uneasiness about the unsatisfactory way in which traditional grammarians had dealt with the question of defining the basic units of grammar. These definitions, it was felt, did not meet the rigorous standards demanded of a twentieth-century science, and this defect should be remedied. The remedial task, however, proved much more difficult than anticipated.

Two developments during the nineteenth and early twentieth centuries had contributed to a certain narrowing of the grammarian's province. One was the successful elaboration of methods of phonetic and phonological analysis. These methods facilitated the description of consonant and vowel systems without reference to the occurrence of sounds in linguistic units of any rank higher than the word. The phonetician and the phonologist in this way established for themselves a more or less self-contained area of study within linguistics. Its effect was to divorce the study of sounds from the study of morphology.[1]

The other development was the compilation and publication of impressively authoritative dictionaries of the major European languages. The work of Littré and Godefroy in France, and of the brothers Grimm in Germany, together with the publication of the *New Oxford English Dictionary*, all contributed towards establishing another independent sub-domain of linguistic inquiry, belonging to the lexicographer. Between the phonetician or phonologist on the

---

[1] The approach to phonology taken by some schools, e.g. glossematicians and generativists, deliberately attempted to bridge this gap; but it was a gap none the less. Languages were treated as systems having 'double articulation', one articulation being that of meaningless units (phonemes) and the other articulation being that of meaningful units (morphemes and words).

one hand and the lexicographer on the other, the grammarian was restricted to the unoccupied territory in the middle.

Thus it came about that modern linguistics inherited a concept of grammar which had been reduced, in effect, to whatever in language was not pronunciation, nor orthography, nor vocabulary. This reduction underlies the typically tripartite organisation of language descriptions which has continued throughout the present century.

Unquestioning acceptance of the 'fixed code' fallacy led linguists to devote their efforts to developing ways of identifying the fixed forms which supposedly underlay speech activity. They sought (i) at fixed set of sounds for each language, and (ii) a fixed set of grammatical units, combinable according to a fixed set of grammatical rules.

The search for the fixed set of sounds issued in the development of phoneme theory. It became, in effect, the search for phonic units which would play for speech the same role as the letters of the alphabet played for writing. Not until the mid 1930s was it pointed out that, given any set of utterances in a language, it will always be possible to derive conflicting analyses of the underlying set of phonemes.[1] This conclusion, one might have supposed, would have devastating consequences for the 'fixed code' hypothesis, and for the language myth in general. Far from it. Competing phonemic analyses continued to proliferate, on the confident assumption that what now needed to be determined was which one of the analytically possible phoneme systems the speakers of the language were 'really' using.

Thus the spectre of the phoneme continued to haunt phonetics laboratories long after the corpse should have been laid to rest. In 1970 phoneticians were still supposing that 'recognising the sounds in a spoken message requires that the listener should perceive sounds and place each item in one of a number of categories which correspond . . . to the phonemes or phonological units of the language system'.[2] By the end of the decade, however, experimental studies had repeatedly shown that how a listener identifies a specific

---

[1] Y. R. Chao, 'The non-uniqueness of phonemic solutions of phonetic systems', *Bulletin of the Institute of History and Philology, Academia Sinica*, 1934, vol. IV, pt. 4.
[2] D. B. Fry, 'Speech reception and perception', *New Horizons in Linguistics*, ed. J. Lyons, Harmondsworth, 1970, p. 33.

acoustic stimulus linguistically (what he hears a sound 'as') may be influenced by many different factors, and vary from one occasion to another. Thus the evidence which would have supported most convincingly the postulation of the phoneme as an invariant unit of linguistic form was not forthcoming. Similarly, as regards speech production, doubts were being raised about so-called 'translation theories' of phonation, which postulate underlying phonological units and a programme whereby these units are translated into muscular movements of the vocal apparatus.[1] In short, the notion of a fixed set of basic speech-sound units could no longer be seen as providing the unquestionable basis for a convincing account either of the speaker's or of the hearer's activities.

What is surprising is that the conviction that somehow there must 'really be' fixed phonological inventories for speakers and hearers had lasted so long. For what the history of phoneme theory makes abundantly clear is that phonological units were originally postulated to provide a description—and specifically a notation—for the differences between minimally contrasting pairs of words, when compared in isolation from their occurrence in any context of discourse. Once isolated words are no longer implicitly accepted as the basis for comparison, the fixed set of phonemic oppositions thus exhibited becomes unstable. For example, the initial alveolar [l] of *leaf* and the final velar [ɫ] of *feel* do not contrast phonemically in English, provided we restrict the comparison to what the dictionary treats as 'single words'. For then we can find no examples of pairs of words which differ merely in respect of one of these two sounds contrasting with the other in the same position in the sound-sequence. But as soon as we are allowed to compare, for example, *pylon* with *pile on*, the picture changes. The [l] and the [ɫ] which were formerly allophones of 'the same phoneme' become contrastive elements.

Once it was realised that identification of basic phonological units is a function of what utterances are compared with what other utterances, the temptation to believe in a fixed inventory of phonemic invariants should have diminished accordingly. That it did not bears witness to the influence of the language myth both inside and outside the laboratory.

[1] P. F. MacNeilage, 'Speech production', *Proceedings of the Ninth International Congress of Phonetic Sciences*, Copenhagen, 1979, vol. I, p. 26.

As regards the search for a fixed set of grammatical units, modern linguistic orthodoxy simply carried on where traditional grammar left off. But the determinacy of grammar was inextricably bound up with the question of how grammar was determined, and in particular to what extent it was determined by meaning.

A break had to be made with traditional grammar on two main points. First, the definitions on which the traditional terminology was based often appealed overtly to extralinguistic factors. This jarred with the modern claim that languages were autonomous systems, defined by their own internal structuring. Secondly, the assumption of the traditional grammarian was that the same descriptive apparatus would fit a language at all periods in its history. This contained an implicit rejection of the modern distinction between the synchronic and the diachronic. In the name of the new linguistic science, traditional grammar had to be condemned on both counts. So it was natural to identify these as the reasons why traditional grammar had failed to do what modern linguistics was now in a position to do.

Thus emerged an 'official doctrine' about traditional grammar, which identified 'two besetting sins of traditional grammar that have hindered and distorted its operations and the development of theoretical consistency'. The first sin was the attempt 'to base grammar and the categories of grammar on alleged types of meaning, or on notional, conceptual, or philosophical categories'. The second sin was 'the description of a language in terms found suitable, or assumed to be suitable, for another language, usually one carrying cultural prestige, such as Latin or Sanskrit, or for an earlier stage of the language in question, which for the purposes of grammatical description counts as a separate language also'.[1]

In accordance with this doctrine, and to show the world that the twentieth-century linguist was not tainted with the 'besetting sins' of his academic forebears, the definitions of traditional grammar were arraigned on a motley variety of charges. These ranged from plain 'inaccuracy' (that is to say, failure to give a correct classification of forms and constructions) to 'circularity'. These charges and the evidence adduced to support them are worth examining. They throw interesting light on the dilemma of a linguistic science which still needed the traditional descriptive apparatus, but could no

[1] R. H. Robins, *General Linguistics: an Introductory Survey*, London, 1964, p. 183.

longer afford to subscribe to the theoretical presuppositions which that apparatus seemed to imply.

The charge of inaccuracy was often based on the claim that there was only an imperfect correspondence between a grammatical distinction and its traditional definition. Thus, so the argument went, such forms as the English *oats* and *wheat*[1] are counter-examples to the proposition that 'singular' and 'plural' may be defined in terms of the distinction between the notions 'one' and 'more than one'. For *oats* is a plural (having the plural ending *-s* and being followed by plural verb forms, for example, *The oats are*...), whereas *wheat* is a singular (having no plural ending and being followed by singular verb forms, for example, *The wheat is*...). None the less, it was claimed, *oats* does not mean 'more than one oat'. Similar examples cited were the singular *foliage* vs. the plural *leaves*, and the case was sometimes supported by interlingual comparisons, for example, between the English singular *hair* and its French plural counterpart *cheveux*.[2]

Arguments of the above kind start from this assumption: the thesis that the distinction between singular and plural may be explicated in terms of the numerical difference between 'one' and 'more than one' entails that every noun is either singular or plural according to whether it stands for 'one' thing or 'more than one' thing. Examples are then adduced which are alleged to show the latter proposition to be false. This in turn is taken to disprove the original thesis. Thus the *oats-wheat* argument is basically analogous to the following. The distinction between 'lower class' and 'upper class' cannot be explicated in terms of 'low' vs. 'high' incomes. For this entails that all members of the lower class have low incomes and all members of the upper class have high incomes. But there are certain cases in which two individuals have comparable incomes, yet one is lower-class and the other upper-class. A penurious baronet may have no greater income than an agricultural labourer. Therefore the explication of 'class' in terms of income is untenable.

What is wrong in both cases is the supposition that a defender of the thesis needs to claim that for any particular *x* in question, the classification of *x* is uniquely determined by the explicatory criterion. This begs the question against the thesis under criticism.

[1] L. Bloomfield, *Language*, London, 1935, p. 190.
[2] F. R. Palmer, *Grammar*, London, 1971, pp. 34–5.

What the critic needs to establish in the first place is that the thesis criticised does in fact entail this application of the criterion. Unless this can first be demonstrated, the argument collapses. Moreover, even if it is granted that this can be demonstrated, all the defender of the thesis need do to salvage his case is simply to concede the contentious examples. In other words, he will admit that if *oats* is plural then *wheat* is plural, whereas if *wheat* is singular then *oats* is singular. Either will involve also conceding an exception to the grammatical rule that subjects and verbs agree in number, and at this point his critic may urge that the concession is itself a defeat for the notional definition. But it is at this point also that the full extent of the critic's question-begging becomes clear. For the critic has given himself the advantage of assuming that an independent criterion is available which establishes beyond question that *oats* is plural and *wheat* singular. The criterion appealed to is the variation in the accompanying form of the verb: *The oats are* . . . . *vs. The wheat is* . . . This criterion, however, invites two objections. In the first place, it is not clear why it should be preferred to the notional criterion. It would be quite legitimate for the defender of a notional definition to object that the critic is simply insisting on giving the terms 'singular' and 'plural' a different interpretation from the interpretation they receive under the notional definition. Secondly, if we take the critic's criterion at its face value, it appears to call in question the validity of a simple binary distinction between singular and plural altogether, at least as far as English is concerned. For in English there are nouns which may be followed either by *is* or by *are*: *The government is considering the proposal, The government are considering the proposal; The crew is on strike, The crew are on strike,* etc. Adopting this criterion, therefore, gives at least a tripartite classification of English nouns in respect of the category of number; and, arguably, a more complex classification when we take into account the related behaviour of demonstratives. (*This is* . . . *vs. These are* . . . appears to establish *this* as an '*is*-form' and these as an '*are*-form'. But whereas we say *This government is* . . . but not *These government are* . . ., we say both *This personnel is* . . . and *These personnel are* . . .) At the very least, if *wheat* is singular and *oats* is plural, then *government* must be either both or neither; and whatever merits or defects that classification may have, it does not accord with the usual application of the terms 'singular' and 'plural'. This is rather typical of the way in which attempts to retain the terminology of traditional grammar while rejecting its notional definitions turn out in the end to be self-defeating. The reasons for refusing to accept the definitions tend to call in question the validity of the terminology.

Moreover, in rejecting a notional definition of singularity and plurality no reason was offered for assuming the definition to entail that objective similarity between referents guarantees similarity of grammatical classification for the words designating the referents. Whatever plausibility the case of *oats* and *wheat* may appear to have as a counterexample depends a great deal on this assumption; that is to say, it is based on the objective similarity of the cereals in question. The same is true of such examples as *foliage* and *leaves*. But what these examples show is that the argument they are invoked to support misrepresents the thesis under attack. What matters in these cases is not objective similarity of the referents, but what the relevant unit is. It would be just as absurd to suppose that if the notional definition were correct then *foliage* 'ought' to be plural, on the ground that foliage comprises more leaves than one, as it would be to suppose that likewise *rain* ought to be plural because rain consists of many drops. All the defender of a notional definition need do here is point out that the fact that there is more than one drop involved does not make it more than one rain, any more than the fact that more than one minister is involved makes it more than one government.

Somewhat different considerations apply to misleading equations such as that of English *hair* with French *cheveux*. This equation is based on the fact that a normal French translation of such a sentence as *His hair is black* would be *Ses cheveux sont noirs*. In other words, these sentences would be used to describe the same state of affairs. But this fact provides no evidence against a notional definition of number. French does have a noun which offers an appropriate parallel to *hair* in *His hair is black* (= *Ses cheveux sont noirs*), and that noun is *chevelure*. Where the two languages differ is in the following respects. First of all, idiomatically it is more usual to say *Ses cheveux sont noirs* than *Sa chevelure est noire*. Secondly, French does not employ *cheveu* to designate a head of hair as well as a single strand of hair, whereas English employs *hair* to designate both. Thus what the equation of English *hair* with French *cheveux* ignores is that *His hair is black* may need to be translated not by *Ses cheveux sont noirs* but by *Son cheveu est noir*.

Arguments adducing counterexamples of the kind discussed above make the mistake of assuming that notional definitions are based on very simplistic claims about the correspondence between language and reality, or between language and some logical classification of things. They then try to show that these claims, although apparently borne out in many instances, are not borne out in others. What is puzzling is how anyone who believed that this was the basis of the traditional distinctions could also have believed that those distinctions would none the less turn out to be appropriate for purposes of describing the structure of *la langue*, and merely needed redefining on more scientific grounds. But combining those beliefs made it possible to have the best of both worlds—a ready-made descriptive apparatus, but no commitment to the unwelcome implications of its definitional basis.

How exactly to distinguish singular from plural will doubtless strike most non-linguists as an exceedingly trivial issue. But it reveals a great deal about the problems modern linguistics brought upon itself by opting to retain the terminology of the traditional grammarian, while trying to opt out of the traditional definitions.

If a traditional distinction like that between singular and plural cannot be defined notionally in the traditional way, it is unclear that it can be defined at all: for at least two reasons. One is that if the distinction is taken to be determined by the structure of the language, it must vary from language to language. Plurality in English cannot correspond to plurality in French or in Latin: for these have inherently different morphological and syntactic systems. Consequently there is no common grammatical basis to support a general definition.

The second reason is that even within a given language, there is no guarantee that the traditional distinction corresponds to any unambivalent principle of grammatical structuring at all. On the contrary, it often appears to be the case that terms like 'singular' and 'plural', once divorced from their traditional notional basis, are left embracing a variety of different and sometimes obscure cases which ought to be distinguished. For instance in English, if *dog vs. dogs* is taken as a standard exemplification of the distinction, it seems fairly clear that *fish vs. fishes* is different. For while it is characteristic that *dog* and *dogs* are not freely interchangeable in examples such as *How many dogs are there?*, precisely that substitutivity is characteristic of the relation between *fish* and *fishes*. Or again, if *dog vs. dogs* is the paradigm, it is unclear whether the nouns in *No smoking* and *No admittance* are singular or not. For they certainly do not seem to admit pluralisation. (One sees no notices which read *No smokings* or *No admittances*.) Likewise, it is not clear whether the distinction between *a dish of carrot* and *a dish of carrots* is a singular-plural distinction, or a different distinction which merely happens to take a similar form. For there is no analogous contrast to be drawn for *dog* and *dogs*. In short, where the morphology of a language does not correlate systematically with its syntax, we are left uncertain how to apply the traditional distinction without covert appeal to notional factors.

This is not an isolated case. We see the same ambivalence over that part of the traditional descriptive apparatus known as the 'parts of speech'. Modern theorists still wanted, for example, to talk about 'nouns'. But they could not afford to accept the traditional account of what nouns were.

Definitions like 'A noun is a word which names things' might be criticised on various counts. Even if the definition were accompanied by supplementary explanations of what 'things' were (for example, that 'things' included persons, places, qualities, actions, and so on) these explanations usually left room for the critic to ask awkward questions. (Is fire really a 'thing'? Or peace? Or hope? Or intention?)[1] He might also question the correlation between nouns and what they were said to name; for example, if nouns are said to name qualities, it might be pointed out that there are words for qualities which are not nouns, but adjectives (*brave, foolish, good*, etc.).[2] Furthermore, it might be represented that a definition of nouns by reference to what they name falls foul of the fact that two sentences of identical meaning may differ in the number of nouns they have (for example, *He suffered terribly* and *His suffering was terrible*).[3] Finally, it could be claimed that we identify words as naming 'things' by examining the grammatical contexts in which words are used, for example, by looking for

---

[1] Palmer, op. cit., p. 39.
[2] C. C. Fries, *The Structure of English*, New York, 1952, p. 67; Palmer, op. cit., p. 39.
[3] Palmer, op. cit., p. 39.

accompanying forms such as *his* or *this*, or by ascertaining whether or not certain words may be made the subject of a sentence.[1] In short, we look for the grammatical characteristics of nouns. Thus the definition of nouns in terms of what they name is a circular one.[2]

Such objections turn out on closer examination to be less damaging than might at first sight appear. For instance, questions as to whether fire is a 'thing', or peace, or hope, or intention, are quite legitimate insofar as they draw attention to the fact that notional definitions of a 'noun' do not usually make explicit reference to physico-chemical changes, or states of affairs, or psychological conditions. None the less, no reason is offered why in principle a notional definition could not be broadened to include these 'things' too. On the other hand, an objection to the inclusion of qualities in the list of 'things' named simply attacks the notional definition by distorting it. Doubtless *brave, foolish* and *good* in expressions like *John is brave, John is foolish* and *John is good* may be described as words for qualities. But it is here open to the traditional grammarian to object that they are not names of qualities in the sense of his definition (as are *bravery, foolishness* and *goodness*). From his point of view the function of adjectives like *brave, foolish* and *good* is to characterise an individual as possessing a certain quality. But they are not on that account names of the qualities in question, any more than *long-necked* is the name of the giraffe.

Similarly, the traditional grammarian will have no great difficulty defending himself against the argument from supposedly synonymous expressions. If challenged to identify the nouns in *He suffered terribly* and *His suffering was terrible* on the basis of a notional definition, his answer will be quite straightforward. The first sentence of the pair tells us that some animate being suffered terribly, but the individual who suffered remains unidentified. The word *he* merely tells us that this individual was male. But there is no part of the sentence which contains the name of that individual or the name of any specific class of individuals to which he belongs. Therefore one may conclude on the basis of the notional definition that in this first sentence there are no nouns. The second sentence of the pair, however, tells us that something was terrible, and it identifies what was terrible by means of an expression which

---

[1] Fries, op. cit., pp. 70–72; Palmer, op. cit., p. 39.
[2] Palmer, op. cit., p. 39.

includes the name of a certain mental or physical condition. The name in question is *suffering*. There is no other name, either of a mental or physical condition, or of anything else. We may conclude, then, that the second sentence contains just one noun, which is the word *suffering*. In short, one sentence of the pair includes an expression (*his suffering*) of a type which is absent from the other. If we were to substitute for it an expression of the type which occurs as subject of the first sentence, we should change *His suffering was terrible* into *It was terrible*. This analysis even suggests a counter-attack available to a defender of the notional definition. The analysis in terms of names, it might be argued, shows us why it was a mistake to suppose in the first place that the two sentences are identical in meaning. What is predicated in the first is not the same as what is predicated in the second: nor is that of which the predications are made the same in both cases. Thus although both sentences might occur in a description of the same event (for example, John's last illness), and the same facts about that event might make both statements true, to conclude on those grounds that the sentences are synonymous would simply be a mistake. The occurrence of a noun in one but not the other is a grammatical reflection of their non-synonymity.

Nor need the traditional grammarian be unduly worried by the claim that identifying nouns by determining whether they name 'things' comes down to looking for the morphological and syntactic features associated with nouns. He will be able to point out that these strategies will not always give the same results, even though they may do so in many cases. For example, in *John wanted to learn why*, the morphological and syntactic evidence for determining whether *why* is a noun is inconclusive. Here *why* occurs in a position which can in principle be occupied by nouns or noun phrases (cf. *John wanted to learn mathematics, John wanted to learn Greek, John wanted to learn the answer*), but also by adverbs (cf. *John wanted to learn quickly*). On the other hand, *why* does not usually combine with articles, possessives or demonstratives, but may occasionally do so (for example, *the why and wherefore*). For similar reasons it would be unclear by these criteria whether *he* in the sentence *He suffered terribly* counted as a noun. If we adopt the notional defini-tion, however, it becomes quite clear that in these examples neither *he* nor *why* are nouns. *He* is not the name of the person who suffered, and nor is *why* the name of what John wanted to learn.

Finally, the charge of circularity seems to be founded on an argument which may be analysed as follows. 1. The notional definition defines nouns by reference to two classes ('words' and 'things') and an asymmetrical relation ('naming'). If we represent the two classes by '*x*' and '*y*', and the relation by 'ϕ', then the definition is of the form: 'Nouns are members of *x* which ϕ members of *y*.' 2. However, this definition does not tell us how to identify members of *y*. 3. In fact, we are able to identify members of *y* by determining what may be ϕ-ed by those members of *x* which are nouns. 4. Therefore, the definition offered is circular.

The conclusion, however, is a mistake. The argument is exactly parallel to the following. 1. Uniforms are defined as dresses of the kind worn by soldiers, policemen and postmen. 2. But this does not tell us how to identify soldiers, policemen and postmen. 3. In fact, we can identify soldiers, policemen and postmen by their uniforms. 4. Therefore, the definition is circular. But the trouble is that how we identify soldiers, policemen and postmen has nothing to do with whether the definition of uniforms is circular. Circular definitions are definitions like 'A twin is a person who has a twin brother or sister', 'An ounce is the weight exactly equivalent to half of two ounces or twice half an ounce', 'Glass-blowing is the art of blowing glass'. These are definitions in which a prior understanding of the definiendum term is required in order to understand the definiens expression. But it can hardly be seriously maintained that one has to understand the term 'noun' as a prior condition for understanding the term 'thing' (or the terms 'person', 'place', 'quality', etc.).

What the argument is really directed against is not the circularity of the notional definition (for there is no circularity), but rather the difficulty of applying the definition in particular instances. This, however, is quite a different matter. Judges or juries may occasionally find it difficult, on the basis of the legal definition of a certain crime, to decide whether or not defendants are guilty of it. That does not show that the legal definition is circular. Nor does it mean that the definition is inadequate. It may simply be in the nature of the offence that the kind of evidence available is often likely to be contentious or inconclusive. *Mutatis mutandis* the same problem may arise for grammatical definitions.

It is therefore difficult to believe that objections of the kind which modern theorists raise would have caused any intelligent traditional grammarian much embarrassment. Whether in practice reliance on notional definitions made the traditional grammarian more prone to confuse questions of grammar with questions of meaning may perhaps be doubted. Certainly, such confusions are by no means always avoided by present-day theorists. Even those who take care to distinguish between the grammatical and the semantic implications of classificatory terms are sometimes misled by the traditional terminology. For instance, a distinction may be drawn between [+ Masculine] and [− Masculine] as semantic feature specifications and as grammatical feature specifications. In some languages both specifications may be utilised, but are not to be equated. Thus in French the noun *femme* ('woman') must be classified as [− Masculine] in two different respects. In one respect, *femme* would thus be classed with *fille* ('daughter'), *tante* ('aunt'), *impératrice* ('empress'), and all other French nouns for which the feature [− Masculine] is part of the specification of the meaning of the lexical item. But in the other respect *femme* would be classed not only with *fille*, *tante*, and *impératrice*, but also with *sentinelle* ('sentinel'), in which the feature [− Masculine] reflects the fact that the accompanying form of the definite article is not *le*, the corresponding form of the adjective is not *beau*, and so on. In French a noun like *table* ('table') will be classified as [− Masculine] in the second respect, but not in the first, for as far as the semantic feature specification of this noun is concerned, the distinction between [+ Masculine] and [− Masculine] does not apply. None the less, it is sometimes claimed that a sentence like *Le professeur est enceinte* ('The teacher is pregnant') breaks a grammatical rule.[1] Such cases arise when a noun which is semantically unspecified in terms of the distinction between [+ Masculine] and [− Masculine], but grammatically [+ Masculine], happens to be coupled with an adjective which occurs only in what is traditionally regarded as the Feminine form, for example, *enceinte*. What has happened here is that the traditional classification 'Feminine' has been translated as grammatically [− Masculine] as well as semantically [− Masculine]. Once this translation is questioned, it becomes obvious that it is absurd to claim that *Le professeur est enceinte* involves a

[1] D. T. Langendoen, *The Study of Syntax*, New York, 1969, pp. 39–40.

non-agreement between noun and adjective. There is no more infringement of a grammatical rule here than in a case like *La dame est incroyable* ('The lady is incredible'), where, equally, no distinctive form of the adjective is available to match the gender classification of the noun, *incroyable* being an invariable singular form.

To sum up, the cudgels which modern linguistics seized in order to give notional definitions a ritual beating turn out on examination to be suspiciously fragile. This is no accident. Had they been stouter, or more vigorously wielded, there might have been serious damage to the traditional framework of grammatical description, which it was in everyone's interests to preserve. That may explain the half-hearted apologies for traditional grammar which are occasionally offered by modern theorists. For example, it is sometimes said that what was wrong with the use of notional definitions is not their irrelevance, but rather that grammatical analysis was thus tackled 'the wrong way round'. In other words, to base grammatical analysis on semantic criteria was to work from what is inherently less systematisable towards what is more so, instead of vice versa. 'The objection to traditional grammar in this respect is not so much that it did the wrong thing, as that it went about it the wrong way . . .'[1] At least one modern writer has defended notional definitions of the traditional parts of speech, with the proviso that they be understood as terminological labels and not as criteria for determining membership of syntactic classes. On this view,[2] once a syntactic class has been established on distributional grounds, if it is found that all or the majority of lexical items designating persons, places and things fall within this class, then the members of this class may be termed 'nouns' in accordance with the traditional notional definition. In other words, if the linguist can establish that the 'formal' word class X and the 'notional' word class A are related in such a way that A is mainly or wholly included in X, then it is reasonable to give X the designation suggested by the notional definition of A.

This view comes perhaps closest to recognising the role which the notional definitions fulfilled in traditional grammatical studies. In most cases it would be simply a mistake to suppose that such definitions were intended to provide criteria for classifying forms and

[1] Robins, op. cit., pp. 276–7.
[2] J. Lyons, *Introduction to Theoretical Linguistics*, Cambridge, 1968, pp. 317–18.

constructions. To this extent, the questions about the validity of these definitions which modern theorists are fond of asking fall into the same category as 'When did you stop beating your wife?' The character of the notional definitions of the parts of speech was pointed out in 1892 by Henry Sweet: they are for the most part etymologies. Sweet illustrates his point by showing that four out of five definitions of the term *preposition* given by contemporary grammar books included reference to the fact that prepositions precede the words they govern; whereas no one, as Sweet observed, would suppose that Latin *tenus*, which is normally postposed, is on that account not a preposition.[1] The fact is that traditional grammarians were not the dupes of notional definitions in the way that some moderns like to suppose, but were for the most part well aware of the discrepancies between the notional components in question and the corresponding grammatical facts.

As regards the view that traditional grammar, in adopting notional definitions, embarked on linguistic analysis from 'the wrong end', an important distinction must be drawn. It is essential not to confuse analytic procedures with definitional theory. The preference for starting from the phonic side in linguistic analysis is sometimes defended on the ground that 'expression' phenomena are directly observable, and hence statements about them can be more easily checked than statements about semantic aspects of language. What is doubtless true is that the sounds a person utters or the words he writes are public phenomena, whereas what is going on in his mind is not a public performance of any kind. Thus in one sense linguistic analysis must start from what is said or what is written. But it does not follow that the formal features of a language are available to inspection, whereas the semantic features are hidden. From a Saussurean point of view, that would not only be a naive assumption, but a confusion of *langue* with *parole*. The consonant phonemes of English are no more 'directly observable' than are, for example, the meanings of English prepositions. Whether it may be more convenient to begin one's analysis of English with the consonant phonemes or with the meanings of prepositions is a quite different matter. Similarly, although it may be useful to take the notion 'more than one' as a guide to the identification of plural forms in English, Saussurean structuralism in no way admits the

[1] *A New English Grammar*, pt. I, Oxford, 1892, pp. vi–vii.

legitimacy of defining English plurals in terms of the notion 'more than one'. For 'more than one' is a notion which can be given a precise interpretation independently of the structure of any particular language. From a Saussurean standpoint, whatever the grammatical difference may be between, for example, *horse* and *horses*, or between *cheval* and *chevaux*, it cannot be stated in terms of a language-neutral distinction which simply contrasts designating a single item with designating more than one. Whoever may be guilty of confusing methodological convenience with theoretical principle, this is not a mistake that can be laid at the door of Saussure. His position is quite clear. In defining the elements and relations of *la langue*, no priority can be given either to form or to meaning.

The remarks on the traditional parts of speech in the *Cours de linguistique générale* summarise with admirable clarity the whole dilemma of linguistics *vis-à-vis* traditional grammar. Saussure picks on the problem of whether, in the French sentence *Ces gants sont bon marché* ('These gloves are cheap'), the expression *bon marché* is an adjective. From one point of view, we can say that it consists of an adjective *bon* ('good') plus a noun *marché* ('market'). But this analysis, as Saussure observes, explains nothing. From another point of view, a logical point of view, *bon marché* does on the other hand function adjectivally to say something about the gloves. But yet, from another—morphological and syntactic—point of view, it does not behave in the manner typical of French adjectives: it is invariable, it never precedes its noun, etc. What conclusion can be drawn? It must be, says Saussure, that the traditional division of words into nouns, verbs, adjectives, etc., does not correspond to any undeniable linguistic reality. And yet, of necessity, linguistics is condemned to work constantly with 'concepts forged by the grammarians, without knowing whether or not they really correspond to constituent elements in the system of *la langue*'.[1]

Saussure's view of traditional grammar makes an interesting contrast with that of his generativist successors half a century later. In place of Saussure's reluctant acceptance of the old pedagogic distinctions *faute de mieux*, we find instead their confident endorsement: not merely as providing a convenient basis for descriptive

---

[1] *Cours*, pp. 152–3.

presentation, but as capturing essential facts of a speaker's knowledge of grammar.

The longevity of the traditional grammatical terminology and its facile adaptation to the requirements of modern linguistics is nowhere more strikingly illustrated than by the kind of account that transformational theorists were still offering in the mid-1960s of examples like *Sincerity may frighten the boy*. The transformationalists' analysis concurred entirely (on their own estimation) with that of the traditional grammarian on at least the following points:

    (i) *Sincerity may frighten the boy* is a 'sentence',
    (ii) In that 'sentence', *frighten the boy* is a 'verb phrase',
    (iii) In this 'verb phrase', *frighten* is the 'verb',
    (iv) *sincerity* is a 'noun phrase',
    (v) *the boy* is a 'noun phrase',
    (vi) In the 'noun phrase' *the boy*, *boy* is a 'noun',
    (vii) In the 'noun phrase' *the boy*, *the* is a 'determiner',
  (viii) *sincerity* is a 'noun',
    (ix) *the* is an 'article',
    (x) *may* is a 'verbal auxiliary',
    (xi) *may* is a 'modal',
    (xii) *sincerity* is the 'subject' of the 'sentence',
  (xiii) *frighten the boy* is the 'predicate' of the 'sentence',
  (xiv) *the boy* is the 'object' of the 'verb phrase',
   (xv) *frighten* is the 'main verb',
  (xvi) *sincerity* is the 'subject' of the 'verb' *frighten*,
 (xvii) *the boy* is the 'object' of the 'verb' *frighten*,
(xviii) *boy* is a 'count noun',
  (xix) *boy* is a 'common noun',
   (xx) *boy* is an 'animate noun',
  xxi) *boy* is a 'human noun',
 (xxii) *frighten* is a 'transitive verb',
(xxiii) *frighten* is a 'verb' that does not freely permit 'object deletion',
(xxiv) *frighten* is a 'verb' freely used in the 'progressive aspect',
 (xxv) *frighten* allows 'abstract subjects',
(xxvi) *frighten* allows 'human objects'.

This impressive list appears to demonstrate that, given even a minute fragment of English as a sample, modern linguistics can straight away confirm the traditional grammarian's analysis on at least twenty or so specific points. According to Chomsky,[1] all the

---

[1] N. Chomsky, *Aspects of the Theory of Syntax*, Cambridge, Mass., 1965, pp. 63–4.

above 'information' supplied by the traditional grammarian is 'without question, substantially correct'.

This is a very instructive pronouncement. Whether or not it does justice to the traditional grammarian, it reveals a great deal about the status of the descriptive statements which contemporary linguistics has to offer. The example itself, *Sincerity may frighten the boy*, yields a number of significant clues. Unlike Saussure's *Ces gants sont bon marché*, it is not something one can readily imagine being said in everyday circumstances. Asking a random selection of non-linguists what they think the example means produces an interesting variety of answers. Some people appear to think it means that the boy in question may be frightened if someone else shows sincerity. Others appear to think it means that the boy may be scared to say what he really thinks. Others doubt whether it means anything ('meaningless', 'nonsense', 'gibberish'). Still others simply 'don't know' what it means. Even those who think they do know sometimes appear to find it puzzling in some way. The fact is that the example has, as Firth would have put it, 'no implication of utterance'. It thus seems clear that what the statements (i)–(xxvi) above must be about, in the final analysis, is not something which English speakers do say, or have said, or have heard said, or even understand; but about a decontextualised abstraction of some kind, represented by a sequence of English words. '*Sincerity may frighten the boy*' is what this abstraction is called.

If this is right, it follows that one must first of all identify the abstraction in order to be in any position to assess exactly what the statements (i)–(xxvi) are claiming. Secondly, it will be essential to discover whether the abstraction the transformationalist is talking about is the same as the abstraction the traditional grammarian is alleged to have been talking about, irrespective of whether transformationalist and traditional grammarian both refer to it in the same way. If not, any contention that transformational theory 'confirms' the traditional grammarian's analysis becomes a very curious one. The atom of Rutherford was manifestly not the atom of Democritus, in spite of going by the same name. Hence it would be very curious to maintain, for example, that modern physics confirms as 'without question, substantially correct' the account of matter given in *De Rerum Natura*.

As to what abstraction '*Sincerity may frighten the boy*' might perhaps designate, there are many possibilities: a class of utterances, an utterance-type, a statement-type, a class of written word-sequences, a class of strings of printed letters, an abstraction somehow 'in between' speech and writing, and so on. But without going into the complex question of the extent to which the traditional grammarian's conception of what he was making statements about corresponded to the transformationalist's conception, what can more easily be ascertained is that different grammarians themselves defined such terms as 'noun', 'verb', 'sentence', etc., in different ways. Consequently, to assume that statements of the type 'x is a noun' had one standard interpretation throughout the Western tradition, and hence that traditional grammarians who used the classification 'noun' were all really 'saying the same thing', is to move to yet a further plane of meta-abstraction. That any equation at all should be set up between the 'information' allegedly supplied by traditional grammar and the 'facts to be accounted for by a grammatical theory'[1] is itself the most eloquent indication of the kind of thinking about language which is involved.

The transformationalist's claim to be at one with the traditional grammarian makes no sense except in the context of a certain metaphysics of language studies, which is best described as the counterpart of Platonic realism. Ideal realities are postulated to fit existing abstractions. Hence ideal grammatical entities are postulated in order to underwrite the grammarian's generalisations. But all ideal realities need a heaven where they can exist in tranquillity, accessible to contemplation but immune from observation. For such linguistic realities, heaven could have no better location than the mind of the (ideal) language-user.

A development of this kind is not altogether surprising. Once Saussure had redefined the science of language as being first and foremost a science of synchronic systems, only two plausible courses were open. One course would have involved a complete break with the academic past, and left the new science with the enormous task of constructing its own methodology and descriptive apparatus *ex nihilo*. Unfortunately, one cannot claim to have a science if none of its practitioners is quite sure how to do it. The alternative was to accept the descriptive legacy of the Western grammatical tradition, and rehabilitate the efforts of its much maligned pedagogues. It was

---

[1] Chomsky, op. cit., p. 208.

eventually the adoption of a Platonic metaphysics of language studies which made this rehabilitation theoretically respectable. Retrospectively, it could now be claimed that there were certain unchanging linguistic realities which validated the work of the traditional grammarian all the time, without his realising it. In order to teach his pupils Latin, he had been obliged to devise descriptive classifications which respected those realities. Thus was the debt owed by modern linguistics to the Western pedagogical tradition ultimately justified.

It is not the spuriousness of the justification which matters here, but the *de facto* continuity which such a justification both acknowledges and seeks to validate. By taking over the basic framework of analysis which the Western grammatical tradition offered, modern linguistics took over also—and unavoidably—a certain way of looking at linguistic ability, for which this analytic framework had originally been designed. The perspective is one which effectively precludes any representation of language as a creative process, because it is not the normal perspective of the language-user. It is restricted to looking at languages 'from the outside', as the traditional grammarian had to. His task was to reduce languages to systematised bodies of information and instructions, which can be taught to a learner. The learner is presumed already to understand—or to be able to find out for himself—what language is. All he needs to be taught are the specific details of the particular language he is learning. His grasp of the communicational requirements intrinsic to language is simply taken for granted. One does not inquire into his creative capacity for language, because it is presupposed. Furthermore—and this is the crux of the matter—it is presupposed in a certain way: namely, as a capacity for using languages. The distinction between a language and its use, like the distinction between a language and its acquisition, is a theoretical artifact of the tradition.

*　　*　　*

The conflict between traditional grammar and the requirements of the new scientific theory of internalised linguistic knowledge shows up clearly when it comes to explaining what it is for an utterance to conform to a 'grammatical rule'. On the old view, grammatical rules were simply do's and don'ts to follow if you wanted on the one hand to avoid the linguistic mistakes typical of children, foreigners or the uneducated, and on the other hand to use the language with the authenticity characteristic of the 'best' speakers. A linguistics which rejected normative pedagogy and at the same time internalised linguistic knowledge created for itself the problem of devising a new explication of 'grammaticality'. Saussure never solved this problem, and it has continued to pester his generativist successors. Some have claimed to be able to distinguish 'degrees' of grammaticality. Others have held grammaticality to be relative to certain assumptions about the nature of the world. Those who reject this 'grammatical relativism' contend that the grammaticality or otherwise of an utterance is inherent 'in the language' and does not depend on extralinguistic facts or beliefs. But these disputes tend to obfuscate rather than clarify the issue.

To speak of the 'grammatical intuitions' of the native speaker merely transposes the obfuscation on to a psychological level. For it is quite unclear what it means to say that native speakers have 'intuitions' of grammaticality, unless these intuitions can be distinguished from, for example, semantic intuitions, stylistic intuitions, or any other kinds of intuition about what it is appropriate to say and in what circumstances. Consequently to maintain, as generativists have done, that the principle aim of a descriptive grammar is to specify all and only the grammatical sentences of the language becomes quite vacuous. It is to treat a language as if it were, on the formal plane, a closed logistic system of the type devised for purposes of mathematical logic, within which the 'well-formedness' of a formula can be 'proved'. But the fact is quite simply that the languages used in everyday life are not enormously blown-up logistic systems. On the contrary, logistic systems are drastically cut-down versions of everyday languages. And an essential purpose of the cutting-down is to provide the logician with a limited, self-contained decontextualised system within which the procedures of mathematical proof can be manipulated.

Thus to interpret 'grammaticality' as some psychophysical counterpart to well-formedness in a mathematical system is to foist a grotesquely inappropriate analogy upon linguistic behaviour as a whole. Furthermore, it is not even an analogy which provides a viable solution to the problem it was supposed to deal with.

To take a very simple example, suppose Pierre is learning

English under the hypothetical tutelage of some archetypal 'traditional grammarian' of the old school. Pierre comes across for the first time the word *dealer*. It occurs in a book he was looking at, in the sentence 'He bought the clock from an antique dealer'. What, Pierre asks his tutor, is this word *dealer*? His tutor then explains to him that *dealer* is a noun, based on the verb *deal* meaning 'to trade, to do business', and that just as the noun *singer* means 'one who sings' so the noun *dealer* means 'one who deals'. The term *antique dealer*, therefore, means 'one who trades or does business in antiques'. Pierre is also told by his tutor that the noun *dealer* has a regular plural in -*s*, admits anaphoric pronouns and possessives of either gender, and so on. When Pierre has assimilated all this information, he will know everything there is to know about the grammar of the word *dealer*, in the traditional sense, and he will also know what the dictionary gives as one of the meanings of this word.

Anxious to make good use of his newly acquired piece of English, in his next composition exercise Pierre proudly produces the sentence: 'I order my newspaper from the newspaper dealer.' He is then crestfallen to learn at correction time that this is not what an Englishman would say.[1] But now, he wants to know, where did he go wrong? According to what his tutor had told him, he had carefully observed the grammatical rules pertaining to the noun *dealer*, and also its meaning.

At this point, any old-fashioned grammarian—if honest—would have to tell Pierre that there is much more to learning English than just learning the grammar of the words and their dictionary meanings. Anyone who wants to be able to speak English like an Englishman and not like a foreigner also has to acquire a great deal of information about how English is used, including *inter alia* that the man who runs a newspaper shop is not called a 'newspaper dealer', but a 'newsagent'.

Information of this kind is extremely difficult to accommodate convincingly in any theory which treats a language as the product of a decontextualised system of rules generating all and only the sentences of the language. If *I order my newspaper from the newspaper dealer* is to be excluded from the set of English sentences, it has to be shown that it infringes some rule of English (phonological,

---

[1] More exactly, not what a speaker of British English would say. (The expression *newspaper dealer* is used in American English.)

grammatical, or semantic). On the other hand, if it is allowed to be included in the set of English sentences, then the rules manifestly do not provide a fully adequate theory of English, in the sense that they fail to distinguish between the utterances of a native speaker of English and the utterances a foreigner might produce but a native speaker would not.

The decision to exclude *I order my newspaper from the newspaper dealer* from the sentences of English is tantamount to claiming that the information supplied by Pierre's tutor does not capture the 'internalised rules' which native speakers of English have mastered. In other words, the string of words is in some way ungrammatical or semantically anomalous. But then the question arises: what grammatical or semantic rule of English does the phrase *newspaper dealer* violate? For it certainly appears to conform to all the requirements governing the syntax of animate agent nouns.

For example, *Smith is a newspaper dealer* is not at all like, say, *Smith is a courage dealer*, or *Smith is a Germany dealer*, or *Smith is a thirteen dealer*, each of which might be held to infringe a rule prohibiting the occurrence of a noun of some syntactically definable subclass (that is to say, abstracts, proper names, and numbers) in the slot before *dealer*. But if the three examples just cited are ungrammatical in English, they are ungrammatical for exactly the same reasons as, respectively, *Smith is a courage owner*, *Smith is a Germany owner*, and *Smith is a thirteen owner*. Whereas *Smith is a newspaper dealer* no more violates these rules than does *Smith is a newspaper owner*. So it seems that what is happening if it is claimed that *Smith is a newspaper dealer* breaks a grammatical rule of English is simply that a rule is postulated prohibiting just the combination of *newspaper* and *dealer*. The explanatory value of such a move is nil. It merely devalues the notion of a 'grammatical rule'.

Nor would it be any more plausible to treat *newspaper dealer* as analogous at the phrase level to a form like *blick* at the morpheme level; that is to say, as a 'possible' or 'potential' expression of the language, which is none the less not an 'actual' expression. This would not do because, in the first place, it simply amounts to conceding that *Smith is a newspaper dealer* is, after all, grammatical; and that leaves no explanation of its oddity that a grammarian can give. But, secondly, the comparison is false in any case. For the reason why *blick* lurks in the shadow world of 'non-actual morphemes' is that although it conforms to the phonological rules of English, it has no morphological status: we cannot say whether it is a noun, or a verb, or a suffix, or what it is; whereas it is perfectly clear exactly what the morphological and syntactic characteristics of the elements in *newspaper dealer* are, and also what the status of the resultant combination is.

A different possibility would be to treat *newspaper dealer* as the normally unrealised member of a neutralisation; that is to say, as analogous to a form like /sbin/ which may be regarded as the unrealised counterpart of *spin* (since the phonemes /p/ and /b/, according to orthodox analyses, do not stand in opposition after initial sibilants in English). But this analogy will not hold up either. For the non-occurrence of /sbin/ is a particular example of a more general rule governing the phonemes in question. Whereas there is no comparable generalisation from which the non-occurrence of *newspaper dealer* could have been predicted.

Finally, it would not be very convincing either to claim that *Smith is a newspaper dealer*, although syntactically well formed, is semantically anomalous. For there is no apparent incompatibility between the meanings of the words *newspaper* and *dealer*. Thus *Smith is a newspaper dealer* is not on a par with semantically dubious combinations like *Smith is a surcharge dealer*, or *Smith is a conclusion dealer*, or *Smith is a climate dealer*. If it were, then it ought to be the case that *Smith is a dealer in newspapers* is equally dubious from a semantic point of view, as are *Smith is a dealer in surcharges*, *Smith is a dealer in conclusions*, and *Smith is a dealer in climates*. But in that case it would be hard to account for the definition of the word *newsagent* given in the *Shorter Oxford English Dictionary*, which is: 'a regular dealer in newspapers and periodicals'.

This appears to exhaust the possibilities of excluding *Smith is a newspaper dealer* from the sentences of English on linguistic grounds. The alternative would be to try to explain its non-occurrence on extralinguistic grounds. The difficulty here is that there are no obvious extralinguistic reasons for its non-occurrence either. That is to say, *Smith is a newspaper dealer* is not like, say, *Smith is a pollen dealer*. The latter is also a form of words which does not normally occur in English. But that is because there happen to be no pollen dealers; that is to say, our commercial system has no use for the organised marketing of pollen. Whereas the fact that English speakers say *Smith is a newsagent* and not *Smith is a newspaper dealer* is not to be explained by reference to the nature of our commercial system. The non-occurrence of *Smith is a newspaper dealer* is in some sense a linguistic fact; but it is not a linguistic fact which can be satisfactorily explained within the confines of a bi-planar theory of language.

Examples like *newspaper dealer* might be multiplied endlessly. There are very many combinations of English words which native speakers of English never spontaneously use, even when apparent opportunities for using them occur, and despite the fact that their use would not run counter to any general patterns or regularities of English word combination. That *newsagent* and not *newspaper dealer* is the usual expression employed in (British) English to describe someone who runs a shop where newspapers are sold is something which has no explanation in terms of syntactic or semantic rules. It is simply a fact of English usage: a fact of the kind which grammarians of antiquity sometimes referred to by the terms *consuetudo* or *usus loquendi*. The attempt to subsume such facts under 'grammar', and thus place them on a par with, for example, rules of agreement for gender and number, merely illustrates the confusion produced by attempts to reinterpret the traditional notion of grammaticality in terms of some internalised principle of combinatorial structuring which organises the totality of the formal content of a native speaker's knowledge of his language.

A complementary aspect of this confusion is to be seen in the insistence by some generative theorists that certain combinations of words are grammatical, even though nonsensical. The classic example of this in modern discussions of the topic is: *Colourless green ideas sleep furiously.*[1] Whether or not it is a good example, it shows the rather desperate extremes to which modern linguistics was driven to try to justify treating grammaticality as an independent formal property. At the same time it shows all too plainly the self-defeating character of such attempts. For whatever else may be said about *Colourless green ideas sleep furiously*, what is obvious is that only by regarding it as not (entirely) nonsensical is there any hope of detecting grammatical structure in it at all.

If such an example is to be taken seriously, the first question

---

[1] N. Chomsky, *Syntactic Structures*, The Hague, 1957, p. 15.

which it raises is to what extent it conforms to English usage. It certainly conforms to English usage inasmuch as, individually, the words are English words. But in that respect *Colourless green ideas sleep furiously* is no different from *Furiously sleep ideas green colourless* (which, so it is claimed,[1] is both nonsensical and ungrammatical).

If we go on to ask whether the combinations *green ideas* or *sleep furiously* (as distinct from *ideas green* or *furiously sleep*) conform to English usage, we shall doubtless be able upon investigation to ascertain such facts as the following. In the English-speaking community, talk which involves distinguishing the colour of ideas occurs mainly in political contexts, and talk which involves distinguishing various ways of sleeping is mainly concerned either with distinguishing different positions of the body during sleep, or with whether the sleep is complete, interrupted, disturbed by dreams, etc. We may go on to inquire which English colour-words are commonly used to talk about the colour of ideas, and we shall find that *green* is not among them. Similarly, we shall find that the English words commonly used to distinguish various positions of sleeping and qualities of sleep do not include *furiously*.

This presents a difficulty for the thesis that *Colourless green ideas sleep furiously* is both grammatical and nonsensical. For if the concept of *Colourless green ideas sleep furiously* as a sentence is not the concept of some unit of which *green ideas* and *sleep furiously* (as combinations distinct from *ideas green* and *furiously sleep*) form part, then it is quite unclear how the words *Colourless green ideas sleep furiously* are to be taken as forming a sentence, and hence even less clear what is involved in the claim that they are grammatical. If there just are no such expressions as *green ideas* and *sleep furiously* in English usage, then *Colourless green ideas sleep furiously* can hardly be even the formal half of a non-existent English sentence. But if, on the other hand, the contention is that although this is not commonly the case in English discourse, certain ideas none the less 'could'—perhaps poetically, metaphorically, or jocularly—be described as green, and sleep 'could' likewise be said in some circumstances to be furious, then the claim that the phrases *green ideas* and *sleep furiously* are nonsensical in English fails. In short, we cannot tell whether words are grammatically appropriate

[1] ibid.

to what they were intended to say unless we can tell what that was: and if we think we can tell from the words themselves what it was they were intended to say, then to that extent we have already demonstrated that they were not just nonsense. The grammarian cannot have it both ways.

To ask whether combinations of words which are *ex hypothesi* nonsense none the less conform to grammatical rules simply begs the question of whether it is coherent in such cases to talk about language rules at all. It is rather like asking whether, when football is played by teams of convicts chained together round the ankles to prevent their escaping, the chain counts as part of the boot for purposes of deciding fouls. The fact is that football is not played by teams of convicts chained together, so the question does not arise.

There is, of course, nothing to prevent a philosophically inclined sports enthusiast from asking what would be the rule if football were played under such conditions. But the only way an answer can be obtained is by writing to the F.A. for a ruling, and the chances of obtaining one will be slim. Analogously, someone who is speculatively inclined can, if he so wishes, ask whether, if to utter the words *green ideas* were to talk nonsense, it would none the less be in conformity with the grammatical rules for English nonsense. But it is difficult to see who decides the grammatical rules for English nonsense, or indeed what point there is in having any. Being able to encode and decode many different pieces of English nonsense is not one of the tests by which we recognise a fluent speaker of English, any more than knowing many possible ways of getting sums wrong is one of the tests by which we recognise a competent mathematician.

Of recent years, determinacy of linguistic form at the grammatical level has been questioned even within the generativist school, by advocates of 'non-discrete' or 'fuzzy' grammar. The implicit assumption of orthodox generative theory had been that the traditional word classes, such as 'noun', 'verb' and 'adjective', were 'discrete' classes; that is to say, that a word either is or is not a 'noun', either is or is not a 'verb', either is or is not an 'adjective', and so on for as many classes as the grammarian recognises. But this assumption, its critics argued, forces an arbitrarily rigid classification upon the facts. In many instances, a word exhibits only a certain number of the shared syntactic properties which are held to be typical for membership of a given class. Thus it will be only 'up to a point' classifiable as a 'noun', 'verb', 'adjective', etc.

For example, the words *near* and *opposite* have a status intermediate between that of the typical English verb and the typical English adjective. Like verbs, they can take an object complement without a preposition:[1]

> *The shed is near the barn.*
> *The Post Office is opposite the bank.*

On the other hand, like adjectives, they can also take an object complement introduced by a preposition:

> *The shed is near to the barn.*
> *The Post Office is opposite from the bank.*

In this respect, they are neither 'true' verbs nor 'true' adjectives, but share syntactic properties with both.

Likewise, it has been argued that the distinction in English between 'auxiliary' and 'verb' is non-discrete, for there are words which are intermediate in status. These include what is traditionally treated as the commonest 'verb' of all, *to be*. For this behaves like a typical 'auxiliary' in having contracted forms with a negative (e.g. *isn't*: cf. *can't*), but like a typical 'verb' in taking *to* before an infinitive (e.g. *They are to arrive tomorrow*: cf. *They can arrive tomorrow*), and in showing inflection for person and number in the present tense.[2]

Many examples of grammatical indeterminacy of this kind have been adduced in support of replacing the concept of discrete grammatical classes by the concept of 'category squishes'; a squish being a continuum or scale, along which the syntactic behaviour of words may be plotted as 'more nouny' or 'less nouny', 'more verby' or 'less verby', and so on.

Analogous considerations hold for the application of grammatical rules. Just as different words may exhibit different 'degrees' of belonging to a grammatical class, so rules may apply in different degrees in different types of case. It has also been argued not only

---

[1] J. R. Ross, 'The category squish; Endstation Hauptwort', *Papers from the Eighth Regional Meeting, Chicago Linguistic Society*, Chicago, 1972, pp. 316–28.
[2] A. Radford, 'On the nondiscrete nature of the verb-auxiliary distinction in English', *Nottingham Linguistic Circular*, 5, 1976, pp. 8–19.

that differences between grammatical classes are non-discrete, but that, for example, the difference between nouns and clauses is one of degree.[1] These indeterminacies are held to explain uncertainties and variations in speakers' judgments concerning what can and cannot be said in their native language. 'Almost every syntactic or semantic phenomenon,' it has been claimed, 'has a shadowy area in which speakers become unclear with respect to judgments about meaning and well-formedness.'[2]

Various options are open to theorists who wish to defend a discrete model of grammar against the charge that it cannot account for 'squishy' or 'fuzzy' phenomena. One is to reinterpret such phenomena as the complex products of a variety of discretely defined factors. Another is simply to increase the number of discrete distinctions and rules available, until all allegedly intermediate cases are separately accommodated. In this respect, the argument between partisans of non-discrete grammar and their opponents ultimately ends in stalemate.

Of more interest in the present context is to observe how the partisans of non-discrete grammar, for all their criticism of the traditional distinctions, cling to two notions. One is that grammaticality is still measurable (albeit approximately) by taking the traditional parts of speech as reference points. 'Nouns' and 'verbs' are abolished, only to be replaced by 'nouniness' and 'verbiness'. The other is that grammaticality is measurable in some kind of communicational vacuum. Hypothetical utterances are compared without any reference to the kind of context in which they would be likely to occur, or their appropriateness to that context. Usages of different styles, registers and periods are juxtaposed. (The improbable example *Sarah is like unto a bumblebee* has been compared to *Sarah is like a bumblebee* in order to demonstrate that *like* is a 'preposition-deleting adjective' of the same kind as *near* and *opposite*.)[3] The grammatical properties of an arbitrary string of words are believed to constitute a subset which forms the basis of speakers' judgments, independently of any other properties the

[1] J. R. Ross, 'Nouniness', *Three Dimensions of Linguistic Theory*, ed. O. Fujimura, Tokyo, 1973.

[2] G. Lakoff, 'Fuzzy grammar and the performance/competence terminology game', *Papers from the Ninth Regional Meeting, Chicago Linguistic Society*, Chicago, 1973, p. 271.

[3] Ross, 'The category squish...', p. 317.

example may have, and even though no one is clear about which the grammatical properties are. Thus vaguely defined 'degrees of grammaticality' make the normative legacy of Priscian and Donatus scientifically respectable after all. The language myth is decried in one form, only to be immediately acclaimed in another.

Chapter Four

Form and Meaning

By abandoning the historian's perspective, but at the same time being unwilling to accept the consequences of adopting entirely the language-user's perspective, modern linguistic theory involved itself in a number of awkward compromises. The most crucial of these concerned the contents of this abstract system of linguistic knowledge (*la langue*) which hypothetically underlay verbal communication between members of a given community. The key question here was to decide how much of the communicational process was supposed to be accounted for by knowledge of the language.

The Saussurean answer to this question takes a very simple view of the communicational process itself. It is a view in all essentials analogous to that put forward in the seventeenth century by Locke, which assumes that communication is a matter of transferring thoughts from one person's mind to another's. Accordingly, the function of a language is seen as being to provide the mechanisms for this transference. In Locke's estimation, the universal purpose of speech exchange is to reach a common understanding, and this is achieved when the words uttered by the speaker 'excite the same ideas in the hearer which he makes them stand for in speaking'.[1] Moreover, Locke held that this was also the language-user's view. Men 'suppose their words to be marks of the ideas in the minds also of other men, with whom they communicate; for else they should talk in vain, and could not be understood, if the sounds they applied to one idea were such as by the hearer were applied to another, which is to speak two languages'.[2]

Saussure's unquestioning acceptance of this telementational

[1] *An Essay Concerning Human Understanding*, 1690, III, ii, 8.
[2] ibid., III, ii, 4.

model is epitomised in the well-known diagram of the 'speech circuit' (*circuit de la parole*) in the *Cours de linguistique générale*. Its interpretation is given as follows:

The starting point of the circuit is in the brain of one (person), call him *A*, where facts of consciousness, which we shall call concepts, are associated with representations of linguistic signs or acoustic images, by means of which they may be expressed. Let us suppose that a given concept triggers in the brain a corresponding acoustic image: this is an entirely *psychological* phenomenon, followed in due course by a *physiological* process: the brain transmits to the organs of phonation an impulse corresponding to that image; then sound waves are propagated from *A*'s mouth to *B*'s ear—a purely physical process. Next, the circuit continues in *B* in inverse order: from ear to brain the physiological transmission of the acoustic image; in the brain the psychological association of this image with the corresponding concept. If *B* speaks in turn, this new act will follow—from his brain to *A*'s—exactly the same progression as the first, and will pass through the same consecutive phases . . .[1]

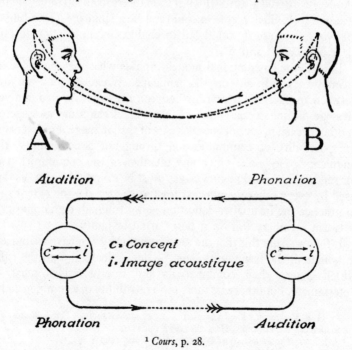

Audition   Phonation

c ▪ *Concept*
i ▪ *Image acoustique*

Phonation   Audition

[1] *Cours*, p. 28.

Saussure's diagram could well stand as an illustration of what has been called Locke's 'translation theory' of understanding.[1]

The same telementational model survives as a basis for transformational grammar. According to Katz, 'linguistic communication consists in the production of some external, publicly observable acoustic phenomenon whose phonetic and syntactic structure encodes a speaker's inner private thoughts or ideas and the decoding of the phonetic and syntactic structure exhibited in such a physical phenomenon by other speakers, in the form of an inner private experience of the same thoughts or ideas'.[2]

One immediate consequence of accepting the Lockean view of verbal communication is that it imposes very strict constraints on what a language is conceived to be. For communication could not work in this way at all without a predetermined plan, which ensures in advance that the hearer will be able to receive exactly the idea which the speaker intends to convey. It would not do to have a system under which, typically, when *A* wished to convey the idea of a knife, he uttered a word which *B* then interpreted as conveying the idea of a fork. Such a system could not be a language, according to this view, because it would fail to enable communication to take place between *A* and *B*.

Thus the telementational model imposes what may be called an 'invariance condition' on the language. Whatever may vary as between speaker and hearer, or between the conveyance of a given message on one occasion and conveyance of the same message on another occasion, cannot count as part of the language. For to ensure the possibility of communication throughout a community, the linguistic 'code-book' which any member of the community uses for sending and receiving messages must be exactly the same as that used by every other member, at least in theory. To the extent that in practice the invariance condition is not fulfilled, communication between members will be at best partial or faulty.

It follows from this that the ideal community will have a language in which all the basic units must be determinate and all the rules which govern their combinations and interpretations must be determinate. For otherwise there is no possibility of a common code-

[1] G. H. R. Parkinson, 'The translation theory of understanding', *Communication and Understanding*, ed. G. Vesey, Hassocks 1977, pp. 1–19.
[2] J. J. Katz, *The Philosophy of Language*, New York, 1966, p. 98.

book for the whole community. This stipulation is entirely in accordance with the tenets of the language myth concerning synchronic systems. But it does not in itself resolve the problem of deciding how much of the communicational process knowledge of a language accounts for. What it does settle in advance is that the expressions of a language in some sense have to be determinate in respect both of 'form' and of 'meaning'. That is to say, there must be fixed rules for deciding whether a given sequence of sounds does or does not represent an expression of the language and, if it does, for identifying that expression; and there must also be fixed rules for assigning the correct interpretation to any expression thus identified.

Thus before any decision has been made about what in principle is to count as 'form' or 'meaning', the communication model already imposes a bi-planar structuring upon the language system, in the sense that no expression with a determinate meaning can fail to have a determinate form corresponding to that meaning, and no expression with a determinate form can fail to have a corresponding determinate meaning. Although for descriptive purposes the two planes of form and meaning may be considered independently, it is the network of specific correlations between them which makes communication possible. It would be of no avail for the language-user to know all the forms of his language, and all the possible meanings those forms had, but not to know which forms had which meanings.

Posed in these terms, the problem of explicating 'form' and 'meaning' is a problem typical of the social sciences, and of lay-oriented science in general. It is already clear in advance what the theoretical requirements for 'form' and 'meaning' are: for these are determined by the communication model adopted. A different communication model would have imposed different theoretical requirements. But in addition, there are conditions which have to be met for a satisfactory explication of 'form' and 'meaning' which are of a characteristically different kind from those encountered in the natural sciences.

The natural sciences in general have no essential interest in relating their inquiries to the layman's understanding of the world in which he lives, except insofar as the capacities, mechanisms and afflictions of the body provide data for research. This is not to say that the natural sciences have no interest in improving the layman's everyday lot. But although, for example, medical research into cancer is directed towards prevention and effective treatment of the disease, it is in no way restricted by a need to keep within the bounds of what the layman understands or believes about cancer. It would be manifestly absurd to criticise such research because it availed itself of methods and concepts not directly translatable in terms of the cancer patient's own experience of his condition, or because it developed methods of treatment based on theories not easily grasped by the man in the street. In this and comparable cases, the layman's view of the matter is, as far as the scientist is concerned, more or less of an irrelevance.

Other areas of science, on the contrary, have just such an interest in the layman's view. These are areas which may be described as 'essentially lay-oriented', in the sense that it is the lay-man's everyday experience of the world which provides both the point of departure and the ultimate explicanda. These are areas which include most of the social and behavioural sciences, and it is here that a science of language might seem to have a place reserved as of right. In such disciplines, many key terms and concepts are necessarily calqued upon familiar terms and concepts used in the ordinary business of discourse concerning everyday experience.

It is characteristic of lay-oriented science that the things to which the key terms and concepts refer are problematic in ways which affect the very nature of the inquiry. Whereas any layman can point to uncontroversial examples of houses, trees, chairs and other things which go to make up the physical furnishing of his environment, he cannot similarly take for granted uncontroversial exemplification of things which go to make up the social and psychological furnishing of his environment; for example, intentions, attitudes, personalities, cultural values, or political policies. One is not here, as Frege put it, 'in the happy position of a mineralogist who shows his audience a rock-crystal: I cannot put a thought in the hands of my readers with the request that they should examine it from all sides.'[1] Such intangibles are just those on which the layman is likely to find himself in disagreement with other laymen. The paradoxical situation thus arises that much of what lay-oriented science claims to investigate is in no way uncontentiously 'given' to

[1] G. Frege, *Logical Investigations*, ed. P. T. Geach, Oxford, 1977, p. 13 fn.

lay experience: whereas whatever is thus 'given' falls for the most part outside its investigatory purview. This does not mean that the layman is himself less certain about whether he lives in a democracy or thinks rationally or speaks English than about whether there are flowers in his garden and a roof over his head. But it does mean—to say the least—that such doubts as might be entertained about questions of the former kind are intrinsically different from doubts which might be entertained about the latter.

The problem of explicating 'form' and 'meaning' falls into this category. The distinction involved is a layman's distinction in the sense that the ordinary individual clearly recognises the difference between, for example, asking how to spell the word *entropy*, or asking how many letters it has, or what it rhymes with, and, on the other hand, asking what it means, or whether it has the same meaning as the word *energy*. Furthermore, he knows that it is perfectly possible that someone might know how to spell the word, or how to pronounce it, without necessarily knowing what it means; and vice versa. The layman may not be clear about the basis of this distinction, and there may be other questions about words which he would hesitate over putting in one class or the other. But there is no serious reason to doubt that his view of language accommodates such a distinction, however vague it may be. Consequently, it would be both pointless and perverse for a science of language to fail to respect this distinction in assigning an interpretation to the terms 'form' and 'meaning'. This is not to say that, either in this particular case or in general, it is the sole task of lay-oriented science to give a theoretical account of the concepts which enter into the layman's view of the world. On the other hand, it is typical of analysis in lay-oriented science to rely on such concepts.

Respecting the layman's distinction, however, still leaves room for manoeuvre, and scope for controversy too. This is because the behaviour which we recognise *grosso modo* as 'linguistic behaviour' offers no obvious sameness of form or sameness of meaning, but a variety of possible criteria for classing together features which, considered otherwise, differ. The linguist's task would be a simple one if the observable facts enabled him straight away to draw conclusions of the type 'Every time sound-sequence x is produced, the meaning conveyed is y', or 'Every time the meaning to be conveyed is y, the sound-sequence x is produced'. But the more carefully he attends to language in action, the more inevitably he is driven to the conclusion that no two sound-sequences which come up for analysis turn out to be precisely the same. It appears to be beyond the vocal control of the average speaker to replicate his own utterances exactly, even when endeavouring to do so; much less to replicate exactly a sound-sequence uttered by someone else. And yet this seemingly offers no hindrance to communication.

At this point, the linguist who is working within the framework of a Lockean model of communication is obliged to conclude that the sameness of form which his model demands lies not in the sounds themselves, but in their relevance to the communication situations in which they are produced. However, the exact communicational relevance that sounds have also appears to vary from one occasion to another, and the range of information that speech may convey is very wide. From the sounds we hear when we listen to an utterance, we have learned to derive information about the speaker's wants, beliefs, expectations, emotional state, health, social status, educational background, sex, age, regional provenance and personal identity. Furthermore, information concerning any of these may be conveyed in a great variety of ways on different occasions. In short, there is no simple system of correlation between phonetic contrasts and informational distinctions. Thus the linguist must select a dimension of communicational relevance which holds out the best prospect of identifying that sameness of meaning which his model demands, and without which he would have no criterion for identifying sameness of form. Linguistic analysis is thus automatically focused, under the aegis of this model of communication, on a search for invariants of meaning which are unaffected by differences between one communication situation and another.

The linguist's decision to choose one dimension of communicational relevance as the basis for recognising sameness of meaning is itself greatly influenced by the lay-orientation of his discipline. There is strong cultural pressure on him to make a choice which respects the layman's view of what 'a language' is. Thus he is likely to exclude, for example, the analysis of how listeners are able to distinguish the voices of different individuals, simply because this does not fall within the layman's concept of linguistic knowledge. If a man is unable to identify his wife's voice over the telephone, this is not attributable in the layman's view to any kind of linguistic ignorance on her husband's part, nor to any kind of linguistic defect on hers. On similar grounds, the communicational relevance of phonetic distinctions relating to sex, age and health will be excluded from the linguist's consideration. Differences relating to regional provenance and social status may occupy a more controversial position. Depending on the cultural context, the lay view may be inclined to treat any systematic variations from a given standard of speech as linguistic deviations. But the least controversially 'linguistic' dimension of communicational relevance will include those respects in which the layman regards himself as able to understand for all practical purposes what another speaker says, and hence identifies himself as a member of a linguistic community ultimately delimited by reference to the kind of incomprehension associated with foreigners who have never 'learned the language' at all.

Given a literate society, and a cultural context where the layman's assumptions about language were shaped by an educational programme based on the authority of grammar books and dictionaries, the strategy favoured by modern linguistics was unsurprising. The identification of sameness of form and sameness of meaning was tackled by borrowing the traditional criteria of the grammarian and the lexicographer. Thus, roughly speaking, sound sequences would be counted as formally identical if they received identical transcription in standard orthography. At the same time, the basis for determining sameness of meaning was taken to be word-meaning as identified in the conventional monolingual dictionary. The problem with this solution was not how to operate it, since it had been in operation for centuries, but how to justify it theoretically.[1] Thus modern linguistics became, as a science, less concerned with the discovery of new facts about language than preoccupied with the justification of old analytic methods.

The chief difficulty lay in reconciling the traditional pattern of linguistic analysis with the new tenets of synchronic structuralism. One illustration of this is provided by the Saussurean and post-Saussurean attempts to identify the invariant form-and-meaning units which are required for an account of linguistic structure conforming to the telementational model. It is ironical, moreover, that

[1] Sevareid's law yet again.

some structuralists who, like Bloomfield, overtly rejected a telementational model none the less continued the same search for
these invariants. Not until the introduction of avowedly 'mono-
planar' analysis by the post-Bloomfieldian distributionalists was the
search (temporarily) abandoned, eventually to be taken up once
again by the theorists of generative grammar.

The descriptive apparatus of traditional grammar consisted
basically of (i) a set of distinctions pertaining to word classes (the
so-called 'parts of speech', 'conjugation', 'declension', etc.); (ii) a
set of distinctions pertaining to word composition ('prefix', 'suffix',
etc.); (iii) a set of distinctions pertaining to grammatical categories
('number', 'mood', 'tense', etc.); (iv) a set of distinctions pertaining
to syntactic relations between words ('agreement', 'government',
etc.); (v) a set of distinctions pertaining to sentence types ('interro-
gative', 'negative', 'hypothetical', etc.), and (vi) a set of distinctions
pertaining to sentence composition ('subject', 'predicate', 'clause',
etc.). The whole of this apparatus rests ultimately on one undefined
concept, that of the 'word'. Traditional grammar assumed that
there was no need for a definition of the 'word'; and the assumption
was correct in that, for pedagogic purposes, it was quite unnecessary.
The paradigms which the grammarian set out for his pupil to learn
implicitly provided all the information necessary for word identification. From the point of view of linguistic theory, on the other hand,
this puts the cart before the horse. Hence a major problem which
arises over the accommodation of the traditional grammatical
distinctions within the framework of modern linguistics is that of
finding a suitable unit which will serve as a basis for them. For it
would be incompatible with the claim that modern linguistics is a
science if it simply left the inquirer to work out for himself the
status and nature of the ultimate elements in terms of which
grammatical statements were formulated.

In order to respect the autonomy of synchronic systems,
criteria for identifying linguistic units had to be sought 'within' the
language, granted the assumption that forms and meanings had no
independent existence. Profusion of terminology may tend to make
it look as though there were many diverse attempts to solve the
problem of setting up a minimum unit for purposes of grammatical description. But in practice only one strategy was ever
seriously considered, and it is that which is outlined in the *Cours de*

linguistique générale. It is a strategy which will here be termed for convenience 'contrastive segmentation'.

Saussure considered only two basic types of relation as pertinent to linguistic analysis. These were 'syntagmatic' relations and 'associative' relations. Syntagmatic relations hold between two or more consecutive signs combined linearly *in praesentia.* Associative relations hold between two or more signs linked *in absentia* by reason of some likeness of form or meaning. Contrastive segmentation operates upon sequences of syntagmatically related signs.

The method consists of segmenting any given utterance so as to satisfy the following conditions:

(i) a one-to-one correspondence between sections in the sequence of acoustic images (α', β', γ'), and particular concepts (α, β, γ) associated with those sections,

(ii) the linear ordering of the acoustic sections matches that of the sequence of concepts,

(iii) the segmentation is without residue, that is to say, leaves no part of the utterance unaccounted for, and

(iv) the segmentation makes sense of the utterance as a whole.

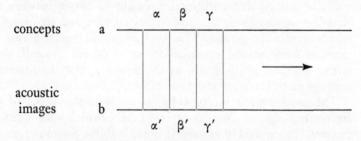

The example Saussure takes is the French utterance

[siʒlaprɑ̃]

Only two segmentations are possible which will make sense of this utterance. One segmentation introduces divisions after [i], before [l] and before [p]. The other introduces divisions after [i] and both before and after [l]. The first of these segmentations corresponds to the written forms *si je la prends* ('if I take it/her') and the second to the written forms *si je l'apprends* ('if I learn it').

It should perhaps be emphasised that contrastive segmentation is not intended to provide a complete grammatical analysis of an utterance. Nor does the identification of signs by this method imply that the phoneme sequences in question invariably function as *signifiants* of the corresponding *signifiés*. But the recurrence of the same signs in other combinations provides verification that a proposed segmentation is correct. Certain sound sequences, for example, [siʒ], never occur as *signifiants* in French. Others, for example, [rɑ̃] (*rend* 'gives back', *rang* 'rank'), do so, although not in this particular instance. For if [rɑ̃] were here taken as a *signifiant*, that would leave the preceding consonant [p] unaccounted for on the plane of content.

Saussure himself was the first to concede that in many cases the practical application of this method was by no means straightforward, and it might be said that he unwittingly supplied an example of one kind of difficulty in his segmentation of [siʒlaprɑ̃]. For he fails to discuss whether his first segmentation requires a further division after [l]. In other words, he unquestioningly takes the pronoun form *la* as corresponding to a single concept, although he does not attempt to state what this concept is. But since the form *la* here stands in opposition to *le* ('him/it', as in [siʒləprɑ̃]), it could be argued that a distinction should be drawn between the *signifiant* which signals the pronominal element and the *signifiant* which signals the gender. This analysis would be supported by Saussure's own second segmentation, where the consonant [l] alone is the *signifiant* which stands as the pronoun, and the utterance conveys no information about gender.

The case raises a much wider issue about the status of the Saussurean *signifié*. Are concepts to be equated with units of information encoded in messages? Since both the pronoun forms *le* and *la* appear without a vowel under certain purely phonological conditions in French utterances, there would be a case for saying that the nonvocalic form is a homophonous *signifiant* since it answers in some instances to the same concept as *le*, but in other instances to the same concept as *la*. On the other interpretation of concepts, however, the nonvocalic form of the pronoun would correspond neither to the same concept as *le*, nor to the same concept as *la*, but to what those two concepts have in common. This is one of a number of important issues which are not adequately clarified in the *Cours de linguistique générale*.

What is clear enough, however, is that contrastive segmentation is a procedure which leaves no residue on the plane of expression, and this is a fact with important consequences in the present context. It means that the Saussurean conception of the linguistic sign excludes the possibility of the same sign having more than one form. Saussure put the matter beyond doubt by citing the two pronunciations of French *mois* ('month'), that is to say [mwɑ] as in *le mois de décembre* ('the month of December') and [mwɑz] as in *un mois après* ('a month later'). The variation depends on liaison; that is to say, on whether or not the following word in the phrase begins with a vowel. None the less Saussure treats [mwɑ] and [mwɑz] as two different signs with identical *signifiés* (on a par, that is to say, with cases of synonymy like *furze* and *gorse*).

In this important respect the Saussurean sign does not accomplish what was accomplished by the word unit of traditional grammar. The forms assembled in the traditional paradigms (*amo, amas, amat* . . . etc.) were always regarded as variant forms of the same word, but they are treated from the Saussurean point of view as separate sign combinations. Moreover, there is no simple way of translating from the traditional terminology into Saussure's; that is to say, no simple way of stating the relationship between the traditional word unit and the sign. For the different forms of a word are not necessarily even linked by sharing a common sign (*walk* and *walked* have a sign in common, but not *go* and *went*). Nor can the link between sign and word be supplied by Saussure's recognition of associative relations. While one would confidently expect that the forms of a given word will enter into associative relations with one another, the word as a unit cannot be defined in these terms. For on the one hand the network of associative relations will often unite more forms than the traditional paradigms include (for example, *walker* as well as *walk* and *walked*). But in other instances it will bring together less. There is an associative relationship between *walk* and *walked* based on identity of *signifiants* and identity of *signifiés*: but in the case of *go* and *went* there is only a partial similarity of *signifiés*.

* * *

The gap between Saussure and Bloomfield as linguistic theorists is not only a generation gap and an intercontinental gap but also a philosophical gap. When Saussure established modern synchronic linguistics as occupying a special enclave within cognitive psychology, he could not have foreseen that psychology was about to undergo a revolution which banished all talk of unobservable mental entities and mental processes as 'unscientific'. The behaviourist approach to language adopted by Bloomfield in the 1930s rejected Saussure's 'internalisation' of the object of linguistic study, in favour of the examination of verbal behaviour as a reaction to external circumstances. None the less, Bloomfield's transatlantic version of synchronic structuralism shared at least one important feature with its European counterpart.

For contrastive segmentation is also the procedure which underlies the theory of the 'morpheme' as developed by Bloomfield. Bloomfield's definition of the morpheme as 'a linguistic form which bears no partial phonetic-semantic resemblance to any other form'[1] implies that what enables us to identify a certain segment of an utterance as having a certain meaning is the possibility of comparing that utterance with other utterances and recognising respects in which they are similar. The example Bloomfield takes is the utterances *John ran* and *John fell*. These we recognise as phonetically alike, inasmuch as they contain a first segment [dʒɔn], but different inasmuch as they contain the second segments [ran] and [fɛl] respectively. But we also encounter utterances such as *Bill ran* and *Dan fell*, which resemble *John ran* and *John fell* in respect of their second segments, while differing both from these and from each other in respect of the first segments. Our practical knowledge of the circumstances in which such utterances occur enables us to correlate the elements [dʒɔn], [bil] and [dan] with particular individuals, and the elements [ran] and [fɛl] with certain kinds of happening in which these individuals were involved. These resemblances are semantic resemblances. Thus the members of each of the pairs (i) *John ran, John fell,* (ii) *John ran, Bill ran,* and (iii) *John fell, Dan fell,* are linked by a partial resemblance in sound and in meaning. For Bloomfield *John ran, John fell, Bill ran* and *Dan fell* are complex forms, a complex form being 'a linguistic form which bears a partial phonetic-semantic resemblance to some other linguistic form'.[2] The complex forms are composed of simple

[1] L. Bloomfield, *Language*, London, 1935, p. 161.
[2] ibid., p. 160.

forms or morphemes. Morphemes are thus presented as the end-products of a process of comparison, reached when it is no longer possible to match smaller phonetic resemblances with smaller semantic resemblances.

However, it does not take a great deal of reflexion upon these examples to detect that what is going on here is not quite what Bloomfield claims. For if partial phonetic-semantic resemblance were genuinely the relevant criterion, then we should not be able to stop at a 'simple form' like *John*. Comparison with *Dan* reveals a phonetic resemblance in respect of the final consonant. This is matched by a semantic resemblance, which rests on the fact that the individuals who are the bearers of those names are animate beings and male. It is evidently no coincidence that Bloomfield's search for phonetic-semantic resemblances stops as soon as we reach units which would qualify as signs according to Saussure. Indeed, Bloomfield's account may be read at one level as an attempt to provide a mechanistic explanation in behaviourist terms of the relationship between *la parole* and the signs of *la langue*. (Saussure refrains from explanation: for him the mental association of *signifiant* with *signifié* is a postulate of linguistics, not an explicandum. Whereas for Bloomfield, who rejects a mentalistic approach to language, this will not do.)

It might perhaps be objected against the further segmentation of a form like *John* that 'male animate being' is not part of its meaning. But this is not an objection which can be raised in defence of Bloomfield, since for Bloomfield meaning reduces to recurrent features of the situations in which forms are used, and in the case of *John* it will be a recurrent feature that this form is used of a male animate being. What is true, on the other hand, is that we do not recognise in the form *John* two phonetic parts, one answering to the concept 'male animate being', and the other answering to the concept of a particular member of the class of male animate beings. But to say this is to offer the rationale underlying Saussure's linguistic sign, not that which allegedly underlies Bloomfield's morpheme. However we look at it, matching sounds with concepts is not, in the final analysis, quite the same as seeking phonetic-semantic resemblances. What Bloomfield does in practice is the former, at the same time claiming that what he is doing is the latter.

For Saussure, the primary link between sounds and meanings is provided by the linguistic sign itself. The fact that, for example, the word *elephant* is not a verb in English does not need to be accounted for in terms of any grammatical structure, since it is already accounted for by the *signifié* of the word in question, which makes it impossible to substitute, say, *elephant* for *like* in *I like ice-cream*. Similarly, insofar as there are signs which fulfil what were traditionally regarded as grammatical roles, for example, formation of plurals by addition of a given suffix, no separate structural apparatus is necessary. Thus, granted an inventory of signs, grammar is concerned with abstractions which arise on the one hand from associative relations between signs, and on the other from syntagmatic relations between signs. For example, the notion of 'genitive' may arise from an appreciation of associative similarity between certain suffixes which show no identity of *signifiants*;[1] or the notion of a syntactic function, for example, 'subject' may arise from an appreciation of the syntagmatic contrast between *John hit Bill* and *Bill hit John*. Such abstractions, although important, are none the less secondary in the sense that they could not exist except in virtue of the prior existence of linguistic signs.[2]

Bloomfield, on the other hand, treats grammar as the phenomena comprising 'the meaningful arrangement of forms in a language'.[3] From a Saussurean point of view it could be objected that the notion of 'arrangement' conflates various quite different linguistic relations. Bloomfield's four types of arrangement are 'order', 'modulation', 'phonetic modification' and 'selection'. The first of these involves contrasts of the type *John hit Bill vs. Bill hit John*; the second contrasts of the type *John! vs. John?*; the third contrasts of the type *I do not vs. I don't*; and the fourth contrasts of the type *drink milk vs. fresh milk*.

There is, however, a major difference between the Saussurean sign and Bloomfield's morpheme. For Bloomfield allows morphemes to have alternants. Alternants are the product of one of the four types of grammatical arrangement which Bloomfield recognises: it is the type termed 'phonetic modification'. This is defined as 'a change in the primary phonemes of a form'.[4] In other words, the same morpheme may appear in different phonetic forms. For Bloomfield *run* and *ran* are alternants, as are *keep* and the first three

---

[1] *Cours*, p. 190.   [2] ibid., p. 191.
[3] *Language*, p. 163.   [4] ibid.

phonemes of *kept*. The result is that what emerges in Bloom-fieldian analysis as a class of alternants looks in many instances very like part of the word paradigm of traditional grammar. To this extent, the theory of the morpheme presents a more plausible attempt to rescue the 'word' of traditional grammar than does the Saussurean theory of the linguistic sign. But what is of interest in the present context is to identify the types of difficulty which applications of contrastive segmentation leave unresolved.

Suppose *A* and *B* are holding a conversation. What is happening, according to the orthodox view, is that each is encoding his thoughts into a sequence of sounds, which the other then decodes into thoughts matching those originally encoded by his inter-locutor. The fact that *A* and *B* are able to do this is explained by their knowing the same language. Doubtless they can perform the encoding and decoding operations very rapidly and without much conscious effort. It is not how they do this which linguistic analysis proposes to explicate. The aim, rather, is to recover the invariants which underlie the encoding and decoding of the messages.

It is important to note in this connexion that full recovery of the underlying linguistic units is essential. If *B* arrived at an interpreta-tion of the sounds in some other way, which bypassed some or all of the units involved in *A*'s encoding, he would to that extent not be using his knowledge of their common language. Nor would he strictly speaking have understood *A*'s message, in terms of the Lockean 'translation theory' of understanding. So the task for the linguist is to try to identify, in the first instance, what the linguistic invariants might be which underlie the encoding and decoding.

The application of the method of contrastive segmentation encounters three major types of problem. These are:

(i) problems involving the 'location' of meanings. That is to say, although it may apparently be clear to the analyst what meanings are present in a given stretch of discourse, it is not clear to which phonological segments of it these meanings are to be assigned.

(ii) problems involving the 'comparison' of meanings. That is to say, although it may seem clear that two segments each have a meaning, it is not clear whether the meanings are the same or different.

(iii) problems involving the 'characterisation' of meanings. These

are problems where it is not clear what meaning a given phonological segment has, or whether it has a meaning at all.

Problems of the first type arise as follows. Suppose *A* says to *B*:
'Do you like your tea stronger?' What *B* will hear at the end of this
utterance is the sequence of sounds [strɔŋgə]. Perhaps *B* replies:
'Yes, I like it fairly strong', concluding this utterance with the
sequence of sounds [strɔŋ]. The problem for the analyst is that
comparison of the two forms shows that in [strɔŋgə] he is dealing
with a combination of two units. But it is by no means clear where
the boundary between them lies. Specifically, he must ask himself
whether the consonant [g] belongs to what would in traditional
grammar be called the 'stem', or to the 'suffix'.

An argument from 'subtraction' would give the result that [g]
belongs to the suffix, since it does not occur in the simple form of
the adjective in this variety of English. On the other hand, an argument from 'elegance' would give the result that [g] belongs to the
stem, since this provides a suffix which is identical in form with
that found in the great majority of other comparative adjectives. If
the analyst examines related evidence, the upshot is still inconclusive. The pair *long* and *longer* behave in an exactly similar way,
as do *young* and *younger*. It might be doubted whether *wrong* has a
comparative *wronger*: but if it has, it is not clear that the comparative has a consonant [g]. There are certainly other cases where the
comparative involves an alternation of the stem in English, perhaps
the most striking being *good : better*. But as against the superlative
strongest, the adverbial suffixed form *strongly* has no [g]. Nor can it
be maintained that the occurrence of [g] in *stronger* is an automatic
phonological consequence of adding a vocalic suffix to a stem ending
in a velar nasal; for pairs such as *sing : singer* disprove this. In short,
a case can be argued for either solution, so that one cannot tell
exactly which is the *signifiant* corresponding to the *signifié* 'strong',
nor which is that corresponding to the *signifié* 'comparative'.

What should perhaps be pointed out is that if we are applying a
Saussurean analysis there is no room for a third solution, and
certainly for no solution which treats the segment [g] as what later
theorists dubbed an 'empty' morph. For the notion of an empty
morph implies precisely that there is no identifiable *signifié*.
Whether a third solution is viable within Bloomfieldian morphemic

analysis is debatable, inasmuch as it might be argued that it is possible that there should turn out to be something semantically common to all the types of comparison where a [g] is inserted between stem and suffix. Alternatively, if the intrusive [g] appears in no other instance, it could be argued that it signifies whatever is unique in the comparison in question, as against all other comparisons. The point is worth mentioning since it shows up an interesting difference in linguistic epistemology between Saussure and Bloomfield. For Bloomfield, meanings are not identified as concepts, but as features of the situations in which forms are used. Thus it is not in principle incompatible with Bloomfieldian behaviourism that language-users might be unaware of the meanings of certain forms, whereas for Saussure this would be a contradiction in terms.

The particular examples analysed may seem to involve very trivial difficulties, which ultimately make no difference to *B*'s understanding of what *A* said. It is in part precisely for this reason that they are of considerable theoretical significance. For they show, first, that if indeed messages are in some sense based upon invariant form-and-meaning units, those units are not unambiguously identifiable at the level of the sounds *B* actually hears. The units in question must be units of a more abstract kind; which in turn implies that *B* must engage in not just one decoding process, but at least two (from sound-sequences to forms, and from forms to meanings). Secondly, what is shown is that it is of no importance whether or not *B*'s 'code-book' differs in certain respects from that used by *A*. Both conclusions indicate important questions which must therefore be asked about the language myth and the model of communication associated with it. What exactly is meant by the claim that communication requires the reception by the hearer of 'the same' ideas as the sender transmitted? What would count as empirical confirmation that sender and recipient were in fact using 'the same language' for communicational purposes on any given occasion?

The relatively humdrum, unexciting nature of many questions about the segmentation of sound-sequences does not allow a defender of the language myth to brush them aside as irrelevant. They are just as central to his thesis as more obvious contentions, such as that if *B* mistakenly supposed that the word *sun* was another name for the moon, then what A was saying would have been in part misunderstood. For if this theoretical position is to be taken seriously as a thesis about how human beings communicate by means of language, it must be taken as claiming that A's code-book and B's code-book have exactly the same text. If A uses in encoding a message any form which does not occur in B's code-book, it follows that B must literally be unable to comprehend what A is saying at that point. Otherwise the thesis collapses into the vague and hence uninteresting observation that there must somehow be 'sufficient similarity' between B's interpretation of the sounds and A's.

Problems of the second type, involving 'comparison' of meanings, arise in cases like the following. Suppose A says at one point: 'Go down the street and take the second turning on the left, and that is where John and his wife live.' In this utterance, B will hear three segments [and], which the traditional grammarian would treat as three examples of the same 'conjunction' *and*. But it is far from clear whether these three segments have the same meaning. The first appears to mean more or less the same as *then*. The last appears to mean more or less the same as *together with*. The *and* in the middle seems to mean something different again, providing a less explicit link than the other two between what precedes and what follows. Are there then (at least) three different conjunctions *and* in English? Or is there a common meaning which all three examples share? (It may be noted in passing that how many meanings *and* has is a rather crucial question for the analysis of inference, and one which has occasioned clashes of opinion among philosophers.)

Problems of the third type, involving the 'characterisation' of meanings arise typically with forms like the definite article. If A says 'Did you see the film?', it is clear enough that he is asking B a different question from the one he would have asked by saying 'Did you see a film?'. This difference is clearly a difference of meaning, and it depends on the contrast between the segments [ðə] and [ə]. But it is not at all clear how exactly to characterise the meaning of the segment [ðə]. Nor is the question made easier by comparing this use of the definite article with its use in cases such as: 'The older he gets, the less he goes out.' Here there does not even seem to be a possibility of contrasting the definite and indefinite articles: for no one says, for example, 'An older he gets, a less he goes out.' A similar quandary arises from cases like the segment [tə] in 'I like to hear it'. There is no alternative form which can be used in this construction in English, and it is never omitted. But it is extremely difficult to decide whether this [tə] has any meaning or, if it has, what that meaning is. Here the method of contrastive segmentation appears to break down for want of viable contrasts which will reveal the meanings involved.

If when *A* had certain ideas and encoded them into a particular sequence of sounds, *B* operating with a different procedure of analysis was none the less able to segment *A*'s sound-sequence into units which happened to represent the same ideas that *A* originally encoded, that would simply be by good fortune. In one sense, one could still claim that *A* conveyed his ideas to *B* successfully. But this success is no longer attributable to a common system shared by *A* and *B*.

The move typically made in modern linguistics to salvage the 'common language' thesis is, in essence, to allow *A* and *B* to have superficially different encoding and decoding procedures, provided the underlying units match. The 'common language' is thus removed in yet another sense from the level of what is directly observable, and relegated to some deeper level of identity. Thus even if *A* forms the 'comparative' of the adjective *strong* by adding a suffix [ə] to a stem [strɔŋg], while *B* decodes the result by subtracting a different suffix [gə] to leave a different stem [strɔŋ], although *B*'s procedure is not the mirror image of *A*'s this will not matter as long as we postulate two underlying units {*strong*} and {*er*}, and rules which permit either *A*'s mode of combined realisation or *B*'s disjunctively. Thus the theorist can still claim that at this 'deeper' level *A*'s morphology and *B*'s morphology are identical, and it will be in virtue of this underlying identity that when *A* utters the sound-sequence [strɔŋgə] *B* is able to understand what *A* is saying.

It should be noted in passing that the traditional grammarian had no need of complicated manoeuvres of this kind, because it served his purpose simply to list the form *stronger* as the comparative of *strong* and to make sure that his pupil knew how both were pronounced and when each was used. For the traditional grammarian, that was all that knowledge of the language involved. The elaboration of competing analyses of the comparative form would have been simply an irrelevance. If he wished to state a general rule about the formation of comparatives, what would suit his pedagogic purpose best would be to state a rule in a simple form which covered the greatest number of instances, and then list the exceptions to that rule as 'irregularities'. He had no need to con-sider the problem as a problem about the 'location' of meanings.

By postulating underlying units which may be variously related to 'surface' forms, the problem of locating meanings is in effect banished by fiat. More precisely, a deeper level of linguistic struc-ture is envisaged, where that particular problem simply does not arise. This is a strategy characteristic of the model of grammar which came to be known as 'IP' ('Item-and-Process'), as distinct from the typically Saussurean model, which was designated 'IA' ('Item-and-Arrangement'). 'The essence of IA,' it has been said,[1] 'is to talk simply of things and the arrangements in which those things occur.' Probably one reason, as Hockett has pointed out, why structuralism in both its Saussurean and Bloomfieldian manifesta-tions favoured the IA model was that 'process' terminology was uncomfortably reminiscent of the approach taken by the nine-teenth-century historical grammarians, and was thus felt to be incompatible with synchronic analysis. Thus 'if it be said that the English past-tense form *baked* is "formed" from *bake* by a "process" of "suffixation", then no matter what disclaimer of historicity is made, it is impossible not to conclude that some kind of priority is being assigned to *bake*, as against either *baked* or the suffix. And if this priority is not historical, what is it?'[2] The query does not apply to any corresponding IA description, which would treat *baked* as a linear concatenation of two separate and equipollent grammatical units, two independent signs in the Saussurean sense.

The advantages claimed for the IP model over IA are often presented as advantages of simplification. Thus in respect of an English past tense form like *took*, a contrast is drawn between five different analyses possible under IA, every one of which is in some way unsatisfactory,[3] and the simple IP solution, which treats *take* as the underlying form, and derives *took* by a process of replacing the stem vowel. However, the contrast is one which calls for comment.

[1] C. F. Hockett, 'Two models of grammatical description', *Word*, vol. 10, 1954, p. 212.
[2] ibid., p. 211.
[3] ibid., pp. 223–4. The problem is essentially where to locate the meaning 'past', which apparently distinguishes *took* from *take*.

First, the IP solution is itself no simpler than any one of the IA solutions: the apparent gain in simplicity results from not having to puzzle over which of the various IA solutions is preferable. Secondly, the IP solution is not equivalent to proposing an arbitrary answer to the problem of analysing how the meaning of the form *took* is distributed, if at all, over component parts of the form. What the IP solution does is dissolve the problem of locating meaning in the surface segments altogether, by postulating an underlying unit and a process which jointly produce the desired result.

The consequences of this strategy for characterising a speaker's knowledge of the language should be noted. In effect, the IP solution claims that it is not part of our knowledge of English to know where to locate the meanings 'take' and 'past' in the surface form *took*. *A* and *B* are allowed to have different, idiosyncratic views about this (not merely in the sense of openly proclaimed analyses, but also in the sense of psychological procedures for encoding or decoding the meaning) without prejudice to the claim that both know exactly the same morphological facts. What the IP solution holds is that *A* and *B* are both using the same morphological system, provided only that both correlate the same underlying unit or units with the same surface form or forms, by way of the same linking process or processes.

The linch-pin of the IP solution is the identification of 'the same' underlying units and processes. This applies not merely to the analyses of isolated word-forms like *took* or *stronger*, but to the analyses of all word combinations. Transformational grammar, which is essentially IP grammar, as distinct from Bloomfieldian phrase-structure grammar based on the IA model, typically requires the postulation of 'deep structure' items, and of related processes ('transformations') which convert these items and their combinations into the 'surface forms' which language-users produce.

At the same time, it is necessary to divorce the underlying units and processes from psychological or neurophysiological events, because room must be left for allowing *A* and *B* to conduct their encoding and decoding procedures differently. Thus the distinction between 'linguistic competence' and 'linguistic performance' as drawn by transformational theorists is ultimately required in order to preserve intact the postulate that speaker and hearer are using the same language. In this respect its theoretical role differs from that of the Saussurean distinction between *langue* and *parole*, which rests upon the simpler but less plausible assumption that in a homogeneous speech community there is no scope for speaker and hearer to be at variance in their handling of the linguistic system.

None the less, transformationalists are not infrequently tempted by the prospect of having their theoretical bun and eating it as well, implying that the processes and units postulated in order to differentiate deep structure from surface structure also have a rather vaguely defined psychological or neurophysiological reality. This has led some psycholinguists to complain, not unjustly, of a 'systematic ambiguity'[1] about transformationalists' use of the notion of linguistic competence. The ambiguity is between a 'weak' or 'neutral' definition, according to which competence comprises merely the rules hypothesised to account for observed and projected regularities in the linguistic output of a native speaker; and a 'stronger' definition, according to which the rules in question are assumed to be 'actually represented in the speaker's head'.[2] The phraseology transformationalists often use is consistent with the stronger interpretation: for example, the language-user is commonly said to have 'internalised' the rules of his native language.[3] It is difficult to see what this means if it does not mean that the rules are internally present in some form of neurophysiological programming. On the other hand when, as the result of psycholinguistic tests, the validity of some of the postulated rules has been challenged, the reaction of transformationalists has been 'to retreat to the more neutral definition of competence: arguing that transformational grammar "is not a model for a speaker or a hearer"[4] and therefore is immune to psychological evidence about the activities of actual speakers and hearers'.[5]

An ingenious compromise between these two positions has also

---

[1] J. Greene, 'Psycholinguistics: competence and performance', *Communication and Understanding*, ed. G. Vesey, Hassocks, 1977, p. 87.

[2] ibid.

[3] N. Chomsky, *Language and Mind*, N. York, 1968, p. 23: 'The person who has acquired knowledge of a language has internalised a system of rules that relate sound and meaning in a particular way.'

[4] N. Chomsky, *Aspects of the Theory of Syntax*, Cambridge, Mass., 1965, p. 9.

[5] Greene, loc. cit.

emerged, which endeavours to identify the internalised rule system as just one of the factors which combine to determine what the speaker says and how the hearer interprets it.[1] This allows the transformationalist to have the best of both worlds. That is to say, his hypotheses about the language rules remain immune from counterevidence produced by psychological experimentation (because the counterevidence can always be explained away as due to the interference of other factors). At the same time, however, the rules can claim to be descriptions of neurophysiological realities, and not merely elegant formulae invented by the linguist to summarise his observations and predictions of patterns of linguistic usage.

This is not the only respect in which deep structures turn out to be difficult to pin down. Their explanatory status is no clearer than their ontological status. As Rundle observes, 'for deep as well as surface structures, the question would arise as to why a combination of elements should have the meaning it has. That there is such a question is perhaps overlooked because of the common assumption that the meaning of a phrase is something mental, an idea perhaps, which is required merely to occur in association with either a word or a deep-structural element'.[2] For example, it is quite unclear how the synonymity of two sentences (whatever that might be) is explained or 'accounted for' by specifying just one deep structure for both, as is usual in transformational grammar. Certainly a theorist is at liberty, if he wishes, to represent relations between expressions by adopting certain notational conventions; for example, setting up a notation which he calls a 'deep structure representation', from which two or more sentences can be 'derived' by processes also notationally represented. But this is no more an explanation of the relations in question than choosing the colour green on a diagram to mark certain similarities of function between the parts of a machine provides an explanation of those similarities. Setting up a common deep-structural notation, just like choosing the colour green, is meaningless in the absence of an explanation of what it is intended to show: and explanations of what exactly synonymity is are hard to come by in the writings of linguistic theorists. Usually, one has to be content with the assurance that

[1] *Language and Mind*, loc. cit.
[2] B. B. Rundle, *Grammar in Philosophy*, Oxford, 1979, pp. 25–6.

native speakers of a language intuitively recognise synonymous expressions, or even that they 'know' as native speakers that synonymous sentences have the same deep structure. Now if such an assertion had some clear neurophysiological interpretation, at least one would be on the way to seeing what kind of explanation the postulation of a common deep structure might purport to be offering: even though, for practical reasons, it were never empirically testable. (For example, if having a common deep structure meant having a single source in some identified neurophysiological subsystem, it would begin to emerge in very general terms how that might explain the availability of certain patterns of paraphrase.) But since there are indefinitely many types of semantic similarity between expressions, and they can hardly all be represented as separate notational identities underlying the surface forms, it becomes difficult to see what the claim that speakers and hearers have 'knowledge' of deep-structural identities amounts to. If it is not even clear what a common deep structure represents, it is even less clear how it offers an explanation of anything at all.

What is abundantly clear, on the other hand, is how common deep-structural notations came to play a part in the development of the language-game of transformational semantics. A theory which postulates that deep and surface structures differ, so that identical surface structures can be generated from different deep structures, automatically creates for itself the problem of finding a role to be filled by the complementary notational device which will allow divergent surface representations to be derived from a common deep-structural notation.[1] Identity of deep structure is a concept projected by the theory itself, not by any conspicuous feature of observable linguistic usage. It is a classic case of finding work for an idle description to do.

What is no less clear is that the device of a common deep-structural notation is iconic of the belief that similarities and differences of meaning should ideally be perspicuously mirrored in similarities and differences of form. It is another facet of the illusion of an 'ideal language' where, as envisaged in the *Tractatus*, expression would be pictorial of that which is expressed. It is equally a reflexion of presuppositions built into the Lockean model of communication, which requires a determinate repertory of thoughts or

---

[1] Sevareid's law once more.

ideas shared by speakers and hearers. Failure to indicate whether or not two sentences were synonymous would be failure to identify the constitution of part of that repertory, and hence failure in principle to explain how communication works.

Chapter Five

Language and Thought

The language myth supports and in turn derives support from the ways in which we ascribe conceptual capacities to others on the basis of the words they use or do not use.

Not long ago the following story appeared in the columns of the *New York Herald Tribune*:[1]

> Tex Doe, the marshal of Harry City, rode into town. He sat hungrily in the saddle, ready for trouble. He knew that his sexy enemy, Alphonse the Kid, was in town. The Kid was in love with Tex's horse, Marion. Suddenly the Kid came out of the Upended Nugget Saloon.
>
> 'Draw, Tex,' he yelled madly.
>
> Tex reached for his girl, but before he could get it out of his car the Kid fired, hitting Tex in the elephant and the tundra.
>
> As Tex fell he pulled out his own chessboard and shot the Kid 35 times in the king. The Kid dropped in a pool of whisky.
>
> 'Aha!' Tex said. 'I hated to do it but he was on the wrong side of the queen.'

The most remarkable fact about this story is that its author was not a human being, but a computer at Brazosport College, Texas. But in some ways a no less remarkable fact is the following. The production of the text by a non-human-being may be treated, by at least some human beings, as a reason for denying that the text is really a story at all, and indeed for denying to it the status of language altogether.

That is a reflexion of the extent to which belief in the language myth has come to be one of the most central beliefs in Western civilisation's understanding of man. That belief is also the under-pinning of the reluctance by many philosophers, psychologists and

[1] 10 March 1979.

linguists to accept that, for example, chimpanzees can be taught to be language-users. But the case of machines is even more critical, because machines are *ex hypothesi* mere assemblages of inert matter. They are not even alive. Thus it is felt profoundly unacceptable and disturbing to attribute linguistic acts to machines (other than 'metaphorically' or in some other less-than-literal way). Machines have no minds. Therefore they have no thoughts to convey to us. Therefore their production of sequences of symbols, although in certain respects 'language-like', cannot genuinely be language.

It would follow, on this reasoning, that however ingeniously a computer might be programmed to simulate the verbal output of a human being, its capacities could at best be described as capacities for 'handling language'. It could still be denied to have linguistic knowledge.

This position is sometimes championed by linguists because they feel that anything less is a concession of victory to behaviourism. Katz, for example, imagines 'two giant computers with no ability to formulate thoughts and ideas or understand them but with the ability to produce speech sounds alternately in such a fashion that verbal exchanges between the computers replicate the publicly observable phenomena that occur when human speakers communicate in a natural language'.[1] Katz denies any inclination to regard such computer exchanges as 'genuine linguistic communication', and denies by the same token any inclination to accept the behaviourist's claim to be investigating linguistic communication.

He contrasts the computer exchanges with what might be the case if there were a 'pre-established harmony' that made speech unnecessary. This pre-established harmony would ensure that whenever an individual wished to impart one of his thoughts to an audience, that thought would occur in the minds of the members of his audience, accompanied by an indication of who had sent it. Such a system, in Katz's view, has 'decided advantages over linguistic communication', but it is 'no more genuine linguistic communication than the denatured process envisaged by behaviorists'. He concludes that in order 'to understand the ability of natural languages to serve as instruments for the communication of thoughts and ideas we must understand what it is that permits

[1] J. J. Katz, *The Philosophy of Language*, N. York, 1966, p. 99.

those who speak them consistently to connect the right sounds with the right meanings'.[1]

What is interesting about this comparison is the way in which the computers are taken as archetypally mindless contrivances even though they have the capacity to engage in verbal exchanges which are indistinguishable from the verbal exchanges of human beings. The question of whether it is coherent to attribute mindlessness to any device which can engage in verbal exchanges indistinguishable from those of human beings is not allowed to arise. If it is a coherent supposition, then linguists are in a rather difficult position. For example, they will never be able to tell whether chimpanzees have really mastered language, because even if the chimpanzees appear to be engaging in verbal interaction of a kind behaviourally indistinguishable from language, it could still be the case that this simian interaction is not telementation. Even more problematic will be deciding when human beings are engaging in language, and when they are just indulging in mindless verbal behaviour. On this view, the key question for linguistic science must be: What evidence do we have that human beings have mastered language?

Although it is not difficult to see how the alleged mindlessness of machines may be felt to stand in the way of granting that a machine could have linguistic knowledge, what may be less obvious is that the language myth itself is the source of the dilemma. For the language myth is responsible for assimilating the linguistic behaviour of human beings in certain important respects to the operations of machines. Since recurrent instantiation of invariants is in principle exactly the kind of process a machine can be built to handle, this makes it difficult to claim that language is beyond the capacity of machines in any technical sense; for just this kind of capacity is allegedly the basis of human linguistic activity. On the other hand, since the essential function of the human activity is allegedly telementational, it is equally difficult to concede that mindless processing of symbols can ever be equated with language. Hence the one thing the language myth cannot afford to dispense with is the mystical distinction between linguistic programming-cum-execution on the one hand, and linguistic knowledge on the other.

*   *   *

[1] ibid., p. 100.

The counterpart of the principle 'no language without telementation' is 'no telementation without language'. The telementational transference of a concept *x* becomes dependent on finding a language which has an expression for concept *x*. But the criteria for being a linguistic expression for concept *x* remain mysterious.

When Gulliver was taken prisoner in Lilliput, the two officers charged with drawing up an inventory of the Man Mountain's possessions described one of the items they found in the following terms:

> Out of the right fob hung a great silver chain, with a wonderful kind of engine at the bottom. We directed him to draw out whatever was at the end of that chain; which appeared to be a globe, half silver, and half of some transparent metal: for on the transparent side we saw certain strange figures circularly drawn, and thought we could touch them, until we found our fingers stopped with that lucid substance. He put this engine to our ears, which made an incessant noise like that of a water-mill: and we conjecture it is either some unknown animal, or the god that he worships: but we are more inclined to the latter opinion, because he assured us, (if we understood him right, for he expressed himself very imperfectly) that he seldom did anything without consulting it. He called it his oracle, and said it pointed out the time for every action of his life.[1]

The inventory of the Man Mountain's possessions is typical of Swift's method in *Gulliver's Travels*, which repeatedly forces the reader to look at things from an unaccustomed perspective; or perhaps to look at things which the reader may not at first recognise at all, so bizarre is the way in which they are presented. The disparity between different descriptive standpoints becomes a mechanism exploited throughout the book, and is central to its satirical purpose. It is a mechanism which constantly invites the reader to compare what things seem to be when described in one way with what they might seem to be if described in another way; and to reflect upon the implications of that difference. The exploitation of such a method relies on a degree of linguistic sophistication which should not be taken for granted.

The account just quoted will serve as a paradigm example of what one may call, for want of a better term, 'description from ignorance'. It is not that the Lilliputian officers overtly confess

[1] Jonathan Swift, *Gulliver's Travels*, part I, ch. II.

their uncertainty about what it is they have found in Gulliver's fob pocket. Even had they thought it best to conceal that uncertainty, for fear of being held incompetent or for any other reason, their ignorance would still be comically obvious to Swift's reader from the actual descriptive terms they use. To speak of an engine in the form of a globe, half silver and half of transparent metal, with figures circularly drawn upon the transparent side is, from the point of view of anyone acquainted with the English language, *ipso facto* to speak of a familiar object as if it were an outlandish one. We recognise immediately that these are not the terms which would be used except by someone who did not understand what it was he was describing.

The way Swift creates this impression here is based upon a calculated linguistic trick. The inventory he presents is allegedly translated from the Lilliputian. In other words, what the Lilliputians say in their own language we are invited to judge as if they had said it in ours. None the less, it is a linguistic trick that works. We readily conclude from the description given that the Lilliputians have neither the word nor the concept for the thing they are trying to describe. The description from ignorance is indicative not merely of terminological poverty but of a conceptual lacuna as well.

The notion that how people describe things is indicative of how they think—or do not think—about the things described, and thus reflects their very understanding of the world about them, is a deeply entrenched idea. It manifests itself in many different versions and guises. Taken to one extreme, it appears both to lend support to and in turn derive support from the thesis that thinking and talking ultimately amount to much the same thing, or at least are different modalities of the same activity. Variant forms of this thesis differ according to whether priority is assigned to language over thought, or vice versa. Either thought is held to be internalised language, or else language is held to be externalised thought.

Among evidence often invoked in this connexion is the psychological phenomenon of 'interior monologue'. In *The Concept of Mind*, Gilbert Ryle wrote:

> Theorising is an activity which most people can and normally do conduct in silence. They articulate in sentences the theories that they construct, but they do not most of the time speak these sentences out loud. They say them to themselves. Or they formulate their

thoughts in diagrams and pictures, but they do not always set these out on paper. They 'see them in their minds' eyes'. Much of our ordinary thinking is conducted in internal monologue or silent soliloquy, usually accompanied by an internal cinematograph show of the visual imagery.

This trick of talking to oneself in silence is acquired neither quickly nor without effort; and it is a necessary condition of our acquiring it that we should have previously learned to talk intelligently aloud and have heard and understood other people doing so. Keeping our thoughts to ourselves is a sophisticated accomplishment. It was not until the Middle Ages that people learned to read without reading aloud. Similarly a boy has to learn to read aloud before he learns to read under his breath, and to prattle aloud before he prattles to himself. Yet many theorists have supposed that the silence in which most of us have learned to think is a defining property of thought. Plato said that in thinking the soul is talking to itself. But silence, though often convenient, is inessential, as is the restriction of the audience to one recipient.[1]

The complementary phenomenon to 'interior monologue' is 'thinking aloud'. It sometimes happens that a person absorbed in his own thoughts is quite unaware that he has spoken at all until someone else asks him what he said, or comments upon it. The fact that we sometimes catch other people or ourselves thinking aloud leads naturally to the supposition that in such moments we glimpse merely the iceberg tip of an immense amount of verbal activity which never breaks the surface of audibility.

Given the evidence from 'interior monologue' on the one hand and 'thinking aloud' on the other, it seems to be merely a matter of everyday observation that thinking may be, and quite often is, 'done in words'. This phraseology appears expressly designed to deny that the words, whether audible or silent, are merely an accompaniment to the thinking. Yet it is an odd phrase, and perhaps not an entirely comprehensible one. With human activities generally, it makes little sense to ask what they are 'done in'. What is running done in? What is eating done in? Or gardening? Or smoking? As soon as one realises the oddity of such questions, the temptation is to interpret the claim that thinking is done in words as a claim about the medium which the activity involves using.

---

[1] G. Ryle, *The Concept of Mind*, London, 1949, pp. 27–8.

Thus, potting is done in clay. Painting is done in oils or water-colours. And so on. The claim that thinking is or may be 'done in words' appears to commit us to the view that thinking is a kind of productive manipulatory activity, and language is the manipulable medium in question. But then the puzzle arises that the role of the activity corresponding to the use of words seems to be already filled. Speaking, listening, writing and reading are already recognised as the word-using activities. So is thinking another one? Or is it just another name for any or all of these? And this question brings us to face an important issue.

It is but a short step from the safe if slightly obscure claim that thinking may be done in words to a much stronger and more con-tentious one. This stronger form of claim would involve an equation between thinking and some form of verbal activity. One variety is the behaviourist claim that thinking simply is, essentially, sup-pressed verbalisation: or, as one of the leading exponents of this view formulated it, '*what the psychologists have hitherto called thought is . . . nothing but talking to ourselves*'.[1] What is championed here is a reduction of thinking to verbalisation. The opposite reduction, going in the direction from language to thought, would presumably take some such form as the following: 'What the linguists have hitherto called speech is nothing but thinking out loud.' In both cases, the weight of emphasis lies on the words 'nothing but'.

On either of these two possible reductions, it would follow that if the Lilliputian language has no word for the kind of engine found in Gulliver's pocket, then in a very fundamental sense Lilliputian thinking about this object must be radically defective. For Lilli-putians do not have and cannot have—as long as they remain monoglot speakers of Lilliputian—the concept required. Descrip-tion from ignorance is therefore the best they can do. The difference between the behaviourist reduction and the conceptualist reduction amounts simply to this. According to the conceptualist reduction, description from ignorance is necessitated by a concep-tual lacuna in Lilliputian thinking. Whereas according to the behaviourist reduction, description from ignorance is imposed on the Lilliputians by a deficiency of language, which in turn reflects a lack of appropriate behavioural experience.

It would be a mistake to attack such reductions simply by trying

---

[1] J. B. Watson, *Behaviorism*, 2nd ed., London, 1931, p. 238 (author's own italics).

to discredit the specific philosophical or psychological positions which appear to favour them. The reductive urge in this instance is simply one manifestation of something more deep-seated. It will survive independently of the fate of particular reductions. For example, the rejection of behaviourism in contemporary psychology leaves more or less undiminished the persuasiveness of the view that language is so central to thought that our linguistic resources cannot fail to mould our patterns of thinking. What is needed in the first place is inquiry into the sources of this persuasiveness.

One source that has been suggested is the feeling that, given our awareness of the close connexion between patterns of thinking and patterns of saying, 'it is redundant to take both patterns as basic'.[1] Furthermore, whichever is taken as basic, the other falls conveniently into a dependent role for which it appears naturally suited. 'If thoughts are primary, a language seems to serve no purpose but to express or convey thoughts; while if we take speech as primary, it is tempting to analyse thoughts as speech dispositions.'[2] The sense of redundancy attendant upon the idea of two basic patterns is enhanced by the well-tailored fit we observe everywhere between words and concepts.

The natural neatness of fit between mankind's words and mankind's concepts is further brought home to us by the difficulty of finding convincing examples of lexical synonymy in a language. Two words answering to but one concept seems to be a situation which languages have no room for. Even terms which seem etymologically destined for synonymy, such as *seaman* and *sailor*, or *left-hander* and *left-handed*, manage in the final analysis to avoid it. However many contexts allow us to substitute one term for the other, there always seems to be an obstinate residue of contexts where the substitution will not work. It is not merely the rarity of candidate synonymic pairs which seems convincing, but the striking evidence from historical linguistics that even when two words originate merely as variant pronunciations of the same lexical item, the speech community will eventually find a way of distinguishing semantically between the two. Whereas the opposite process, which brings two originally distinct words into semantic competition with each other,

[1] D. Davidson, 'Thought and talk', in S. D. Guttenplan (ed.), *Mind and Language*, Oxford, 1975, p. 8.
[2] ibid.

usually concludes with the elimination of one or other of the two contenders.

Linguistic theorists have, however, taken the matter further than this. There have been claims not merely that lexical synonymy is rare, but that it never occurs. And further still, it has been claimed that the impossibility of synonymy follows from a postulate necessary for the science of linguistics.[1] Non-synonymy has been hailed as a 'principle of semantic analysis'.[2] All these claims reflect a deep conviction that ultimately thinking and speaking are one and the same. Idle linguistic machinery, unnecessary duplication of verbal resources, clearly have no place in this scheme of things.

This is one reason why it is so profoundly embarrassing to a linguistics based upon the telementational model to discover that there arise quite elementary problems about the location and characterisation of meanings, as soon as an attempt is made to analyse sequences of sounds systematically and exhaustively from the point of view of their semantic function. Apparently trivial questions like whether *to* in *was obliged to confess* has a meaning, and if so what that meaning is, conceal a potential threat to the notion that linguistic structure can ultimately be explained in terms of the ideas expressed. The stark alternative appears to be that the ideas we imagine ourselves to be expressing are merely reflexions of the linguistic structures we happen to be acquainted with. Far from language being a vehicle at the disposal of thought, thought itself is a projection from language. Thus the concept of putting thoughts into an appropriate verbal form would itself be a mistake: for the verbal resources themselves determine the availability of the thoughts. But such a conclusion goes against the grain of a whole educational tradition which represents language at the service of thought, rather than thought as a slave to language.

One important influence on the view we take of the matter is a realisation of the limitations of translation. We recognise that it is nonsensical to ask for Latin translations of sentences like *Do tachyons exist?* or *Chromosomes contain DNA*, or even *Bugging is an invasion of privacy*. Doubtless it would be possible to invent some pseudo-Lucretian rephrasing of the first question, or some pseudo-Galenian version of the second. But then the original

---

[1] L. Bloomfield, *Language*, London, 1935, §9.5.
[2] E. A. Nida, *Morphology*, 2nd ed., Ann Arbor, 1949, §6.11.

problem arises at one remove. It is unclear what sense it could make, for example, to speak in Lucretian Latin of particles travelling faster than light, if the notion of light travelling at a determinate speed goes itself beyond the conceptual boundaries of Lucretian science. Nor do we need such remote examples to illustrate the nature of the problem. If we are trying to explain to a foreigner what an Englishman understands by the expression *fair play*, and it turns out that the foreigner's own culture allots no place to playing organised games of any kind, then we shall find that it is unhelpful to try to find in his language a translation of the words *fair play* which will help him to grasp what that expression means.

Strategies for explaining things to foreigners depend crucially upon what can be taken for granted about their background. It is one thing to make up a fourth at bridge by pressing into service a visitor from overseas who protests he has never played bridge before, but who admits to having played whist. For it is no insuperable task to explain the rules of bridge to such a person. But it is quite a different matter to enlist a foreigner who protests he has never played bridge, but omits to add that he has never played any other card game either. However anxious he may be to conceal his ignorance, it will not take long to emerge once the cards are dealt. Good luck and astuteness may perhaps see him through for a little while. If he succeeds in getting through a hand without having his bluff called one might perhaps, taking a charitable view, say that for a man who had never seen a pack of cards in his life he played bridge extremely well. A less charitable but probably more reasonable view would be to say that, with the best will in the world, he was just not playing bridge at all. For how can a man play bridge, if he does not know how to play cards?

In analogous linguistic cases, it seems intuitively clear to us what is causing the difficulty. It is not just that this or that language has no word for *tachyon* or *chromosome* or *bugging* or *fair play*, true though that may be. It is not lack of the right expressions, so much as lack of acquaintance with the relevant concepts. The absence of words on which to base a sensible translation is simply a reflexion of the more fundamental absence of ideas.

It seems natural, and reasonable enough, to suppose that the Lilliputian language should have no word for any type of artifact that the Lilliputians had never before encountered. Languages just do not have words for unknown things. Hence, initially, the first account of an unknown type of artifact must necessarily proceed by means of descriptions which are in the nature of tentative exploratory classifications of the new object. To this extent, the linguistic psychology of Swift's description appears unexceptionable. Precisely what would have been implausible, it might be argued, would have been to find the vocabulary of Lilliputian already equipped with a word for precisely the kind of unknown engine discovered in Gulliver's pocket.

Admittedly, one cannot rule out the possibility that some influential Lilliputian seer or prophet might once have dreamed of such an engine, and his vision given rise to a corresponding Lilliputian word, for which most speakers of the language had no practical use whatsoever until Gulliver's arrival. One can then imagine the astonishment of the Lilliputians on discovering in Gulliver's possession an engine previously considered mythical. The situation would be analogous to the unexpected discovery of a herd of unicorns in some unexplored Himalayan valley. But, outside the realms of mythology and science fiction, the occurrence of words like *unicorn* is a rare phenomenon in language. They are luxuries which a speech community rarely indulges in.

There seem, then, at first sight to be two radically different types of translation problem. One can be solved by linguistic knowledge; whereas the other cannot. It only takes a competent bilingual to turn *Sit down on that chair* into French on a given occasion of utterance. Whereas no extent of one's knowledge of Latin will overcome the more basic untranslatability into that language of questions and statements about tachyons or chromosomes. The case of the Lilliputian inventory of Gulliver's possessions would fall into this latter class, where what is missing is the concept, not just the word.

But not all cases look like this. Translation has its limitations even where obvious differences in scientific knowledge or cultural attitudes do not seem to be responsible. Englishmen and Frenchmen are perfectly familiar with broadly the same range of items of domestic furniture, which they use for the same purposes, and value in more or less the same way. None the less, French lacks a single foolproof translation of *Sit down on that chair*, because the vocabulary of French provides no lexical slot for an exact referential counterpart of the English word *chair*. In cases like this, it seems intuitively clear to us that the difficulty is of quite a different order from that which underlies the untranslatability into Latin of *Do tachyons exist?*, *Chromosomes contain DNA*, etc. The difficulty with translating *chair* into French lies in the languages concerned. French and English happen to be lexically incommensurable in this particular area; but there is nothing more serious than that. It is not that the French language is lexically incapable of dealing with furniture, in the same sense that Latin is lexically incapable of dealing with modern particle physics and genetics. An intelligent interpreter will deal with the French problem simply by selecting whichever French word, *chaise* or *fauteuil*, is appropriate on the occasion in question, whereas there is no analogous strategy by which an intelligent translator could deal with the Latin problem.

On reflexion, however, doubts may arise as to whether the two types of translation problem are really so dissimilar. If the vocabulary of French is indeed structured in the way just described, does it not follow that the monoglot Frenchman lacks the concept of a chair in precisely the same sense that Cicero and Caesar lacked the concepts of a tachyon or a chromosome? Does the fact that French happens to have a couple of words, one or other of which will usually do duty where English would normally use the word *chair*, make all that difference? Is it not clear that the French vocabulary reflects a different classification of items of furniture, in which a class corresponding to the concept 'chair' simply has no place? This is not to deny that French could have had a word for a chair if, say, the history of French furniture-making or interior design in France had led to a different classification of furniture. But then, equally, if Roman physics had been better, Latin might have had a word for a tachyon. Granted these points, is there anything left of the contention that the two cases are intrinsically different?

Before attempting to answer this question, it may be as well to point out that the kind of translation problem so far exemplified should be put in a broader context. We may be misled if we think that the problem has simply to do with disparities of lexical labelling between different languages, a lack of one-to-one correspondence between entries in dictionaries. There is more to it than that.

Incommensurability between languages often extends also to grammatical structure. This means that even if the appropriate vocabulary is available, it does not follow that the same thing can be said about the same person, or thing, or event, in two different languages. A proposition formulated in language *A* may pose problems of translation into language *B* because although both languages have the requisite words, they do not have grammatical systems which are parallel in the relevant respects. Thus the sentences *The little girl died*, *The little girl has died*, *The little girl is dying* and *The little girl is dead* may all receive identical translations in a language which has words for *little*, for *girl* and for the verb *to die*, but no grammatical apparatus for drawing distinctions which answer to those between English *died*, *has died*, *is dying* and *is dead*. 'Little girl she die' is a sequence of English words in a recognisably English word-order, but it is none the less un-English in its failure to make clear which option is being selected from the obligatory choice imposed by the grammar of English declarative sentences. It thus fails to identify anything that English speakers recognise as a conceptualisable predication about the little girl. The only sense they are likely to make of it involves, in effect, trying to guess which of the available grammatical forms of the verb *to die* a fluent speaker of English would have used in the circumstances. If 'Little girl she die' is the best that can be done to describe the situation, then that too is description from ignorance. The ignorance in this case resides in not knowing what it is that is describable by means of the resources the English language offers.

Nor do lexical disparities and grammatical disparities exhaust the possibilities of interlingual divergence. This can perhaps be made clear by considering a case where no such disparities intervene, but where the question may still be asked whether two translation equivalents do not present different conceptualisations of what is described. The example is of a type familiar to Anglo-French translators.[1] *Il traversa la rivière à la nage* is rendered into English as *He swam across the river*. Here both languages have words and grammatical apparatus to describe the situation. But French would not say what English says, viz. *Il nagea à travers la rivière*, even though it has a verb 'to swim' and a preposition for 'across'.

[1] J. P. Vinay and J. Darbelnet, *Stylistique comparée du français et de l'anglais*, Paris, 1969, p. 105 et seq.

It is neither lack of vocabulary nor of syntax which prevents this.
One is tempted to resort, by way of explanation, simply to saying
that the two languages evidently prefer different conceptual analyses
of the same situation. There is perhaps a certain reluctance to accept arguments from
structural anisomorphism, because of their embarrassing associa-
tion in the past with theses about the mentality of uncivilised or
primitive peoples. One focus of attention was the alleged lack of
means for expressing abstract ideas. For example, Jespersen[1] drew
attention to such facts as the following. The aborigines of Tasmania
had words for every variety of gum-tree and wattle-tree, but no
word for a tree. The Mohicans had different words for cutting
different things, but no word for cutting as such. The Zulus had
words for red cows, white cows, etc., but no word for a cow. In
Bakaïri, a language of Central Brazil, there were words for different
varieties of parrot, but no general term for a parrot. In Lithuanian,
there was one colour term for gray when speaking about wool and
geese, another when speaking of horses, another when speaking of
cattle, another when speaking of the hair of men and some animals,
but no single word for the colour gray. Examples like these were
cited to show that the speakers of such languages are observant of
differentiae, but either fail to notice or take no interest in common
characteristics. One is reminded here of the reason that Frege[2]
advanced for doubting whether a dog could have the concept of the
number 'one'; namely, the dog would fail to grasp what there was
in common between the experience of being attacked by one larger
dog and the experience of chasing one cat. Analogously, it was
supposed that in many cases primitive peoples simply fail to see,
or at least to see as significant, what is common to a range of related
cases. Jespersen regarded this difference as characteristic of how
'we civilised people' express ourselves linguistically, as compared
with 'savages'. 'Civilisation,' he claimed,[3] 'means . . . increase of
abstract terms and decrease of superfluous special words.'
Setting aside the controversial question of whether general concepts are arrived at by a process of ignoring the differences between

---

[1] O. Jespersen, *Language, its Nature, Development and Origin*, London, 1922, pp.
429–31.
[2] G. Frege, *Die Grundlagen der Arithmetik*, ed. and tr. J. L. Austin, Oxford, 2nd ed.,
1953, §31.
[3] O. Jespersen, *Efficiency in Linguistic Change*, Copenhagen, 1941, p. 45.

particular instances and concentrating on common features, the kind of evidence cited by Jespersen fails to distinguish between importantly different types of case, and importantly different conclusions. On the one hand, it would be absurd to deny that there may be cases where a genuine lack of knowledge is what underlies failure in one language or another to adopt a common term to cover subclasses of the same class. Western botany and biology are sophisticated sciences, and the question as to whether different animals or different plants belong to the same species or not is a sophisticated question. Thus it may be correct to describe a situation by saying, for example, 'speakers of Bakaïri do not realise that all these birds are parrots', and in such a case it would likewise be defensible to say 'they do not have the concept of a parrot'. But this does not follow from the absence of a word for that species in their language.

Similarly, we may find a culture in which, as is reported of the Bororo of South America, there are only two distinct number words.[1] The first of these corresponds to English *one*, and the other to English *two*. But for 'three' the phrase is used: 'this pair and this one which lacks a partner.' And so on. In such a case, it is difficult to resist the conclusion that we are dealing with a fundamental weakness in Bororo mathematics, a genuine limitation on arithmetical knowledge. This is borne out by discovering that above the number ten there is no agreement between Bororo speakers upon how to count. Thus far the case is analogous to that of the parrots. We appear to be justified in saying: 'There is something these people just do not grasp, and that is why their language exhibits corresponding terminological deficiencies.' As in the case of the Lilliputians it would be extraordinary to discover that the language already had all the necessary terminology, but the speakers simply did not know how to use it (rather like children who have a draughtsboard and a set of draughts but do not know how to play). To speak of 'this pair and this one which lacks a partner' may seem as much a description from ignorance as the Lilliputian account of the engine in Gulliver's pocket. Only in the case of Bororo mathematics, the ignorance is linguistically institutionalised.

Numbers, however, are not quite like parrots. We are not inclined to take it for granted that just because they have no word for a

---

[1] H. Hoijer (ed.), *Language in Culture*, Chicago, 1954, p. 129.

parrot this means that speakers do not realise that all these birds have something in common. But there is much more of a temptation to suppose that lack of appropriate mathematical terms does mean a failure to grasp the corresponding mathematical concepts. This is because we find it puzzling to understand how anyone could do the mathematics without the appropriate numerals or other symbolic representations. And the difficulty involved is not merely a practical difficulty. We find it hard to see what would be meant by claiming that a person could possibly do the mathematics without the symbols. Our notion of mathematics is essentially a notion of symbol manipulation in some form or other, in a way that grasping a classification of fauna or flora is not. If anyone feels inclined to ask why a human being could not, in theory, do the calculations without employing symbols for that purpose, as if in some way his brain could operate an internalised abacus on which nameless beads were simply moved along nameless strings, the answer is that moving beads along strings is not *per se* calculation: it is simply moving beads along strings. It only becomes calculation when the beads themselves are interpreted systematically as symbols of a certain kind. One must be careful here not to allow the modern prestige of the computer to obscure the difference between thoughts and the mechanised simulation of thought processes.

Both parrots and numbers have to be distinguished from another type of case, where it simply appears implausible on grounds of common sense to explain lack of terminology by appeal to lack of knowledge or lack of intellectual skills. The most obvious example here concerns colour words, which notoriously differ from one language to another, without there being any physiological or psychoperceptual differences between human beings which would account for this diversity. Here one's first inclination is to say that speakers are trained to analyse colour differently in different communities, and if these differences reflect anything they reflect the fact that some communities have found it more useful to draw certain general chromatic distinctions, whereas other communities have found it more useful to draw others. It is satisfying to note that those who equate the absence of general terms with primitive mentality tend in this area of vocabulary to find themselves on the defensive. There are languages like Bassa, which divide the spectrum in two, having one term which covers the yellow-orange-red end, and another term for the rest.[1] But the Englishman finds it hard to accept that he has failed to see what purple, blue and green have in common, and is consequently unable to formulate the requisite abstract colour concept. However, the explanation of colour terminology by reference to cultural utility tends to be circular, inasmuch as it is difficult to establish at all convincingly that needing a given chromatic distinction takes priority over finding a use for one that is already lexically given. It sounds rather like saying that Britain is a monarchy because the British find it useful to have a monarch, whereas France is not a monarchy because the French do not find it useful to have a monarch. But at least colour words differ from numerals and from terms for natural species in that the question is why certain distinctions are lexically recognised in preference to others, rather than whether the community's state of intellectual development is such as to make the distinctions available for recognition at all.

A further reason sometimes advanced for discounting interlingual comparisons as evidence for differences in conceptual thought is the suspicion that such comparisons are often based upon unsympathetic or inadequate translation. Thus Hockett[2] complains of the distortion involved in the claim that the Chinese believe that 'you are a year old when you are born'. The basis of this claim is supposedly a misinterpretation of the Chinese term *swèi*. In English one calculates a person's age in years reckoned to the last anniversary of the date of birth. So if the question is asked 'How old is John?', the answer 'Twenty-four' means that his last birthday was the twenty-fourth anniversary of his birth. Whereas the corresponding numerical expression for the Chinese answer might variously be 'twenty-four', 'twenty-five' or 'twenty-six'. But this is because the term *swèi* does not mean 'year' in English sense, but rather 'calendar year during all or part of which one has been alive'.

Another example Hockett discusses is the Chinese word for a railway train, which is *hwŏchē*. This is a compound of *hwŏ* meaning 'fire', and *chē* meaning 'car, cart, wheeled vehicle'. Thus it appears that Chinese describes a train as a fire-cart and this, from a Western point of view, seems quaintly naive. But the translation, according

[1] H. A. Gleason, *An Introduction to Descriptive Linguistics*, rev. ed., New York, 1961, pp. 4-5.
[2] Hoijer, op. cit., p. 113.

to Hockett, is misleading, and he supports this claim with the following argument. 'Currently, *hwŏchē* means almost exactly what "train" means—there is no necessary image of a fire-spitting locomotive inside the speaker's head when he uses or hears the word. Evidence for this is that "electric train" (as on an electrified railroad) is *dyànlì-hwŏchē*, where *dyànlì* means "electric power"; such a train does not have a fire-spitting locomotive.'[1]

These examples are interesting because they highlight possible misunderstandings about what is at issue in the question of evidence from translation. It is doubtless salutary to point out how misleading it may be to claim that the Chinese believe that 'you are a year old when you are born'. But what this means is not very explicit in the first place. On the face of it, the claim might be that the Chinese believe the normal period of human gestation to be twelve months. But that does not appear to be what is intended. What the claim is about evidently has to do with the Chinese method of reckoning age by the *swèi* measure. However, it can hardly be denied that the English unit of time which corresponds most nearly to this is the year, and the fact is that on the Chinese system an individual is credited with one such unit for every whole or residual part of the calendar year. To put the blame on mistranslation and insist that *swèi* really means 'calendar year during all or part of which one has been alive' is to beg the question. The source of potential confusion is already identified as soon as the proposition 'you are a year old when you are born' is glossed as 'you are counted as being a year old as soon as you are born'. For this, in English terms, is what it amounts to, even though the basis for this way of reckoning age remains obscure until it is explained exactly how many different periods of time may count as adding one year under this system. To insist on a more exact English translation of *swèi* would be beside the point once the counting system is understood. Any such 'more exact' translation would arguably be itself a mistranslation, an overpedantic attempt to make sense of the strange Chinese system as seen through English eyes. We would not, after all, regard it as an omission in a correct verbal rendering of the meaning of the English term *year*, as used in reckoning people's ages, to fail to point out the consequences of the fact that on the English system every fourth year has one extra day; that is to say,

[1] ibid., p. 111.

we would not insist on some paraphrase which included the information that people born on 29 February are dealt with in a different way from everyone else.

Likewise, to contend that the Chinese word for a train does not really mean 'fire-cart', and to cite as evidence the fact that electric trains in China run without the use of fire, arguably exhibits a misconception exactly complementary to the misconception allegedly sponsored by the literal translation. Because trains are mechanically the same both in China and the West, and the same term is applied in each culture both to trains driven by steam and to trains driven by electricity, it does not follow that the word *train* means for an English speaker exactly what the word *hwŏchē* means for a Chinese. The reason why the literal translation 'fire-cart' may often be a bad translation has to do with the fact that Western culture has no fire-carts, but does have trains. It has nothing to do, however, with visual images in Chinese heads. When an English speaker uses the phrase *the foot of a mountain*, the word *foot* may or may not conjure up pictures of toes, toenails, socks, etc. But understanding the meaning of the words is independent of such visual imagery. Nor does it tell us anything about the meaning to point out that English speakers use the phrase *the foot of a mountain* in spite of the fact that, as a matter of sober reality, mountains have no legs at all.

Thus arguments directed against evidence from translation may often court the risk of self-defeat; in particular, by exhibiting just as extreme a form of glossocentrism as the glossocentrism they purport to criticise. They accuse translation of distortion whenever it shows up anisomorphism between languages, but often appeal to alternative translations in order to try to show that what is said in foreign languages has been misrepresented. At the same time, they do not propose any serious examination of what the criteria for accurate translation are. So in the end the case against interlingual comparison is pleaded rather than prosecuted, with somewhat curious results.

For if interlingual comparisons are not admissible as data bearing on identification of the conceptual frameworks which thinking utilises, it may well be asked what would be. There seems to be no half-way house between the implausible position that speaking and thinking are quite unconnected in structure and an extreme relativism of the kind represented by the so-called 'Sapir-Whorf hypothesis'. There are in fact various versions of the Sapir-Whorf hypothesis, which a careful critique would need to distinguish. But it would serve no purpose to go into these distinctions here. The general position may be characterised as holding that the language we speak largely determines our way of thinking, as distinct from merely expressing it.

Sapir spoke of each language as providing a 'deft tracery of prepared forms from which there is no escape'. He held that these prepared forms established a definite feeling or attitude to all possible contents of expression, and, through them towards all possible contents of experience, insofar as experience was capable of being expressed linguistically. Thus the framework of linguistic forms of any given language provided a complete system of reference. He drew an analogy between languages and geometrical sets of co-ordinates, offering a complete system of reference to all points of a given space. To pass from one language to another, he said, was psychologically parallel to passing from one geometrical system to another. The world outside remained the same; and yet the formal method of approach to the expressed item of experience, as to the given point of space, was so different that the resulting feeling of orientation could be the same neither in the two languages nor in the two geometries.[1]

Whorf spoke of 'our linguistically determined thought world',[2] and held that 'we dissect nature along lines laid down by our native languages'.[3] Although explicitly rejecting the behaviourist position that thinking is merely silent speech,[4] he maintained that the categories and types we isolate from the world of phenomena are not recognised simply because 'they stare every observer in the face'.[5] On the contrary, experience offered a kaleidoscopic flux of impressions which had to be organised by the mind, and the mind did this largely by means of language. Each language was not merely an instrument for expressing ideas but rather itself the 'shaper of ideas'.[6] Thus the individual is 'constrained to certain modes of interpretation even while he thinks himself most free'.[7]

---

[1] D. C. Mandelbaum (ed.), *Selected Writings of Edward Sapir*, Berkeley, 1949, p. 153.
[2] B. L. Whorf, *Language, Thought, and Reality*, ed. J. B. Carroll, Cambridge, Mass., 1956, p. 154.
[3] ibid., p. 213.   [4] pp. 66–7.   [5] p. 213.   [6] p. 212.   [7] p. 214.

One objection[1] that has been raised against the Sapir-Whorf position is the intrinsic impossibility of demonstrating that there are English sentences untranslatable into, say, Hopi. For any claim that some specific sentence *S* is untranslatable will always be vulnerable to the counterclaim that all this shows is the incompetence of the translator. Had he learned the Hopi language well enough, he would have been able to find a way of translating.

It is perhaps doubtful whether a defender of the Sapir-Whorf position needs to prove his point by finding untranslatable sentences even though, as the examples mentioned earlier indicate, he would probably have no difficulty in doing so. Rather his point is sufficiently made by demonstrating how a translation cast into the preferred mould of the target language often has to break radically away from the mould in which the message was originally formulated. Thus, to take one of Whorf's own examples,[2] it is not that we cannot translate the Nootka sentence *tlih-is-ma* perfectly satisfactorily for everyday purposes as 'The boat is grounded on the beach'. The point is that the English sentence *The boat is grounded on the beach* totally fails to reflect the way in which the message is formulated in Nootka. It fails, for example, to reflect the fact that the Nootka sentence has no word for 'boat'. A literal rendering would be something more like 'Moving pointwise – on the beach – it is'.

Now it is possible to argue about Whorf's contention that the Nootka sentence has no word for 'boat'. It might be urged that Whorf has ultimately pulled the carpet away from under his own feet by conceding at the outset that 'The boat is grounded on the beach' is a viable translation. But the argument would be pointless in the sense that what is thereby demonstrated is that what will count as a 'word for' an item in another language is in this case, as in countless others, debatable. That could hardly be so if the Nootka and the English did merely clothe one and the same thought in two superficially different pronunciations or written forms. In other words, if the encoding process itself were indeed message-neutral, there would be nothing to argue about in respect of translation.

It has been suggested that Quine's case for recognising the

[1] L. J. Cohen, *The Diversity of Meaning*, 2nd ed., London, 1966, p. 86.
[2] Whorf, op. cit., pp. 235–6.

indeterminacy of translation[1] represents 'the most elaborate defence of Whorf's thesis that has yet been advocated',[2] and hence weaknesses in Quine's argument are seen as undermining the Sapir-Whorf position. Such an elaborate defence, however, was unnecessary in the first place. The work of translation, for anyone who is at all familiar with it, itself exhibits the basic fact on which the Sapir-Whorf position is founded: the constant necessity of rethinking and recasting which is imposed by differently structured languages. If defence is needed, it is upon the other side: to support the proposition that thought is in some mysterious way neutral with respect to its verbal expression.

There is an interesting parallel between the problem that is often posed by literal translation between anisomorphic languages and the problem that arises in cases of description from ignorance. Trying to make sense of the Lilliputian description of the engine in Gulliver's pocket is not unlike trying to make sense of 'Moving pointwise – on the beach – it is'. In both cases, something is being described, but it is not initially clear exactly what it is. The task is to piece together, from the clues given, the nature of the object. It is this effort of piecing together the information on offer which doubtless accounts for at least part of the psychological effect which Sapir described as like passing from one geometrical system to another. And yet there is nothing as orderly about it as Sapir's simile perhaps suggests. The puzzle of putting the pieces together is usually solved, if it is solved at all, by the 'eureka' type of discovery, rather than by any systematic procedure. It suddenly dawns on us what the unknown engine in Gulliver's pocket must be, what it is that could be involved in point-wise movement on the beach, what these mysterious electrically powered fire-carts in China really are. But in order to confirm any of these 'eureka' hunches, it seems we have to go beyond the linguistic information immediately available. Gulliver, after all, might have had some different piece of mechanism in his fob pocket which merely resembled a watch. The pointwise movement on the beach might have been caused by an arrow, not a boat. The Chinese fire-carts might have been fire-engines, not trains. In all these cases, the words themselves do not tell us. We need to look further.

[1] W. V. O. Quine, *Word and Object*, Cambridge, Mass., 1960, pp. 26–79.
[2] Cohen, op. cit., p. 91.

Does looking further mean going outside the bounds of linguistic knowledge altogether? A natural response to this question would be to say that this depends on what is counted as linguistic knowledge. But first, if we are to look further at all, where are we to look? In principle, it seems that there are two quite different directions in which the search might proceed: in the direction of further verbal information, or in the direction of non-verbal information.

The search for further verbal information seems unpromising. In the case of the engine in Gulliver's pocket, the problem is that the verbal information which would clinch our hypothesis about the object is not, and cannot be, forthcoming; at least, not from any Lilliputian account of the matter. For the description from ignorance which we are called upon to interpret arose from the very fact that the Lilliputians do not have the word that would settle the issue once and for all, as far as we are concerned. There is *ex hypothesi* no Lilliputian who can tell us: 'Yes, you are right: the object in the Man Mountain's fob pocket was a watch.'

But cannot a Lilliputian with sufficient patience make good this want of a word by supplying further description? There is perhaps at first a temptation to suppose that he could. Surely, if he sat down and made a more detailed examination of the object, and described minutely every observable feature, would he not be bound to produce enough information to decide without any shadow of doubt whether or not our supposition was correct? Unfortunately, no. So long as his description remains a description from ignorance, there is a sense in which the more pages of description he produces the more he is likely to be wasting both his time and ours. Not a little of the humour of Swift's inventory depends precisely on the fact that the simple word *watch* says more about this object than all the circumlocutory groping that the Emperor of Lilliput's officers can manage. It is not merely the cumbersome nature of their description which makes it amusing. We do not laugh at detailed description *per se*. In a Christie's catalogue, one could probably find lengthier descriptions of watches than anything Swift offers. We would not find them funny. But imagine an auction catalogue in which every single item for sale was given a long Lilliputian description, without saying at any point quite what anything was. We should suppose the auctioneers to be either curiously cautious or curiously unable to make up their minds about what they were offering for auction.

It would be a radically different kind of auctioneers' diffidence from the kind we are used to, which hides behind let-out phrases like 'probably eighteenth-century' and 'school of Titian'. This is deliberate hedging, of what we may call the 'Trade Descriptions Act' variety. Whereas 'Trade Descriptions Act' hedging is precisely what a Lilliputian auctioneer of Gulliver's watch could not possibly have recourse to. To be in a position to describe something as 'probably a watch', or 'possibly a watch', you already have to know what an indubitable watch is. Unless, of course, you are not an honest auctioneer, but a charlatan.

There is all the difference in the world between giving a detailed description of something you know or believe to be a watch, and giving a detailed description of a watch when you have no idea what it is. Swift lets his reader off lightly, because he does not wish to spoil a good joke. But we can imagine the descriptive nightmare which would have confronted the Emperor of Lilliput's officers if Gulliver had opened the casing and shown them the complicated system of springs and cogs concealed behind the dial. The point is that the more the Lilliputians learn about the object which requires further description, the further they are from describing what it is. No amount of observation and listing of observations will in itself produce a description which is equivalent to saying 'This is a watch'. In fact, since the Lilliputian officers do not understand what it is they are looking at, the more description they produce the more irrelevant it is likely to be. They do not know what to look for, because they do not know how to look at it. So increase of descriptive detail will simply result in obfuscation. This illustrates a far-reaching general principle which operates in language. One might call it the 'law of diminishing descriptive returns'. It is our intuitive recognition of this law which Swift relies on for the humour of his description. We are amused because we realise that for a Lilliputian to succeed in describing an object as a watch by piling description upon description is not just difficult but impossible. The longer he persists in trying, the more entangled he will get in his own circumlocutions.

The law of diminishing descriptive returns does not at first appear to apply equally to cases like 'Moving pointwise – on the beach – it is' and 'electric power fire-carts'. Here it seems that if only we had a more precise formulation instead of this irritatingly vague 'moving pointwise', or if only we had a more detailed account of these fire-carts, we could easily confirm our guess that it was a question of a boat in the one case and trains in the other. It is not, after all, that the Nootka Indians or the Chinese do not understand what it is they are describing, as was the case with the Lilliputians.

But suppose the further descriptions we elicited turned out to pose problems of exactly the same order as the descriptions from which we started. Suppose 'moving pointwise' was supplemented by 'sharp-ended progress', or 'fire-cart' by 'iron monster'. We might end up with quite lengthy accounts which still left unresolved the interpretation of the originally obscure elements in the first formulations. This possibility is enough to bring home the realisation that what we are looking for if we embark on the search for verbal clarification is a confirmation or invalidation of some translation equivalent we are proposing: 'boat' in the one case, and 'train' in the other. But this is exactly analogous to our unsuccessful fishing for the word *watch* in the Lilliputian example. The only difference is that here there is a reversal of roles. The Nootka Indian and the Chinese presumably described exactly what they wanted to describe in their own words. They gave a description from knowledge, not from ignorance. Our problem is that their description was inadequate for our purposes. It left us unclear as to what exactly they were talking about. Further description from them will allow us to feel we are getting somewhere only insofar as it allows us to zero in on one of the possible interpretations we are proposing. But as soon as a point is reached where further description offers no obvious elimination of any of the remaining possibilities we had in mind, all it can do is arouse doubts as to whether we really understand their way of looking at things.

Would the situation be different if we had sufficient command of the foreign language to be able to ask questions which would narrow down the field? Doubtless that would help. But ultimately we cannot hope to extract the final verbal confirmation that we need, because of the language barrier. Just as it is no use trying to put the question 'Is it a watch you are describing?' to a Lilliputian, so it is useless to try to ask Indians or Chinese if we are right to translate in the way we propose. We simply cannot put that problem to them with the verbal resources available. If we could, there would be no such problem.

To say that the single word *watch* tells us more about the engine in Gulliver's pocket than pages of description from ignorance may appear at first sight to offer something of a paradox. How can just one word say more than many words?

What is relevant here is not more information as such, however it be quantified, but information that is more to the point, information that takes us further. One answer that appears attractive is to suppose that much information can be conveyed by one word because one word may be understood as standing in lieu of many other words. Our acquaintance with dictionaries inclines us to look favourably upon this explanation. A dictionary will tell us, for example, that the word *watch* means 'a small timepiece with a spring-driven movement, and of a size to be carried in the pocket'.[1] If the one word *watch* can say all that, then it looks like a very useful piece of verbal equipment. Very few people, it might be supposed, would normally choose to utter twenty-three syllables when they might achieve the same ends by pronouncing the monosyllable *watch*. Thus the lexicon of a language comes to be viewed as an ingenious system for saving the community time and effort. The dictionary is held to be, in Ogden and Richards' famous phrase, 'a list of substitute symbols'.[2]

According to the 'substitution theory', an essential part of linguistic knowledge must comprise knowing what verbal substitutions are permissible in a given linguistic community. Having a grasp of a word as part of the vocabulary of a language involves knowing what other words it can take the place of. Knowing the right substitutions is knowing the definition of the word. This idea of interverbal definition has become particularly influential in European education from the Renaissance onwards, ever since the monolingual dictionary became a cultural institution and the normal procedure for finding out the meaning of a word was established as being to consult the authority of the lexicographer.[3]

The substitution theory also contains the germ of a more powerful idea. Not just the vocabulary of a language, but the whole of its grammar can be viewed in substitutional terms. For example, we

[1] *Shorter Oxford English Dictionary*, 3rd ed., p. 2391.
[2] C. K. Ogden & I. A. Richards, *The Meaning of Meaning*, 10th ed., London, 1949, p. 207.
[3] R. Harris, *The Language-Makers*, London, 1980, ch. 6.

are acquainted with the word *watch* in sentences like *Gulliver had a watch*. But this word *watch* we distinguish from another word *watch*, which is found in sentences like *Watch the kettle*. We differentiate between these two words, although they are pronounced and written identically, by referring to one as 'the noun *watch*' and the other as 'the verb *watch*'. The terms *noun* and *verb* belong to the traditional technical terminology of the European grammarian. What is the point of this distinction between nouns and verbs? One point of it is that classifying a word as a noun indicates that it can substitute for a large number of other words, also nouns, without producing incomprehensible or outlandish combinations; whereas this is just the result that is likely to ensue when a noun is substituted for a verb, or some other part of speech. So if we take the sentence *Gulliver had a watch* and substitute for *watch* the noun *hat*, or the noun *banana*, or the noun *headache*, we still have perfectly acceptable English sentences, even though the meaning is now different: we have the sentences *Gulliver had a hat*, *Gulliver had a banana*, and *Gulliver had a headache*. Whereas the attempt to substitute these nouns for the verb *watch* leads to curious results like *Hat the kettle*, *Banana the kettle* and *Headache the kettle*. On the other hand, if we take the sentence *Watch the kettle*, and substitute for the verb *watch* other English verbs, such as *bring*, *empty* or *fetch*, we produce *Bring the kettle*, *Empty the kettle* and *Fetch the kettle*, whereas substituting these verbs for the noun *watch* produces results like *Gulliver had a bring*, *Gulliver had a empty*, and *Gulliver had a fetch*.

It is occasionally possible to substitute English nouns for verbs, or vice versa, without blundering into gibberish. But that depends on the individual words and the particular sentence in question. In general, it can be said that nouns and verbs in English are not mutually substitutable. The same goes for other parts of speech. Hence the grammar of a language may be seen as the rules governing substitution classes. Each class of words may be divided into subclasses on the same basis. It is obvious, for example, that not all nouns substitute equally well for one another. *Asthma* is a noun: but one does not say in English *Gulliver had a asthma*. However, it is possible to work out which subclasses of noun and which subclasses of verb can be freely substituted one for another, and similarly for all other word classes. This basic idea of substitution possibilities, extended from lexicon to grammar, underlies the twentieth-century theory of language which came to be known as 'distributionalism'.[1]

The distributionalists' major contribution to the development of grammatical theory was to provide a much more sophisticated and flexible basis for describing the syntax of a language than was offered by the traditional theory of the parts of speech. Perhaps more important was the fact that it offered a methodology which could be applied to any language whatsoever, however far removed the structure might be from the structure of the familiar Indo-European languages, which the traditional grammarian's methods of classification were designed to cope with.

Furthermore, distributionalism supplied also an account of linguistic form at the phonological level. That is to say, the same basic notion of substitution could be made to yield not only an explanation of what it was to have a knowledge of the morphology and syntax of a language, but also an explanation of what it was to have a knowledge of the sound system on which morphology, syntax and lexicon were all ultimately based. The units of the sound system were defined as phonemes, each characterised in terms of a distinction between substitutable and non-substitutable phonetic features. Any sound substitution in a given position which altered the identity of the word in question revealed allophones of different phonemes. Any sound substitution which left the identity of the word intact involved merely variant realisations of the same phoneme.

The economy and elegance of the distributionalist account of linguistic knowledge has an attractiveness which should not be underestimated. The theory proved capable of unifying and interrelating the whole gamut of traditionally recognised structural components of language. One range of substitution possibilities identified phonological form. Another range of substitution possibilities identified grammatical units and classes. Another range of substitution possibilities identified units of vocabulary. Thus the position of any given word in the language could in principle be located by stating (i) what substitutions would or would not effect a change of phonological form, (ii) what substitutions would or would not involve a change of grammatical class, and (iii) what

[1] Z. S. Harris, *Methods in Structural Linguistics*, Chicago, 1951.

substitutions would or would not bring about a change of meaning. A word, according to this theory, can be viewed as a unit defined by the unique complex of substitutions which would alter its identity as an element in the language. One of the consequences of this view has a bearing on the questions previously discussed.

The 'substitution theory' of the word offers by implication an account of the phenomenon of description from ignorance. It is not that the Emperor of Lilliput's men were mistaken in trying to give a description of the engine in Gulliver's fob pocket. It is simply that they did not hit on the right description. Had they reported: 'We found in the Man Mountain's possession a timepiece with a spring-driven movement, of a size he could carry in his pocket', their account would have been unexceptionable. It could hardly be objected that they had omitted to say that it was a 'small' timepiece, since on a Lilliputian scale everything about the Man Mountain was enormous. But in the event, although their report mentioned one essential feature of a watch, namely that it is of a size to be carried in the pocket, it failed to mention the two other components of our dictionary definition: (i) that it is a timepiece, and (ii) that it has a spring-driven movement. These are the omissions which show, according to the substitution theory, that the Emperor's officers did not understand what it was they had found. From this one might hazard two guesses about Lilliputian culture: first, that its chronometrical system had some other basis than mathematical subdivision of the earth's axial rotation, and second, that Lilliputian technology had not yet invented clockwork.

If these guesses are correct, then a simple non-linguistic explanation becomes immediately available not only for why it is that Lilliputian has no word for a watch, but also for why it is that Lilliputian attempts to describe this object are doomed in advance to miss the mark.

The substitution theory of the word has, however, its Achilles' heel. If the word *watch* is a substitute for the words 'small timepiece with a spring-driven movement, etc.', we may ask the following question. For what words are the words which occur in the definition substitutes? If these words in turn are substitutes for longer descriptions, the same question may then be raised concerning the words in those definitions. And so on. Behind the definition of the single word *watch* there thus appears to lie a regress of further definitions, which has no clearly discernible end point. For we cannot envisage what kind of verbal substitution it could be which would render any further substitution superfluous. So although it is satisfactory to have explained how it is that the single word *watch* can say more than the lengthy descriptions of the Emperor's officers, we apparently find ourselves awkwardly committed to the thesis that this one word stands in lieu of a potentially infinite chain of description. At this point the explanation collapses from the sheer weight of its own structure. For it would seem that no final description of what a watch is can ever be given. Any attempt to formulate one will be foiled by the Hydra-headed proliferation of further description required to support it. Thus, ironically, it emerges that the word *watch* itself is another form of description from ignorance. The ignorance is merely less obvious when concealed behind the monosyllable *watch* than it is when exposed in the lame circumlocutions of the Emperor's officers.

Ignorance of the Lilliputian variety is less uncommon than its illustration by reference to Swift's fictional example might suggest. Description from ignorance is a phenomenon of everyday occurrence in cultures which have reached a certain level of technical sophistication and specialisation. Any householder who has had occasion to telephone his plumber or electrician in an emergency and try to explain what has gone wrong with some piece of domestic apparatus of which the construction and workings are a mystery to him will be all too familiar with the experience. He soon realises that he is using clumsy circumlocutions to refer to gadgets, parts and processes for which there must presumably be exact non-circumlocutory terms. Furthermore, when the plumber or electrician uses those correct terms in reply or, worse still, asks questions like 'Well, do you mean the ball-cock?', the embarrassed householder may find that he just does not know whether that is what he means or not.

The solution in such cases is usually to abandon the attempt at further verbal classification. 'Come and see for yourself' is the ultimate recommendation when verbal communication breaks down. Confrontation with the object seems to supply what mere description lacks. Can this solution be generalised?

The case of Gulliver's watch seems to suggest that it can. Someone who is acquainted with the word *watch* and knows what a watch is ought to be able to say, on examination of the engine in Gulliver's pocket, whether or not 'This is a watch' is an appropriate description. Evidently, there may be tricky cases in which doubts arise as to whether a given piece of apparatus counts as a watch or as something else, but in principle we would expect anyone with a sound knowledge of English to be able to tell us whether Gulliver had a watch in his pocket or not. We would not demand that he produce some more detailed description as a warrant for his use of the word *watch*. Any more detailed description would normally be called for only if it were a question of saying what this particular watch is like.

The case of translating the examples from Nootka and Chinese looks at first sight deceptively similar. If we are able to inspect whatever it is on the Indian's beach, we ought to be able to tell whether it is a boat. If we see the Chinese fire-carts, we ought to be able to decide whether they are trains. So it may turn out. But this still does not give us quite the answer the translator wants. For although the object on the beach may be a boat as far as we are concerned, that gives no guarantee that it is (just) a boat as far as the Indian is concerned. The same applies *mutatis mutandis* to the trains of China. Thus to translate simply by the words *boat* or *train* may still omit some significant item of information which the Nootka and Chinese terms convey. There is no way we shall discover this simply by staring hard at the boat or the trains. Confrontation with the object will not serve the purpose. For the information we are seeking does not lie in the object itself at all. It lies in the language.

It would be illusory to suppose that we can identify this information by application of some simple distinction between 'sense' and 'reference', of the kind proposed by Frege[1] in connexion with the expressions *Morning Star* and *Evening Star*. For one thing, such a distinction appears to presuppose an antecedently fixed universe of discourse, in which identity of reference is determined by some culture-neutral counting procedure (as if buttons in a box offered the only valid model of what human beings might want to talk about). But even if, in some magical way, it were possible to establish identity of both sense and reference across languages, this would still leave open the question of translation equivalents. The

---

[1] G. Frege, 'Über Sinn und Bedeutung', *Zeitschrift für Philosophie und philosophische Kritik*, vol. 100, 1892, pp. 25–50.

dimensions of communicational relevance in human discourse are too complex to be captured so easily.

The embedding of language in cultural practices, beliefs and traditions of all kinds, which may differ widely from one society to another, makes it naive to suppose that mere alignment between words and objects affords a universal method for establishing interlingual equivalences. That is not to say that such a method is in all cases bound to fail. The point is, rather, that opting straight away for such a method itself reflects cultural practices, beliefs and traditions of a certain kind. It assumes the validity of a view of language which is itself embedded in a particular cultural matrix. It offers the exact theoretical analogy to the translator who concludes, from his inspection of the object on the beach, that the Nootka word must mean 'boat'. What the translator's conclusion amounts to is that if he were describing the object in English he would have no hesitation in calling it a 'boat'. What the translator's conclusion avoids is facing up to the question of whether the Nootka Indian is engaged in any such enterprise at all.

The translator may defend his conclusion by saying that it really does not matter to him what the Nootka Indian's conceptual analysis of the situation is: all he needs is the nearest English version which will enable an English reader to make reasonable sense of the Nootka words. Such a defence is at least honest. It makes no secret of the fact that the Indian is simply being treated as if he were a surrogate Westerner, speaking a kind of imperfect, phonologically distorted English. But few if any critics of the Sapir-Whorf hypothesis have ever been content to rest their case on a bluff cultural intransigence of this kind. It is too reminiscent of the attitude which advocates shouting louder at the natives if they don't seem to understand you.

Instead, opponents of the principle of linguistic relativity have usually tried to undermine it in one of two ways. One is by seeking to show that even when languages show great diversity in their lexical or grammatical systems, there are always ways of establishing commensurability. These can be used as bridges for gaining access to what appear to be, when considered in isolation, the closed conceptual systems of different linguistic communities. By such means, it is argued, the cryptanalyst's problem facing the ethnographer whose task is to try to understand behaviour characteristic of cultures quite alien to his own can and must be solved.

The bridge argument has been used by anthropologists who feared that the principle of linguistic relativity, carried to its logical conclusion, 'implies the invalidity of the classic "comparative method" '[1] of their discipline. Their case is based on the possibility of discovering 'prime categories' common to different conceptual systems, in spite of the acknowledged differences between the systems. It rejects the alleged incommensurability of systems as being often a simple artifact of relativist methods of analysis. The relativist, it is claimed, usually starts from an erroneous premiss about how the meaning of an expression should be identified. The error in question is the 'total category' error.

The 'total category' error involves the assumption that all designative uses of a term count equally as evidence concerning what the term means. Thus its meaning is taken to be a criterial highest common factor underlying all its various uses. This assumption has obvious connexions with the doctrine of denotation and connotation expounded by Mill,[2] for whom the connotation of, say, the term *virtuous* answered to a criterion or set of criteria in virtue of which individuals are classed as virtuous persons. Any anthropologist who proceeded on Millian lines would not automatically be committed to regarding everything virtuous persons shared in common as being relevant to the connotation of the word *virtuous*. But he would at least be required to suppose that virtuous persons were virtuous by reason of some common qualification other than merely being called, in English, *virtuous*. Furthermore, if he discovered that two quite different classes of person were both designated by this term, and they had nothing in common, or at least nothing which could plausibly be regarded as their common virtuousness, the investigator would be required to conclude that he was dealing with two lexical homonyms, both of which had the form *virtuous*.

Critics of the 'total category' error have contrasted the *impasse* of incommensurability which it produces with the solutions available through the adoption of an alternative approach. This alternative is 'extensionist theory'. It assumes that words have 'primary senses',

---

[1] F. G. Lounsbury, 'Language and culture', p. 11. In *Language and Philosophy*, ed. S. Hook, New York, 1969, pp. 3–29.
[2] J. S. Mill, *A System of Logic*, London, 1843, bk. I, ch. II, 5.

which can be 'extended' in accordance with certain rules.[1] Lounsbury has shown how, by positing just three simple extension rules, it is possible to argue that a native term in the 'Crow type' of kinship terminology, which at first sight appears to have no English equivalent, since it applies to a bewildering variety of male relatives and non-relatives, should in fact be translated as 'father'. For given 'father' as the primary sense, and rules of extension which allow an equivalence (i) between a man's sister and his mother, (ii) between siblings of the same sex, and (iii) between half-siblings and full siblings, it is possible, by various combined applications of these rules, to account for all the males to whom this term can be applied. Lounsbury's same three rules, differently combined, are likewise sufficient to explain how another word in the Crow kinship terminology which applies to an equally bewildering variety of female relatives, can be accounted for on the assumption that its primary sense is 'grandmother'. Elegant demonstrations of this kind appear to show that adherents to the 'total category' error are committed to a theoretical mistake likely to make them overlook or refuse to recognise the facts of lexical structure in the languages they are investigating.

This contrast between 'total category' and 'extensionist' approaches to the analysis of vocabulary calls for three comments in the present context. The first is that postulating primary senses and extension rules leaves unanswered in principle such questions as whether the terms investigated mean 'father' and 'grandmother' *for their users*. In other words, does the Crow Indian regard his own lexical practice as involving an accepted usage by which he calls a whole range of male relatives and non-relatives 'father', in a kind of loose way, as one might in English familiarly call any small boy 'son' even though one were not his parent? Would the Indian say, when taxed about some distant relative, 'Of course, he is not really my father' (just as one might say of the small boy familiarly addressed as 'son' in English, 'Of course, he is not really my son')? Or would the Indian regard all this range of male relatives and non-relatives, including his father, as equally entitled to be called 'father'? Whatever the answers to such questions in any particular case, they are not answers which can be supplied by a set of extension rules. For these are questions about the psychological

---

[1] Lounsbury, op. cit., p. 22 et seq.

reality of the structuring which the extension rules map out. The structuring might have other explanations (for example, of a historical kind) than being a reflexion of the speakers' own semantic classifications.

Secondly, if the systematisation identified by the extension rules is not psychologically real, it begs the question at issue to insist on the term 'father' as a translation equivalent. But if, on the other hand, 'father' is the psychologically real primary sense of the term, the rules postulated by extensionist theory are irrelevant. They neither corroborate nor explain that fact. The systematic analysis of vocabulary structure is one kind of enterprise. The determination of translation equivalents is another. Often the two may run in parallel. It would none the less be a confusion to treat considerations of vocabulary structure as demonstrating the validity of a translation equivalence.

Thirdly, even when all allowances that can be made are made in favour of extensionist theory, it is difficult to see how it offers a generalisable solution to the problem of semantic anisomorphism between languages. For instance, it is not obvious what kind of extensionist account could deal convincingly with such well-known cases as the non-equivalence of French *chaise* and English *chair*. Even to make a start on the programme of generalisation, extensionist theory would need to be supplemented by some doctrine of 'natural' primary senses. In short, it would need to fall back on postulating in some form or other a basic set of invariant concepts common to all mankind. But the plausible candidates for this basic set are so few that one fails to see how it would be possible to 'generate' from them, by whatever universal rules, semantic systems approximating the complexity and diversity found in the vocabularies of the world's languages.

The other popular line of attack on linguistic relativity is to claim that it makes theoretical mountains out of practical molehills. Curiously, this is a line of attack which seems to appeal to philosophers, even though academic philosophy is a subject which might strike the non-philosopher as a surprisingly vulnerable glass house from which to hurl stones of that kind. Critics who reject linguistic relativism on these grounds are wont to point out that in practice the difficulties which the relativist makes so much of are far from insuperable. Translations exist. Bilingualism exists. No theoretical arguments can weigh in the balance against these incontrovertible facts.

The critic who takes this line may be willing to concede that some translations are better than others. None the less, Black rejects what he calls the 'romantic' thesis of 'radical untranslatability', on the empirical ground that 'Shakespeare has been translated with some success into German, even if Pushkin still eludes the English'.[1] Similarly, it is not denied that acquiring bilingual proficiency in two languages may be difficult. None the less, so the argument goes, it can be done if one tries hard enough. Thus Cohen, rejecting Quine's indeterminacy of translation, argues that the ultimate test of translation hypotheses is for the translator to go and live in the foreign community, and take part in all its social activities. If he then discovers that his own communicational efforts are successful over a sufficiently long period of time, and that 'he is not ridiculed for calling the tribe's champion polygamist a bachelor, or for smoking out two rabbits only when he was asked to smoke out two rabbit-warrens; then his grammatical and lexicographical hypotheses cannot be far wrong'. There may be many problems along the learner's way, and certain misunderstandings may come to light only after many years of apprenticeship. 'But in principle this is the way in which most exotic languages have yielded up their secrets to investigators, whether these investigators have been missionaries, traders, administrators, anthropologists or professional linguists.'[2]

The implication behind such arguments is that if a theorist demands more in the way of interlingual equivalence than the practical activities of translators and bilinguals can give, then he is simply asking for too much. In other words, he tacitly appeals to criteria of linguistic competence which are totally unrealistic and unreasonable. Cohen argues that whatever criterion 'is in general adequate to the task of appraising a man's success at speaking his native language, it must also be adequate to the task of appraising his success at speaking any foreign language, however exotic, that he has learnt via the analytical hypotheses of a philological investigator from his own community. And if these hypotheses enable him thus to render his own sentences into

[1] M. Black, 'Some troubles with Whorfianism', *Language and Philosophy*, ed. S. Hook, New York, 1969, p. 32.

[2] Cohen, op. cit., p. 92.

foreign ones successfully, what more can be required of them?"[1]

The answer to this question is that nothing more can be required if indeed it is the case that what accounts for a bilingual speaker's fluency in two languages is his mastery of translation. But precisely that point seems open to question. It may be that the bilingual began by translating from his native language, on the basis of certain rough-and-ready equivalences. But this is a crutch which must soon be discarded if language-learning is to make the progress which will eventually enable him to achieve in his new language the kind of unhesitating proficiency he has already achieved in his own. There is nothing self-contradictory in the supposition that a bilingual equally fluent in two languages, and indistinguishable from a native speaker in either, might still be at a loss to decide whether certain expressions in the two languages are sufficiently alike for purposes of translation. To say that is not to cast aspersions on his proficiency in either language. The difficulty is that the demands placed upon language vary from one communication situation to another, and to this translation is no exception.

Ultimately, there is no gap separating the translator's problem from the kind of problem which may face the participants in any monoglot conversation. If someone asks 'But what did you mean by *tolerance?*' it is no use telling him to go away and learn English. That is not his difficulty. Analogously, it is not necessarily helpful to recommend the translator to go away and learn Hopi. His problem may well remain, however fluent in Hopi he becomes. What he has to decide, in his capacity as translator, is the relevance to a particular communication situation of the words used, and how best to clarify that relevance in a reformulation. That the reformulation has to be couched in another language may make the task more complicated, but it does not affect its essential nature. The mistake fostered by the language myth is in both cases the same. It is to suppose that there 'really is' some context-neutral set of verbal equivalences (interlingual or intralingual) which are determinately adequate to the task of reformulation in all conceivable circumstances, because those equivalences identify the thoughts transferred in the telementation process.

If we are giving instructions to a Frenchman through an interpreter, we do not expect the interpreter to refuse to translate

[1] ibid., p. 93.

'Sit down on that chair', on the ground that French has no word for 'chair'. We expect him to size up the situation and use any French word (*chaise*, or *fauteuil*, or some other) which is appropriate. And if he protests that we are forcing him to mistranslate, we sack the interpreter and try to find one who understands the job better. Provided the Frenchman responds to what the interpreter said by sitting down on the chair we wanted him to sit down on, we do not care exactly how the trick was managed verbally. Nothing succeeds like success. It is the participants' interaction in that situation which makes what the interpreter said a translation. It does not require additionally any certificate of approval issued by the publishers of Harrap's French dictionary. There might have been many other verbal ways of achieving the result required. It would be pointless to ask which of the possible ways was really the 'right' one.

But, it will be objected, suppose the Frenchman does sit down on the chair, but we subsequently find out that what the interpreter did was to recite in French the cardinal numbers from one to ten. Can we still say that our instruction 'Sit down on that chair' was translated?

Rhetorical questions of this kind deserve rhetorical answers; such as 'Why not?'. Perhaps our interpreter has hit upon some hitherto unsuspected way of bridging interlingual gaps. It may turn out that all Frenchmen can be got to sit down on chairs by reciting to them the cardinal numbers from one to ten. Or it may not turn out like that. It makes no difference to the point at issue either way. The general question of what is taken to be subsumed under the term *translation* is a quite different question from whether or not the interpreter did an effective job in this particular instance. Whether or to what extent we subsequently mislead others by describing what he did as 'translating' will in turn depend on the circumstances in which we give that further description. But the misconception that reciting the French cardinal numbers from one to ten just 'could not' be under any circumstances a translation of 'Sit down on that chair' is a distant cousin to the misconception that there just is no French translation of 'Sit down on that chair'. That whole family of misconceptions, which take translation to be a process intrinsically dependent on the decontextualised matching of one fixed code with another, is itself the translator's version of the language myth.

Chapter Six

Linguistics Demythologised?

Why was it that the readers of *The Times* on 31 December 1974, on finding Mr Edward Heath described in the editorial column as 'a doorstep loser', did not unanimously take the Editor to be alluding to the then leader of the Conservative Party's capacity for losing doorsteps? Very probably, the great majority of those readers had never met the expression *a doorstep loser* before. Very probably too, they would have been at a loss to paraphrase that expression exactly: for its concision defies paraphrase. But they had no occasion to puzzle over what was meant. For they knew what was meant. But how?

How is it that the physicists who go to hear a seminar paper in the Department of Theoretical Physics at Oxford entitled 'Stamp Collecting'[1] know that they are not entitled to expect to be addressed on the subject of collecting stamps? More specifically, how do they gather what the paper *can* be expected to be about—as they do—from the title?

How is it that when, on 6 June 1979, the BBC television commentator on the Prudential Cup match between England and Pakistan said at one point during the latter part of Pakistan's innings 'This is a heady field placing', those viewers who speak a variety of English in which *heady* is used only of alcoholic beverages did not suppose that they were being told—either literally or metaphorically—that the field placing was intoxicating? Doubtless because they were quite clear what the commentator did mean. But how could they be, if they had never heard the word *heady* used in this way before?

Why does the journalist who comments (on Alick Rowe's script for the television serial 'Two People') that 'at no point has this been

[1] 26 February 1980.

a love affair in which June has been made to rhyme with moon'[1] not anticipate that readers will write in and point out that this is hardly surprising, because the dialogue is not in verse? Why is the caption 'New York ban on boxing after death'[2] not taken as announcing that corpses are no longer allowed to take part in pugilistic contests in New York? Humanitarians might regard it as a start, at least.

When Dr J. B. Rhine coined the phrase *extrasensory perception*, even the most pedantic of his critics understood what he meant. But if they were right to object that the term *perception* itself implied apprehension by the senses, how could they—or anyone else—have understood what Rhine meant? How can one take a self-contradictory designation seriously, much less argue about whether or not it might be correct?

Why is it that the parents of a teen-aged girl who utters, in the course of a mealtime conversation, the words 'I'm not wearing what I'm wearing' (with rising intonation over the main clause, falling intonation over the subordinate clause, and emphatic stress on the first syllable of the first *wearing*) do not regard her as suffering from hallucinations, or as having taken leave of her senses? Why does this remark not evoke comments from the rest of the family like 'Speak properly', or 'You can't say that', or 'What nonsense!', or 'How can she possibly be wearing something and not wearing it?', or 'Well, it certainly looks as if she's wearing it', or 'You could have fooled me', or 'Don't you find it rather chilly like that?'? Why do none of the hearers treat her words as expressing the self-contradiction they appear to express? Presumably because they knew that she was not contradicting herself. But how did they know that?

How is it that the word *unbeatabix*, which is to be found in no English dictionary, has a synonym which even children can supply, on the basis of hearing the word used just once in a Weetabix commercial? Why does it take a schoolmaster to say 'I don't know what *unbeatabix* means', or even 'There's no such word'?

What did the anonymous contributor to the great corpus of twentieth-century British graffiti mean by his stirring exhortation to the public: 'Be alert. Your country needs lerts'?[3] If anyone

---

[1] *The Times*, 15 December 1979.
[2] *The Times*, 15 December 1979.
[3] N. Rees, *Graffiti Lives, O.K.*, London, 1979, p. 14.

knows, we know. But how can we know, or even think we know, if we cannot find the word *lert* in our dictionaries?

When the little girl standing knee-deep in the long grass said 'Look, mummy, it comes right up to my hinges', what did she mean? Her mother knew, in spite of never having heard *hinge* used in that way before. But how did she know?

When this morning I said to my next-door neighbour 'It's going to be a nice day', he knew what I meant. Or I presume so. But since he had no other mode of access to my thoughts, how could he have known? Perhaps what I had in mind was the fact that it was my birthday.

Questions like these might begin to receive plausible answers if linguistics were demythologised. To treat them as non-frivolous questions would be a first step.

The answers, in one sense, are already familiar. For they emerge naturally from that renewal of language which is our living inheritance. But in another sense they will be strange answers. For they cannot be squared with a language myth that denies the renewal of language, ostensibly in order to make possible a scientific explanation of what language is.

Orthodox linguistics puts a safe distance between the linguist and the need to take such questions seriously. It does so by invoking two standard doctrines of the language myth, which between them can cover all cases of apparent discrepancy between linguistic behaviour and postulated language rules. One is a doctrine of ellipsis, which allows speakers not to mean what they actually say, but to mean something else which they could have said if only they had taken the trouble to express themselves in a fuller or more explicit form. The other doctrine is one which distinguishes between linguistic knowledge on the one hand and contextual knowledge, pragmatic knowledge, knowledge of the world, knowledge of history, knowledge of cricket, etc., on the other.

A judicious combination of these two doctrines will allow any awkward questions of the kind the above examples raise to be fobbed off with no trouble. Mr Heath's doorstep-losing will be a result of editorial concision, combined with knowledge of the extralinguistic fact that at election time canvassers go round knocking at people's doors. Talks to physicists on stamp collecting will be put down to reliance on prior knowledge of Rutherford's famous dictum, together with the abbreviatory licence permitted in titles. And so on. Thus creativity is denied to be part of language, except insofar as linguistic behaviour may involve the instantiation of sentences which although waiting to be used, have never—or rarely —actually been used.

There is need for a linguistics which does not demote creativity to the level of mere statistics. Whether or not a particular sentence has ever been uttered before, or how many times it has been uttered, are irrelevant matters. But these are the only criteria of creativity available in a linguistics which treats the production of utterances as the theoretically predictable output of a determinate system of rules. Anything else 'novel' must be a performance error, or else deliberate infringement of the rules, or else a desperate attempt to invent a new rule. Thus the fixed-code fallacy fails to come to terms with linguistic creativity on both fronts. It cannot acknowledge the creativity of saying 'It's going to be a nice day' because the sentence *It's going to be a nice day* has supposedly been used millions of times before. But nor, on the other hand, can it acknowledge the creativity of coining the word *unbeatabix*, because according to the fixed-code theory there just is no such word: so *unbeatabix* must 'really' be a substitute for something else.

It is not merely that, as Richard Henson puts it, 'innovation is often possible in language without prior notice'.[1] If we are to talk in these terms, then prior notice is the exception, not the rule. The rule is innovation. Innovation is so commonly expected that it becomes noteworthy only in cases where the novelty of what is said for some reason strikes us. The fixed-code fallacy trades upon taking as much as possible for granted, and may thus be able to persuade us that the noticeably novel cases are novel because they involve departures from a prearranged agreement. But there never was any prearranged agreement that this morning I should say to my next-door neighbour 'It's going to be a nice day' provided certain meteorological conditions obtain. There may perhaps be a consistent practice of verbal exchange which has become established between two neighbours. But that is a different matter, and one which in any case the fixed-code theory of languages in no way accounts for.

None the less—the fixed-code theorist will object—there must

[1] 'What we say', reprinted in *Linguistics and Philosophy*, ed. C. Lyas, London, 1971.

surely be a prearranged agreement at some level. Not between you and your neighbour. Nor between neighbours in general. But at least between members of a language community. For anyone who speaks English can understand what you mean if and when you say to your neighbour 'It's going to be a nice day'. To *that* extent, surely, your remark to your neighbour relies for its intelligibility upon a prearranged agreement.

The answer to the fixed-code theorist is quite simply that since there is no such agreement the communicational success or failure of my remark can hardly depend on it. Moreover, the further we move away from considering relations between individuals in specific communication situations towards generalisations about the language community as a whole, the less coherent any talk about prearranged agreements becomes. It is not only with respect to linguistic behaviour that this is so. We can sensibly ask about whether *A* and *B* had a prearranged agreement to dress for dinner, or about whether the members of a dining club had such an agreement; but hardly about what the agreement was for English society as a whole. To think otherwise is to confuse agreements either with conventions or else with laws.

This is not to deny that participants can—and do—negotiate tacit or even overt agreements about the use of words, in the course of linguistic interaction. Their ability to do this is one of the most important aspects of linguistic creativity. And if they could not do it themselves, it is hardly likely that they could ever come to appreciate that art when it is exercised with consummate skill by poets, prophets and sages; nor, by the same token, fall victim to the propagandist.

To see this is already to see that there is something vital missing from a linguistics which cannot show how the alleged banalities of discourse and the alleged novelties are twin products of the same repertory of communicational strategies.

* * *

The question about time which Saussure should have asked holds the key to an understanding of language as a continuously creative process, and also to a linguistics of a quite different stamp from that which developed under the aegis of the modern orthodox tradition. Succession in time, as part of the individual's everyday experience of language, has nothing to do with relating the usage of one generation to that of its remote ancestors, as it does in the historian's perspective. The basic function of succession in time, for the language-user, is to provide a unique contextualisation for everything that is said, heard, written or read. What this unique contextualisation means is fundamental to a grasp of how the language-user's tasks in actuality differ from those assigned to him under the language hypothesis constructed by Saussure and his followers.

The contextualisation provided by succession in time ensures that every linguistic act is integrated into the individual's experience as a new event, which has never occurred before and cannot occur again. This fact is sometimes formulated, misleadingly, as a claim to the effect that nothing that is said can be repeated. When this was on one occasion put to a well-known linguist, he is reported to have replied laconically 'Well! Well!'. If his reply was intended as a sarcastic rebuttal, it shows that he missed the point, quite apart from not providing a very convincing counterexample. (The two halves of 'Well! Well!' are intonationally different, and the range of substitution possibilities for each 'well' differs.) The claim is not that speakers cannot produce or recognise instantiations of the same expressions on different occasions, but rather that this ability does not yield a criterion of demarcation between the linguistic and the non-linguistic, nor imply that whatever we say is decontextualisable. Repetition, to put the point somewhat differently, is only partial replication, and even that partial replication is context-bound by succession in time. In what respects one utterance is a replication of another cannot be assessed independently of their sequentiality.

If succession in time played no such role, the individual's experience of language would be entirely different, and languages would need to be structured on radically different principles in order to fulfil their communicational purposes. The nature of the contextualisation provided by succession in time derives from the more basic fact that we recognise no separate interpretation of chronological occurrence for linguistic as distinct from non-linguistic events. Language does not have its own time scale in our experience. But our experience allows imagination sufficient scope to realise that it could be otherwise. Communication systems operating on a different basis, such that linguistic acts are interpreted as having a different chronological relevance from non-linguistic acts, are not inconceivable. Conceivably even, such systems might at certain times and places have evolved in human society to serve restricted social purposes. It would follow, however, that the structure of discourse using such a system would be quite unlike, for example, the structure of an ordinary conversation in English, which depends essentially on there being no specially elaborated set of conventions which supply a separate time scale for interpreting the situational relevance of what is said. The consequences of this fact permeate language at every level.

Whatever might be the case in hypothetical communication systems, it is characteristic of language that the conversational sequence

A: 'Can you meet me at seven o'clock?'
B: 'I'm afraid I have to work late.'

differs from the sequence

B: 'I'm afraid I have to work late.'
A: 'Can you meet me at seven o'clock?'

in ways which depend ultimately on the fact that we interpret chronological succession for linguistic acts in exactly the same way as chronological succession for non-linguistic acts; for example

A: opens the window
B: shuts the window

as opposed to

B: shuts the window
A: opens the window.

These interpretations manifestly have to do with human intentions, and rest upon certain assumptions about people intending the probable consequences of their own voluntary actions (including probable reactions of others), in the light of their insertion in an apprehended sequence. But the particular point to be noted here is that linguistic acts have no special status *vis-à-vis* non-linguistic acts in respect of their integration into the sequentiality of experience. Our understanding of human behaviour does not merely not require that they should have, but requires that they should not have.

Someone who suddenly says 'It's turned very cold' when we are sitting out in the garden in our shirt sleeves on a hot July afternoon is accounted as behaving in a way which calls for explanation just as if, in the same circumstances, he had said nothing, but hastily put on a heavy overcoat and wrapped a woollen scarf around his neck. Linguistic acts are assumed to be immediately relevant to the current situation, unless there is reason to suppose otherwise, just as non-linguistic acts are. We do not suppose that the unsolicited remark 'It's turned very cold' might relate to some quite different circumstances, any more than we suppose that anyone would suddenly don an overcoat on a hot afternoon in anticipation of a fall in temperature later that night, or as a belated attempt to counteract the rigours of last winter. The principle of chronological integration between linguistic and non-linguistic events plays an important part in our picture of human rationality. The picture would be strikingly different if that principle did not hold.

It is symptomatic that modern linguistics provides no term for this crucial parity of status between the linguistic and the non-linguistic; an omission easily explained by the fact that modern linguistics acknowledges no such concept. But since without such a concept there is no hope of being able to analyse the creativity of the linguistic process, some justification may be seen for adding to the already overpopulated technical terminology of language studies in this instance. The lacuna could be filled if the parity just referred to were designated by the term 'cotemporality'. Linguistic acts could accordingly be said to be cotemporal in our experience with non-linguistic events and circumstances of all kinds.

Cotemporality is the ultimate basis of the distinctions we feel obliged to draw in order to deal metalinguistically with a whole range of so-called 'type-token' ambiguities, and is also intrinsic to our understanding of such everyday notions as asking questions, stating facts, and giving instructions. What has often happened in the history of linguistic and logical theorising is that some of these derived distinctions and notions have been accorded a quasi-axiomatic status which cuts them off from their experiential basis. Consequently, all kinds of academic enigmas have been generated which serve to obscure that experiential basis still further, and lead even to refusal to recognise it.

Acknowledging that cotemporality is central to our experience of language must not be misconstrued as a denial of what is sometimes called 'displacement'.[1] By 'displacement' is meant that feature or complex of features distinguishing communication systems which are not tied to the present from communication systems which are. One of the great assets, it is claimed, that man derives from language is the wherewithal to free himself from the limitations of the present, by being able to exchange messages which relate to the past and the future. Language enables him to recapitulate events which have long since taken place, and to anticipate what has not yet taken place, and perhaps will never take place. This facility, it might well be thought, has given *homo sapiens* a considerable advantage in the struggle for survival, since it makes possible a type of co-ordination and planning which is independent of the continuing face-to-face participation of the individuals concerned. Whereas other animals rely on communication systems which lack displacement. Even the honeybee, it has been pointed out, although having a communication system which allows the formulation of messages concerning spatially displaced objects, namely sources of nectar, has no means of dealing communicationally with temporal displacement.[2] No time lag can be accommodated between return to the hive and transmission of the message, nor between the message and its being acted on. Bees do not regale one another with reminiscences of the nectar they found last week, nor discuss together the nectar they might find tomorrow.

Far from denying the importance of displacement, acknowledgement of cotemporality as central to our experience of language is what alone makes possible any convincing explanation of how displacement works. It depends on the introduction of devices which suspend or neutralise the operation of the cotemporality principle within certain communicationally useful limits beyond those of intrinsic semiotic efficacy. (All that need here be elucidated concerning the notion of 'intrinsic semiotic efficacy' is the simple point that messages vary in the time they take to deliver. If the manager says to the office boy, 'Go out and buy half a ream of best quality quarto typing paper from the stationery shop on the corner, and ask them to charge it to our account', he will quite understandably be annoyed if he finds that an hour has gone by and the office boy still

---

[1] C. F. Hockett, *A Course in Modern Linguistics*, New York, 1958, p. 579.
[2] ibid.

shows no sign of moving towards the door. On the other hand, he will also understandably be annoyed if the office boy is off through the door by the time the manager has succeeded in uttering the words 'Go out and . . .' Knowing what the limits of intrinsic semiotic efficacy are is a matter of applying the principle of cotemporality to particular circumstances. But the fact that there are such limits is shown by the possibility of transgressing them. For example, in currently popular television quiz games, contestants sometimes press the buzzer in anticipation before the question has been completed, and as a result give an incorrect answer to a question which they probably could have answered correctly had they waited to hear what it was.)

Nor is acknowledgment of the principle of cotemporality to be taken as a denial that in the twentieth century we can understand, for example, the Bible or Shakespeare. On the contrary, again, it is only in virtue of that principle that the Bible and Shakespeare are still available to us. The scholars who warn us that the words may have changed their meanings are of course right. The King James version was not intended for the twentieth century, nor Shakespeare's plays for television audiences. But it is an absurdity to suppose that the re-creation of those texts which we engage in (with or without the help of scholarly footnotes) can somehow achieve a timeless validity. It takes two to make a work of literature, or a work of art of any kind. And it takes many more than two to do the constant re-making which incorporates a work of art into a cultural tradition. The great texts of the past contribute to our existence, but no more than we contribute to theirs.

In passing it may be noted that puzzles of the kind dear to philosophers of language concerning the interpretation of sentences like *This statement is true* when occurring in isolation involve cases analogous to the office boy's rushing out through the door before the manager has told him where to go. In other words, they are puzzles generated by ignoring the limits of intrinsic semiotic efficacy. This is a complex matter which Saussure attempted to deal with, partially and unsuccessfully, by insisting on the 'linearity of the signifier'.[1] It is also a matter which has re-emerged more recently in connexion with attempts to explain stylistic effects of different syntactic arrangements in terms of their linear decoding

---

[1] *Cours de linguistique générale*, 2nd ed., p. 103.

requirements.[1] But the sole point of relevance here is that intrinsic semiotic efficacy provides a lower line of demarcation above which it becomes meaningful to speak of a communication system with displacement.

When a communication system includes displacement devices, of whatever kind, the most primitive of them operates only in virtue of the principle of cotemporality. Otherwise, there would be literally no possibility of contrast available which would allow such a device to become communicationally functional. Presumably the most primitive of such devices in general must go beyond the condition Wittgenstein incorporates into his simple builder's language in the *Philosophical Investigations*.[2] In this language, which has four words only ('block', 'pillar', 'slab' and 'beam'), the order in which the builder calls out these words corresponds to the order in which his assistant is expected to bring the blocks, pillars, slabs and beams which the builder requires. This system can be regarded as achieving an economy over an otherwise comparable system which provided suffixes for the words, indicating the relative order in which the various objects were to be brought.

The example allows one to characterise one aspect of the language myth very concisely, and with it the theoretical position typical of modern linguistics. This would be to say that whereas knowing the correlations between the word-types and the object-types is a matter of linguistic knowledge, of *la langue*, everything the builder and his assistant do on the basis of that knowledge counts simply as their use of the language, as *la parole*. So if the order in which the builder calls out the words is significant, that has to be elevated to the status of linguistic knowledge too, and treated as governed by rules of *la langue*. The misleading conflation which this position involves emerges when we ask what simpler system the builder and his assistant might use to accomplish their given cooperative task.

The implication is that Wittgenstein's builder's language contrasts with an even simpler language in which the same verbal equipment is used, but without the order of calls being significant.

---

[1] G. Dillon, *Language Processing and the Reading of Literature*, Bloomington, 1978; T. J. Taylor, *Linguistic Theory and Structural Stylistics*, Oxford, 1980, ch. 5.

[2] L. Wittgenstein, *Philosophische Untersuchungen*, tr. G. E. M. Anscombe, 2nd ed., Oxford, 1958, §2.

That looks reasonable at first sight. On closer inspection, however, we see that this simpler system fails to meet our expectations of a communication system altogether—even of one with as little equipment as four words. For if, quite literally, it makes no difference in which order the builder calls out the words, and no difference in which order his assistant fetches the objects, then provided there is a guarantee that all four types of object are sooner or later going to be needed in the construction project (as presumably is the case), then the builder and his assistant might as well dispense with words altogether. For there is no sense in which the assistant can be wrong in respect of whatever he brings when a particular word has been uttered by the builder. So the builder may well continue to use the words if he likes, but he is going to need a great deal of patience as well. Patience is a very fine thing, but it is not a linguistic rule, nor any set of linguistic rules. Neither is it any kind of principle on which communication systems may be structured.

In brief, if there is to be a communication system worthy of the name, it has to be the case that when Wittgenstein's builder says, for example, 'Block', that must in some sense mean 'Block now'. This is not governed by any linguistic rule; that is to say, by any rule of the kind which governs which kind of object he is asking for. To say that it must mean 'Block now', on the other hand, cannot be interpreted in any way which would presuppose the availability of a paraphrase or expansion which would make that meaning explicit: for in the builder's language there is no such equipment. But it holds in the same sense as when, groping behind him for a hammer he just dropped, the builder's hand is reaching for the hammer 'now', and not executing some kind of superstitious gesture that might or might not be rewarded with success at some time or other unrelated to the movement of the hand in time. If there were no difference between the two acts, there would be no difference either between language and magic. But there is a difference between language and magic. The essence of it is that you can never tell whether magic works or not.

It is cotemporality which allows non-linguistic acts to combine freely with speech in the organisation of interpersonal exchanges. It is also what underlies the 'substitutivity' which, in many types of situation, permits non-linguistic acts to take the place of speech, and vice versa, in the organisation of discourse. Everyone realises, as Sapir pointed out,[1] that if someone says to you 'Lend me a dollar', then two very general kinds of option are open to you in response. One type of option involves speech, and the other involves a non-linguistic act of some kind. Doubtless the response your interlocutor hopes for is one of the latter variety, namely your handing over a dollar. Whether or not that is accompanied by a linguistic response as well (for example, 'Of course', or 'Here you are') is to him of less importance. What he hopes not to have is a linguistic response of the type 'No' or 'Certainly not', or a shake of the head. Thus, Sapir said, 'in those sequences of interpersonal behaviour which form the greater part of our daily lives speech and action supplement each other and do each other's work in a web of unbroken pattern'.[2] Sapir conceived of mutually substitutable linguistic and non-linguistic responses in an exchange as being 'structurally equivalent'. Similarly Pike, whose work in the post-Bloomfieldian period of American linguistics is unique in attempting to establish a theoretical basis for the systematic integration of linguistic and non-linguistic behaviour,[3] pointed out the implausibility of assuming that the intermingling of linguistic and non-linguistic episodes in everyday life is simply a haphazard mixture which lacks structural coherence; and hence the need for an approach which would 'deal simultaneously and without sharp discontinuities with all human overt and covert activity'. Such views, however, lay conspicuously outside the mainstream of linguistic orthodoxy which continued to insist on the validity of analysing speech, as Firth put it, by 'separating it from the whole bodily behaviour of man'.[4] This separation automatically dispenses with any need to recognise the principle of cotemporality, and thus obscures an essential insight into understanding why languages are structured as they are.

It would make very little sense to suppose that cotemporality reflects merely the behavioural consequences of certain features of the autonomous organisation of languages (although that is, at least by implication, the conclusion which the language myth projects).

[1] D. G. Mandelbaum (ed.), *Selected Writings of Edward Sapir*, Berkeley, 1949, pp. 11–12.
[2] ibid.
[3] K. L. Pike, *Language in Relation to a Unified Theory of the Structure of Human Behavior*, Glendale, 1954–60; 2nd rev. ed., The Hague, 1967.
[4] J. R. Firth, *The Tongues of Men*, repr. London, 1964, p. 19.

For it would then be an endless series of coincidences which had to account for the universality of this particular way of integrating linguistic and non-linguistic behaviour. Or else it would have to be supposed that the relevant structural linguistic features were in some way necessarily present, for independent reasons, in all languages. It is significant in this connexion that an innate 'language acquisition device' was first postulated in modern linguistics by theorists totally committed to a formalised version of the language myth. For the more completely linguistic analysis is isolated from—and treated as prior to—any examination of the external manifestation of language in behaviour, the more tempting it becomes to 'internalise' also the source of structural regularities. The innateness theory, however, in turn would require us to believe in an even greater coincidence: that Providence supplied *homo sapiens* with environments and social circumstances which enabled him to make such good use of his fortuitous genetic endowment. The alternative is to suppose that cotemporality is ultimately a reflexion of the way language evolved behaviourally from the creative adaptation of non-linguistic behavioural patterns. Language cannot be the evolutionary tail that suddenly started wagging a surprised dog.

Recognition of the fundamental role played by cotemporality might perhaps have led linguistic theorists to set about the enterprise of descriptive linguistics in a quite different way. By adopting a genuine language-user's perspective, instead of the disguised historian's perspective which Saussure institutionalised as synchronic linguistics, they might have been led to ask such questions as the following. How can we describe systematically what the speaker and hearer have to do in order to integrate speech relevantly into a temporal flow of episodes which they are jointly co-monitoring? To what extent does this integration depend on (i) linguistic and (ii) non-linguistic techniques? How are these two varieties of technique correlated? To what extent are they interdependent? How far does the employment of verbal devices itself depend upon the availability of non-linguistic information? How far do the non-linguistic techniques employed themselves rely on relevant verbalisation? How do the integrational techniques, verbal and non-verbal, vary according to such factors as the status and number of the participants involved? What assumptions about the past linguistic and non-linguistic experience of the interlocutors do these techniques presuppose? To what extent do different communicational media and different types of situation affect the language of the participants in systematic ways? In short, how do people actually use words to communicate, and how can this be described in ways which yield statements which both correspond to the language-user's experience and are open to the kinds of verification and disproof characteristic of the empirical sciences?

*   *   *

A demythologised linguistics would be an investigation of the renewal of language as a continuously creative process. Awareness of this process is the all-pervasive—and perhaps the only authentic —characteristic of the individual's involvement in language. In this sense, the aim of a demythologised linguistics would be to provide an account of linguistic experience.

Central to that experience is the way in which words link past, present, future and one individual to another, through an open-ended adaptation to communicational requirements. What is traditionally classified as belonging to 'language change' is merely one result of this adaptation, when it becomes visible at the macro-linguistic level of community-wide behaviour. A linguistics based upon the language myth cannot deal with other than macro-linguistic effects, and must distort even these when it identifies them in terms of failure to conform to the practices of earlier generations.

If Lilliputian afforded no possibility of coining some new word to designate engines of the kind found in Gulliver's pocket, then in an important and crucial respect Lilliputian would not be a language. To that extent, renewal of language has implications for the study of language change. The point is that no static descriptive model of the Lilliputian language can accommodate this potentiality, while a history of Lilliputian would take account of it only after it has ceased to be a potentiality and passed into established lexical practice. Synchronic and diachronic models alike are intrinsically incapable of coming to terms with the renewal of language, even at the macrolinguistic level.

Freedom from the constant search for supposed invariants of form and meaning would enable a demythologised linguistics to envisage the role of the individual in a radically different way from that imposed by a telemental model of communication. It would no longer be necessary to reduce speaker and hearer to mere automata, handling pre-packaged messages in accordance with mechanical rules.

A demythologised linguistics (or, to give it a less negative designation) an 'integrational linguistics' would need to recognise that language allows and requires us to do both far more and far less than the telemental model claims. Language is a process of making communicational sense of verbal behaviour. Our training in language is a training to use words in such a way that, in the context of a particular situation, our total behaviour will make the kind of sense to others that we intend it should, and effectively implement our interactional objectives. It follows that language cannot be studied in isolation from the investigation of 'rationality'. It cannot afford to neglect our everyday assumptions concerning the total behaviour of a reasonable person. These include assumptions about his probable utilisation of the linguistic resources available to him, but stop well short of assuming that everyone in a language community uses and interprets words in exactly the same way. On the contrary, it is manifest that if individuals actually behaved in accordance with the principle of mechanical uniformity conjured up by the language myth, most of their attempts to communicate would be bound to end in failure.

On what general principles, then, should an integrational linguistics proceed?

First and foremost, an integrational linguistics must recognise that human beings inhabit a communicational space which is not neatly compartmentalised into language and non-language. The consequences of this 'non-compartmentalisation principle' are basic for the methodology of linguistic studies. It renounces in advance the possibility of setting up systems of forms and meanings which will 'account for' a central core of linguistic behaviour irrespective of the situation and communicational purposes involved. But it is important to note that this consequence does not automatically destroy the concept of a language community. What it does, rather, is to demand that the concept of a language community be reformulated in more realistic terms than those of the regimented sameness postulated by the language myth.

Nor is there any assumption that the communicational space

available to the participants in a given situation is an amorphous area which cannot in principle be mapped out, and its locational features differentiated. What is assumed, simply, is that no such cartography can be divorced from the communicational purposes involved, and the available channels of contact between participants. If that is equivalent to denying that there is any one identifiable system which is 'the language' in question, so be it.

The alternative to a linguistics which concerns itself exclusively with 'the language' is a linguistics which takes as its point of departure the individual linguistic act in its communicational setting. Only by such a change of perspective will it ultimately be possible to do justice to the facts concerning the renewal of language. Any theoretical account which abstracts from the phenomena of communication in such a way as to ignore these facts can have no serious claim to be a theory of the human activities and capacities which we customarily subsume under the term 'language'. It is by this criterion that the orthodox tradition of modern linguistics, from Saussurean structuralism down to contemporary generativism, must be judged; and must be found to fail. Its failure, moreover, is not a failure of omission. There is no question of simply 'adding on' some appendix to the apparatus of modern linguistics, in order to deal with the phenomena which are central to the renewal of language. For the paradigm of modern linguistics makes it impossible to acknowledge them as language phenomena at all. The sterility of modern linguistic orthodoxy is precisely that it relegates the essential features and conditions of language to the realm of the non-linguistic. It treats the renewal of language as a mere accident of the communicational process.

To focus upon the individual act in its communicational setting would be to introduce into the study of language a natural perspective which modern linguistics has so far failed to provide. Such an enterprise might take its thematic text from Austin: 'The total speech act in the total speech situation is the *only actual* phenomenon which, in the last resort, we are engaged in elucidating.'[1] With the proviso that, unlike Austin, it is not content to base the analysis of the total speech act on taking 'linguistic meaning' for granted.[2] For that already presupposes a permanent

[1] *How to Do Things with Words*, ed. J. O. Urmson, Oxford, 1962, p. 147.
[2] ibid., p. 148.

organisation of the communicational space available, in advance of any characterisation of the speech act in question. And what our experience of language tells us is precisely that, as a generalisation, this does not hold.

The basic principle which an integrational linguistics will be concerned to give adequate expression to is that language is continuously created by the interaction of individuals in specific communication situations. It is this interaction which confers relevance upon the participants' past experience with words; and not, as orthodox linguistics would have us believe, past experience (that is to say, mastery of 'the language') which determines the communicational possibilities of their present interaction.

The investigation of the conditions under which this achievement is accomplished requires recognition of certain indeterminacies which underlie all human communication. These indeterminacies are probably to be regarded in the final analysis as intrinsic to the human condition; but it would go far beyond the scope of the present discussion to pursue the point.

The central indeterminacy of all communication is indeterminacy of what is meant. Orthodox linguistics is prepared to concede that on particular occasions of language use, it may be unclear what a speaker's intentions were, or how a hearer understood what was said. But these uncertainties are treated as accidents or defects attendant upon the diverse circumstances in which words are used. What the words themselves mean, on the contrary, is held to be determinate for the linguistic community; as if the very multiplicity of possible individual doubts somehow cancelled one another out and produced collective certainty.

From the standpoint of an integrational linguistics, on the contrary, the reverse must be the case. Insofar as what is meant is determinate, it can be only a provisional determinacy, relativised to a particular interactional situation. One consequence of adopting this standpoint is that linguistic behaviour is thereby placed on a par with all other forms of voluntary human action, in which indeterminacy both of intention and interpretation is the rule. Speculatively, one might entertain the possibility that linguistic behaviour constituted an exception to this general rule. But the reasons why theorists postulate determinacy of meaning have nothing to do with capturing some generally acknowledged fact about the way language differs from other human activities. The postulation is made for purely intratheoretic reasons, to safeguard the viability of other theoretical postulations associated with it.

In philosophy of language, the thesis that the sense of expressions is determinate stands as one of the three basic principles of what has appositely been called 'Classical Semantics'.[1] In that context, the importance of the postulate is that it enables a sentence to be considered definitely true or definitely false in any possible world. Determinacy of sense is what validates the law of the excluded middle and upholds the criterion of substitutability *salva veritate* for synonymy. In terms of Frege's simile, the notion that the sense of a sentence were indeterminate would be 'as self contradictory as the specification of an area by a curve that is not closed'.[2] If some expressions only were counted as having determinate senses, this would have the unwelcome consequence that Classical Semantics would apply at best to only part of the language. Finally, it is arguable that a formal contradiction can be derived from the alternative supposition that the world itself is so constituted that certain identity statements have to be indeterminate in order to be true.[3] In short, determinacy of meaning is one of the logico-linguistic bootstraps by which the whole enterprise of Classical Semantics is able to pull itself up off the ground.

Similarly in the case of linguistics, the assumption of determinacy of meaning for all linguistic expressions is one of the twin assumptions (the other being determinacy of form) which is essential to validate any bi-planar theory of language. Without these two assumptions, such a theory is intrinsically incapable of satisfying the requirement of explicating the concept of linguistic knowledge, in the sense of knowing a particular language. If, for example, it were conceded that the meaning of the word *glory* might vary from one speaker of English to another, or from one occasion of use to another, in ways which depended on extralinguistic factors of unspecified and hence unpredictable kinds, there would be nowhere for bi-planar linguistics to stop, short of Humpty Dumpty linguistics. We might, as bi-planar theorists, lament a Humpty Dumpty's

---

[1] G. Baker, 'Criteria: a new foundation for semantics', *Ratio*, vol. XVI, 1974, pp. 156–89.

[2] Baker, op. cit., p. 165.

[3] G. Evans, 'Can there be vague objects?', *Analysis*, vol. 38, no. 4, 1978, p. 208.

perverseness in choosing to define 'glory' as 'a nice knock-down argument',[1] but there would be nothing we could do about excluding the definition from our dictionary. Furthermore, the dictionary entry for *glory*, and for all other words, would be potentially endless. To verify such an entry would be even worse than trying to check a measurement of distance in feet, under a system in which the length of any man's foot counts as one foot. For at least under that system it is clear how, operationally, one sets about the task of measurement, whereas in the linguistic case it would not even be clear how to set about the task of ascertaining meaning. Even when the assumption of determinacy is made, the bi-planar theorist's problems are not automatically solved. But at least they become in principle capable of solution. Otherwise, since under a bi-planar theory to speak of the meaning of an expression in a language would be simply incoherent, such a theory would inevitably fail to give any satisfactory account of what it was to have a knowledge of the language.

The indeterminacy which is the concern of philosophers is chiefly referential indeterminacy; that is to say, failure to determine whether a given thing *x* and a given expression *E* are related in such a way that *x* counts as one of the things to which *E* may properly be applied or not. Dictionary definitions are often formulated in terms which appear to leave it open in very many cases exactly how the word defined shall be applied. For example, the definition of *weed* as a 'wild herb growing where it is not wanted' appears to leave room for endless dispute in particular instances about whether a given herb is a weed or not. The many instances in which there may be no dispute do not offset the referential indeterminacy of the expression *weed* in borderline cases. Furthermore, the definition seems to make it inevitable that there will be borderline cases, since it does not tell us which herbs count as 'wild', nor who is to decide whether such a herb is 'growing where it is not wanted'.

To avoid tying the notion of referential indeterminacy too narrowly to an approach to language which looks like some form of labelling theory, we may treat referential indeterminacy as one variety of indeterminacy of employment. For referential factors are not the only factors relevant to the appropriate use of linguistic expressions. Thus, for example, we might consider the expression

[1] Lewis Carroll, *Through the Looking Glass*, ch. 6.

hello as of indeterminate employment, at least according to dictionaries, on the ground that although dictionaries define *hello* as an interjection expressing greeting, surprise, etc., they fail to say in exactly what circumstances its use would be appropriate.

Indeterminacy of employment must be distinguished from consensual indeterminacy, which arises when two or more users of an expression do not agree as to its use. In many instances referential indeterminacy and consensual indeterminacy go together. None the less, it is possible that user *A* and user *B* may both be quite clear about whether an expression is applicable in a certain case, but it turns out that *A* treats it as applicable while *B* treats it as inapplicable. Equally, it is possible that all users of an expression agree upon its use, but they are none the less all uncertain as to how to apply it in a particular range of cases. The question which arises in connexion with consensual indeterminacy is how to deal with lack of uniformity in the usage of members of a linguistic community. This is the question which is critical for descriptive linguistics, where it presents itself as one manifestation of the more general problem of linguistic variation.

Referential indeterminacy and consensual indeterminacy are sometimes confused. They are also sometimes regarded as explanatorily connected, consensual indeterminacy being blamed for referential indeterminacy. This seems to have been at one time the view of Russell, who likened the meaning of a word to a target. Language used precisely hits the bull's eye, but there will always be an area surrounding the bull's eye which is an area of doubt.[1] Russell attributed this to the fact that no two individuals have exactly the same experiences on which to base their understanding of what a word means. Hence what a word means will differ, however slightly, from one individual to another, even though they all agree upon an important central area of meaning. Russell denied that the bull's eye ever 'shrinks to a point'. In other words, there must be some area of the target within which it is possible to land shots which score full semantic marks. Thus the problem of indeterminacy is dealt with by acknowledging that it is inevitable in view of the way users learn meanings, and allowing it to stand, provided this does not preclude the possibility of establishing a core of semantic determinacy within the penumbra of indeterminacy.

[1] B. Russell, *The Analysis of Mind*, New York, 1921, pp. 197–8.

One objection to such a view might be that it simply equates linguistic accuracy with maximum consensual agreement. An equation of this kind clearly stands in need of supporting arguments. For on the face of it, it is not absurd to suppose that some users of an expression may be ignorant of its exact meaning. It is, after all, a common experience to find that we are less certain of the exact meaning of certain terms than of others. Were this not so, speakers and writers of English would presumably find little use for English dictionaries. But is the usage of more or less ignorant users to count equally with that of well informed users in identifying the bull's eye by which accuracy is evaluated?

One answer to this question has a very long history. It is the answer embodied in the orthological dogma which is central to the Western grammatical tradition.[1] The orthological dogma holds that not all members of a linguistic community are equal in linguistic knowledge. Some are inferior to others. The usage of the inferior does not count in establishing what is linguistically correct. Hence in identifying the exact meaning of a word, only the usage of the best speakers will be taken into consideration. Linguistic knowledge on this view is to be considered as issuing in practical expertise. Language is a τέχνη. One would no more consider all members of a community experts at language than one would consider them all experts at cooking or medicine. And it is simply foolishness or misguided egalitarianism to pretend otherwise.

This view is evidently still attractive to some philosophers: sufficiently attractive to make it possible to dispense with supporting arguments. Thus, for example, Henson claims that it is a 'fact' that 'some people simply speak more carefully than others, and some have a keener ear for the linguistic proprieties'.[2] Whatever such a claim boils down to in particular cases, it is manifestly a much stronger claim than that linguistic usage differs between individuals, or even that different people have different ideas about what is correct. For this would make sensitivity to the linguistic proprieties no more than a speech-behaviour counterpart to 'good taste' (where 'good taste' is defined as 'what I think *I* have, you know *you* have and we both agree *they* haven't got').[3]

[1] R. Harris, *The Language-Makers*, London, 1980, p. 7.
[2] Henson, op. cit., p. 210.
[3] R. Guild, *The Finishing Touch*, London, 1979, p. 8.

It seems, then, that a 'democratic' view of meaning will be challenged by an 'élitist' view, and one of the attractions of the élitist view may be that it holds out the possibility that indeterminacy of meaning is only apparent. It is an uncertainty which arises from taking into account the conflicting usage of speakers who are not all equally expert. Abstracted on to a theoretical plane, it is the attractiveness of the élitist view which supports the postulation of 'ideal speaker-hearers' of natural languages. For ideal users can be guaranteed to know the exact meaning of every expression about which doubt might, in practice, arise, just as they can be guaranteed to know the correct linguistic forms and the correct grammatical rules.

The democratic view, on the other hand, seems to be based on a Lincolnesque belief that 'you cannot fool all the people all of the time'. If you could, a situation might hypothetically arise in which a word was in use in a given linguistic community and yet no member of that community knew what it meant, even though they all thought they did. Such a hypothesis, on the democratic view, is plainly absurd.

But is it absurd? Certainly there must have been linguistic communities in which erroneous beliefs were entertained without dissent; for example, the belief that the earth is flat. Given such a community, what is one to say about the meaning they attach to the word *earth*? Certainly they will use the word *earth* as if the earth were the kind of body which in fact it is not. Can we say on this ground that they are mistaken about the meaning of the word? A prompting to answer this question affirmatively perhaps comes from the fact that in the case of individuals we would, in appropriate circumstances, have little hesitation over saying that a person was simply in error about the meaning of a word. We might say of a person, for example, that he mistakenly thought that *osmosis* was the name of a skin disease, or that he mistakenly thought that French *parce que* meant 'although'. If individuals can be mistaken or unsure about the meanings of words, it seems not unreasonable to entertain the notions of collective error or collective uncertainty.

Bloomfield held that it was too much to expect the linguist to be able to define the meanings of words like *love* and *hate*, because science had not yet advanced to a point where it understood what love and hate were.[1] But if neither the linguist nor any other scientist knows what these words mean, presumably the ordinary language-user does not know either. A more general scepticism might question whether, even when science does claim to know all about something, that knowledge may not subsequently turn out to have been mistaken. Pursuing the sceptic's challenge to its limit, we might ask what guarantee there is that any linguistic community knows the meanings of the words it uses.

A favourite answer to the sceptic is to accuse him of confusing meaning with reference, or semantic knowledge with knowledge of the world. If a linguistic community uses the word *earth* to mean 'the flat body in space inhabited by the human race', then we may legitimately entertain doubts about their geography and their astronomy, but it is simply a confusion to entertain doubts as to whether they know what the word *earth* means. For them, the word *earth* does mean 'the flat body in space inhabited by the human race', and that is all there is to it. That may not be what the word *earth* means for us; but that is a different matter.

However, countering the sceptic's challenge in this way leaves the theorist with the awkward problem of saying exactly where the boundary which includes meaning but excludes reference, or includes semantic knowledge but excludes knowledge of the world, runs. The one thing the theorist cannot afford to say is that the boundary is indeterminate or undrawable, because then the sceptic will rightly accuse him of begging the question. You cannot accuse your opponent of confusing two separate things and in the same breath deny that there is any clear distinction between them.

Depending on whether the theorist is a democrat or an élitist in semantic matters, he will tackle the boundary question differently. In both cases there are problems. If he is an élitist, he has to decide who the élite are: that is, which speakers in the community are those who do know what words mean and use them accordingly. If he is a democrat, he has to decide how the cases of conflicting usage, which will inevitably emerge, are to be dealt with. In some ways, the democrat may appear to have the simpler task, because he can afford to say that the community is sovereign, and therefore one-hundred-per-cent agreement, or ninety-per-cent, or whatever other figure he chooses down to a simple majority, will decide what counts as the

[1] L. Bloomfield, *Language*, London, 1935, p. 139.

meaning of an expression and what does not; whereas the élitist, by virtue of his élitism, cannot hide behind statistics, but has to reckon with the fact that for different expressions the élite will be different. Lawyers are likely to have a clearer idea of what the term *felony* means than doctors will; whereas doctors are likely to have a clearer idea of what the term *lesion* means than lawyers.

But for both democrat and élitist there is going to be a difficulty over consistency. Unless both are careful, their methods will lead them to represent the linguistic community's semantic knowledge as conflicting with itself. For example, the democrat may encounter what is known to sociologists as the 'Condorcet effect'.[1] This has the disconcerting result that in particular cases a community as a whole may appear to prefer A to B, and B to C, but C to A. The Condorcet effect is the result of adding up a series of quite rational individual choices to produce an apparently irrational collective result. But the fact that this effect is well known will not help the linguist who has to decide on the basis of the evidence he has collected whether to put down the meaning of an expression as 'A', or as 'B', or as 'C'. Similarly, the élitist may be in difficulties over reconciling the fact that the meanings of certain expressions as defined by the usage of one section of the community conflict with evidence from other sections of the community about the meanings of the same or related expressions.

There are important differences, as Harrison[2] has pointed out, between grounds on which one might advance the thesis of referential indeterminacy. One possibility is to propose it on general grounds of epistemological scepticism, as Waismann[3] did. What should we say, the sceptic asks, if this familiar domestic animal we had all along taken for a cat started growing to a gigantic size, or, having been killed stone dead, came back to life of its own accord? We observe straight away that the sceptic's questions are rhetorical. There are perfectly plausible answers to them, but the sceptic is not interested. (One might, for example, say in the case of a feline giant, 'Tibbles seems to be doing remarkably well on that

[1] R. Boudon, *The Logic of Sociological Explanation*, tr. T. Burns, Harmondsworth, 1974, pp. 12–13.

[2] B. Harrison, *Meaning and Structure*, New York, 1972, ch. 8.

[3] F. Waismann, 'Verifiability', in *Essays on Logic and Language*, ed. A. G. N. Flew, Oxford, 1951, pp. 117–44.

new brand of cat food', or when confronted with *felis resurgens*, 'Tibbles couldn't have been run over by that lorry after all.') What the sceptic wants us to concede is that we should be in a frightful predicament about what to say, because of the semantic imprecision of our ordinary noun *cat*. Is it right to call the creature a cat? Perhaps it is something else. Whereas, *pace* the sceptic, that is the last puzzle—the very last—we should be likely to exercise ourselves about in the circumstances depicted; unless, of course, we were linguistic philosophers.

Epistemological scepticism is beyond remedy. But it applies across the board. It is as much an indictment of our eyesight, our hearing, our credulity and our scientific methods as it is of our language. If the human condition is such that we can never be sure that anything is quite what it seems to be, then the human race is simply in no position to have a language which is referentially determinate in the sense of guaranteeing our words permanent job-security. A language with job-secure words presupposes omniscience.

One motivation for developing an integrational linguistics is the recognition that language is misconceived when thought of as a system with which we would refute the epistemological sceptic if only we could. There is no perfect hypothetical language, to which the languages we have are merely clumsy approximations. Where the epistemology of integrational linguistics differs from that implicit in traditional linguistics would be in its further recognition that there is no impregnable position to hold against the sceptic by digging in behind the frontiers which supposedly demarcate one linguistic community from its neighbours. That is a strategy which has often commended itself to linguists. For it is tempting to try to meet the criterion of omniscience required for a language with job-secure words, by treating the language itself as defining omniscience. In a much quoted passage, Martin Joos wrote:

> All phenomena . . . which we find we cannot describe precisely with a finite number of absolute categories, we classify as non-linguistic elements of the real world and expel them from linguistic science. Let sociologists and others do what they like with such things—we may wish them luck in their efforts to describe them precisely in their own terminology, but no matter whether they describe them with discrete categories or not, for us they remain vague, protean,

fluctuating phenomena—in a word, they represent that 'continuity'. which we refuse to tolerate in our own science.[1]

These remarks were intended to apply particularly to grammatical description, but they have much wider implications. The theoretical licence they reflect allows the linguist to deal with epistemologically recalcitrant domestic animals simply by sending them to hell, or to sociology, or to philosophy (whichever seems the most definitive banishment). Likewise they allow him to deal with phonologically and morphologically recalcitrant utterances by relegating them to the limbo of non-language. But the very ways in which these powers of relegation have to be exercised are revealing.

Consider a vocalisation of the type which a trained phonetician might transcribe as [zaaaa], plus an indication of falling intonation. Vocalisations of this type are not infrequently employed by speakers of English in circumstances of the following kind. In the course of a game of cricket, the bowler delivers the ball, and strikes the batsman on the pad. Whereupon the bowler turns to the umpire, throwing his arms in the air and simultaneously shouting [zaaaa] at the top of his voice. The umpire thereupon raises one index finger above his head.

The participants in such an incident are in no doubt about the communicational procedures which have been invoked, about the significance of the various actions, why the sequence occurred in the order it did, what the immediate consequences are for those concerned, and so on. But what is the descriptive linguist to make of this vocalisation [zaaaa]?

Basically, the linguist who is operating within an orthodox descriptive framework has two choices. He can reject the vocalisation as falling on the wrong side of the boundary which separates English from non-English and speech from mere noise. Or else he will in some way seek to relate it to the standard formula for dismissal appeals specified in footnote 1 to Law 47 of the *Laws of Cricket*[2] which is: 'How's that?' In other words, he will treat [zaaaa] as an English utterance by somehow accommodating it within the structural systems set up for his description of the

[1] M. Joos, 'Description of language design', *Journal of the Acoustical Society of America*, vol. 22, 1950, pp. 701–8.
[2] 1947 Code, 5th ed., p. 30.

English language. Two possible strategies of accommodation may be envisaged. One would involve postulating optional phonological rules by which [zaaaa] could be derived from [hawzðat]. The other would be to set up *Zaaaa* as an independent English expression synonymous with *How's that?*

The first of these strategies would be tantamount to treating [zaaaa] as a kind of permissible phonological ellipsis, a substitute for the full form which the bowler could have used if he had taken the trouble. The second strategy would be tantamount to expanding the technical vocabulary of cricketing English.

However, [zaaaa] is merely the iceberg tip of the problem as far as the orthodox linguist is concerned. For there are many other vocalisations which do duty as appeals for dismissal on the cricket field, some of which would probably test even the ingenuity of a phonetician to transcribe. If all of these are to be accommodated within the class of English utterances in the same way as [zaaaa], the number of postulated phonological rules or synonymous expressions must proliferate alarmingly. Furthermore, the proliferation will be uncontrolled, in the sense that there is no limit to the number of different vocalisations that can, by *ad hoc* adjustments, be accommodated in this manner. Somewhere the orthodox linguist has to draw a line which will leave [hawzðat] comfortably on one side as a fully accredited English utterance, but keep out the unwanted cricket-field vocalisations at the same time.

How the linguist justifies drawing this line is a problem for his own descriptive conscience. The point is that wherever the line is drawn it will be, from the cricketers' point of view, an irrelevant and arbitrary one. Whatever the linguist's solution, it has to be found within the limits of a predetermined descriptive system. This system leaves him no option but to impose discrete categorisations upon vocal behaviour which participants recognise as constituting a situationally relevant continuum. The linguist is obliged to look for determinacy of form where there is none—at least, not in the place where he is looking. For his determinacy is of a kind which makes no sense in respect of the participants' experience of their own communicational activity.

For an integrational linguistics, what will count in this as in all other cases is how participants interpret vocal behaviour and intend it to be interpretable, as evidenced by their interaction in the particular circumstances. Even where this produces an account which agrees with that given by the orthodox linguist, it will be an account which has a significantly different theoretical and empirical basis.

The case of appeals for dismissal at cricket points to the basic problem for orthodox linguistics in dealing with any continuum of behaviour. The problem is that there is no possibility of specifying in advance any fixed set of vocalisations which are all and only the recognisable forms of appeal. It would be a mistake to suppose that this is a marginal case merely because it is a very obvious one. What is wrong with orthodox linguistics is that its approach to the identification of linguistic form misrepresents the communicational task of the participants. Umpires do not decide whether an appeal has been made by comparing the sounds they hear to an acoustic image of how the words 'How's that?' might be pronounced by a BBC newsreader. Nor is the bowler who shouts [zaaaa] making some kind of gross performance error in attempting to articulate the appeal formula given in the footnote to Law 47. What matters—and all that matters—is that the shout should be hearable as an appeal. *Mutatis mutandis*, this applies not merely to cricket appeals, but across the entire gamut of vocal and verbal activity. When *A* speaks to *B*, the prime communicational concern which both share in common is not just the audibility but the hearability of what is said; as when *A* writes a letter to *B* the prime communicational concern is not just the visibility but the legibility of what is written. But neither hearability nor legibility are objectively measurable in terms of approximation to some idealised standard, whether of pronunciation or of script. Both are products of the creative activity of the participants, and as such inherently context-bound. To suppose otherwise is to conflate the identification of an essential condition for linguistic communication with the evaluation of possible ways of achieving it.

The risk of conflation is unfortunately not reduced by the metalinguistic terminology commonly used to discuss problems of hearability and legibility. We say, for example, of some dubiously legible word in John's letter, 'It looks like *and*'—as if we were engaged in an actual process of comparison between the scrawl on the paper and some imagined copperplate prototype, whereas what we are in fact trying to do is to determine how the scrawl is most plausibly interpretable in its context, in such a way as to make sense of John's communication. If indeed we had some prototype inscription of the word *and* before us, and attempted a systematic visual comparison between the prototype and John's scrawl, we should rapidly convince ourselves that the question 'Does it look like *and*?' misses the point. For in some respects the scrawl will be similar to the prototype, and in other respects it will be dissimilar. What we need to know is which similarities matter. But the prototype itself cannot tell us this. It does not incorporate in its own visual contours the criteria relevant for matching it with every other written shape. All we have done is to substitute one problem for another. Furthermore, the substitution leads us nowhere. For we now have to decide in which respect the scrawl would need to be like the prototype in order to determine whether the scrawl is indeed 'like *and*'. The answer will be that the relevant respects are precisely those in which the scrawl is legible as *and*. If we can determine that for the scrawl, then we do not need the prototype at all. If not, no amount of visual inspection of the prototype will help.

The fact is that human beings do not inhabit a communicational space which is neatly compartmentalised into the linguistic and the non-linguistic, either on the formal side or on the semantic side.

If problems of semantic determinacy have attracted more widespread attention than problems of formal determinacy, that is doubtless because they raise more obvious and more general epistemological issues.

But it was always a mistake for the linguist to try to keep the forces of epistemological scepticism at bay by bold declarations like 'This may not really be a chair, but that's certainly what it's called in English'. That would be like trying to stop a tank by shouting defiance at it. This is what we may be reduced to doing out of bravado or frustration if there seems to be no alternative available. One senses the futility of trying to prevent the sceptic from scoring the point that, however careful we may be in our application of linguistic criteria, ordinary observational statements like 'There's a robin in the garden' may after all turn out to be wrong. And we seem to have no option but to concede to the sceptic that we may be wrong not only about this particular robin but about robins in general. Unfortunately, the desire to escape from this humiliating retreat before the sceptic may lead to other ill-chosen lines of defence, such as a too hastily drawn distinction between factual and linguistic uncertainty.

The hope is usually to be able to draw this distinction in such a way that the doubts which linguistic knowledge will resolve fall on one side, while the doubts which linguistic knowledge cannot resolve fall on the other. Thus uncertainty which, at least after a certain point very soon reached, cannot be cleared up by further argument or discussion about how a certain expression is or ought to be used will be counted as falling into the latter category.

Harrison[1] exemplifies what he refers to as two quite different senses in which it can be said that a person is in doubt as to whether to call something a cat. On the one hand, it may be recognised that the animal has a general cat-like appearance and behaviour, but nevertheless there is room for speculation about whether further investigation might not reveal facts which would rule out the possibility of its being a cat. On the other hand, it may be that in view of what is known about the animal, an equally good case could be made out for calling it a cat as for not calling it a cat, and it is not clear which to say. Doubts of the latter type, in Harrison's view, are linguistic doubts; whereas doubts of the former type are not. Waismann, according to Harrison, failed to see this distinction. Non-linguistic doubts do not arise as a result of any ambiguity or incompleteness in the rules of our language: they are the product of inadequate knowledge of the thing in question. Whereas in the case of linguistic doubt, the opposite is the case: sufficient is already known about the thing in question, and the trouble lies in the inadequacy of the linguistic rules to deal with the case.

The linguist, for his part, is inclined to welcome this distinction because he is so glad to see the back of those science-fiction cats. But sheer relief at the dwindling cat population is soon alloyed by realising that maintaining the distinction is going to be more troublesome than just conceding victory outright to the sceptic. For what looks like a clear and relatively simple distinction when applied to putative cats, putative chairs, etc., starts to be difficult and unhelpful as soon as we turn to abstract, evaluative and theoretical terms. Even the use of ordinary grading words, like *heavy, good, unusual,* typically involves a simultaneous assessment of facts and terminological appropriateness, correlated in such a

[1] Harrison, op. cit., pp. 137–40.

way that when doubts arise it often makes little sense to ask whether they are factual doubts or linguistic doubts. They may in one sense be a mixture of both, but not necessarily a mixture that could even in principle be sorted out into two separate components. Or if, for example, I am in doubt about whether to describe a certain procedure as 'democratic', it is far from clear that my uncertainty is to be resolved either by careful consideration of what the word *democratic* means, or by further investigation of how the procedure is conducted, how it originated, or what effects it has or might have. It may be that my doubt has more to do with how the facts ought to be looked at, what view to take of them. In such cases, it is easy to be misled about the nature of the doubt, because we commonly express disagreement by saying things like 'That's not what I call "democratic" '—which makes it sound as if it is a linguistic issue. Similarly, if someone says 'Tony Greig was a traitor to English cricket' and someone else violently disagrees, it is not necessarily that they do not see eye to eye over anything orthodox linguistics would treat as the meaning of the sentence *Tony Greig was a traitor to English cricket*, or over the facts of the case either. Of course, they might be at loggerheads over both. But it is more likely that discussion of paradigm cases of treachery, or further information about the negotiations in which Greig was involved will not reconcile them, because what ultimately divides them is the view they take of the best interests of English cricket. In vast areas of everyday discourse, what to say depends much more on 'mere opinion' than can possibly be accommodated by a simple dichotomy between factual doubts and linguistic doubts, however it may be set up by the theoretician.

The Yorkshire local authority at Riccall had a notice erected by the level crossing which reads:

Drivers of
LARGE or SLOW
VEHICLES
must phone
and get permission
to cross.

This evidently was not regarded as adequate, for a further notice was put up beneath it, which reads:

LARGE means

over 55′ long or 9′ 6″ wide

or 32 tons total weight

SLOW means 5 mph or less.

Do they think that in Yorkshire people need to be told what the words *large* and *slow* mean? Or is it that in Riccall these words mean something special? The first notice might indeed have left a lorry driver in doubt about whether he had to phone for permission to cross. But it is very unclear why we have to categorise his doubt as a factual doubt about his lorry, or else a linguistic doubt about the words *large* and/or *slow*, or else a mixture of both.

It should not be part of the programme of an integrational linguistics to improve on the theory by setting up some third category of uncertainties and calling them 'doubts of opinion' or 'doubts of perspective'. That would be doubly misguided. In the first place, separating a third category from the other two would be no less fraught with difficulty than separating the two already on offer. In the second place, for those who are absolutely determined to make do with two categories, two will do. It only needs a certain ruthlessness to make every conceivable doubt factual or linguistic, one or the other. Reasons can always be found. But it needs only a little more ruthlessness to make all doubts linguistic; or, alternatively, to make all doubts factual. It was the ruthlessness of the sceptic, who wanted to make all doubts linguistic, that led to setting up the two-category system in the first place, as a first line of defence. But if instead of trying to dig in somewhere, we simply ask how many kinds of doubt there are about what to say, the answer must surely be that there are very many kinds. And before we start trying to count how many, we need to know what is the purpose of counting them.

A common complaint against the empiricist is that, by yielding too much to the sceptic, he makes it impossible to distinguish between the linguistic and the non-linguistic. The anti-empiricist programme claims to be able to render unto the sceptic the things which are his, while reserving for the linguist the things that belong to language. Thus open texture is surrendered to the sceptic, but questions of vagueness and precision are claimed for linguistics. The first point that must be made is that from the standpoint of an integrational linguistics this debate between the empiricist and the anti-empiricist is entirely misconceived.

Waismann wanted to be able to distinguish between a kind of semantic indeterminacy which could in principle be remedied by providing more accurate linguistic rules, and a kind of semantic indeterminacy which could not. He termed the former 'vagueness' and the latter 'open texture'. Vagueness was exemplified by words like *heap* and *pink*, open texture by words like *gold*. Harrison proposes a redefinition of Waismann's terms. Vagueness will characterise a relation between an expression and a particular state of affairs such that linguistic rules yield ambiguous or conflicting results. Open texture will characterise any expression for which it is logically possible that there exists some state of affairs with respect to which it is vague. Thus vagueness will still, as Waismann intended, be in principle remediable by adjustment of linguistic rules. But what Waismann did, in Harrison's view, was to confuse considerations of epistemology with considerations of linguistic structure, and he did this because he was working within the confines of an 'empiricist theory of language'. Harrison rejects such a theory, but his anti-empiricism still yields a distinction which is remarkably similar to Waismann's. The reasons for this are of some interest in the context of the present discussion.

Harrison is concerned to deny that the expressions we use are for the most part semantically indeterminate in the circumstances in which we use them. They are not vague, but on the contrary precise; and his explication of 'precision' is that the semantic rules of the language provide a determinate answer to the question of whether, given the circumstances, the usage was correct. This thesis offers a useful yardstick for measuring the distance between, on the one hand, an integrational analysis of meaning and, on the other, a set of assumptions about meaning shared by empiricist and anti-empiricist alike.

The reason why can be illustrated by considering Harrison's own paradigm example of vagueness. The situation is one in which a sergeant gives a private the order 'Bring the boomerang'. The soldier picks up the boomerang, takes a few steps towards the sergeant, and then throws the boomerang away from him. He continues to advance towards the sergeant, and by the time he has reached the sergeant the boomerang has returned, so that he is able to catch it and hand it to the sergeant. The question which Harrison poses is whether or not the soldier has executed the order. Harrison assumes that the linguistic rules for the verb *bring* are formulated in such a way as to allow us to test at various points for the question 'Is he bringing the boomerang?', and furthermore that the tests result in different answers at different points. An observer considering what is happening at the point when the private has just picked up the boomerang and is on his way towards the sergeant will reply 'Yes' to the question 'Is he bringing the boomerang?' But a few moments later, when the boomerang has been thrown away, the same observer will reply 'No' to the same question. Finally, if the question is put when the soldier has caught the boomerang again, the answer will again be 'Yes'. So the three successive tests produce two affirmative results and one negative. Here, says Harrison, 'we feel equal and opposite temptations to say that the soldier has—in a way—brought the boomerang to the sergeant and that—in a way—he hasn't. The case is tailor-made for the barrack-room lawyer.'[1]

The vagueness could be remedied, Harrison argues, by amending the semantic rules for *bring*. For example, it could be decided to stipulate that an object must remain in the bringer's possession until he hands it to the receiver. Under such an amendment the case would no longer be vague, because the boomerang was not in the soldier's possession throughout.

If this kind of analysis is a victory for anti-empiricism, the victory must be of the Pyrrhic variety. But it is far from clear that it is victory at all. The concessions implicitly made to the sceptic are every bit as humiliating as those the empiricist makes. The claim that here we see how adjustment to the linguistic rules could in principle remove vagueness rings hollow when it is obvious that the linguistic rules have been set up in advance in such a way as to generate just such remediable vagueness. The real question concerns the setting up of the linguistic rules in the first place. The vagueness is relative to linguistic rules which presuppose the relevance of testing an observer's reactions at a sequence of points in the way described. If the sceptic asks 'How do we know those tests were relevant at all?', there is no answer. It is in general unclear why vagueness should be defined in this way, and why in this instance

[1] Harrison, op. cit., p. 142.

two answers 'Yes' and one answer 'No' have to be counted unsatisfactory. A different but equally arbitrary decision would be to count the tests as satisfactory provided they yielded at least some affirmative answers. Furthermore, the vagueness of *bring* can hardly be removed simply by stipulating that objects must remain constantly in their bringer's possession. That merely shifts the vagueness, and invites a challenge to justify what counts as being in someone's possession. The more insistently we probe the example, the clearer it becomes that it is the sceptic who is still dictating the campaign. The ground which the anti-empiricist claims to hold turns out to be a shifting piece of no-man's land not worth defending.

It is possible to propose a quite different approach to questions of meaning, which does not find itself in constant and wearisome retreat before the sceptic, because it outflanks the traditional sceptical position in semantics from the very outset. Both the empiricist and the anti-empiricist make the mistake of allowing the sceptic to interpret the question of semantic determinacy in terms of a pre-arranged programme for covering all eventualities. Once allowed this interpretation, the sceptic is bound to win. He will win because he is right. There is no pre-arranged programme, but he has bamboozled his challengers into arguing as if there were. He can do this the more easily because they are already committed to the assumption that a meaning is something conveyed from speaker to hearer by means of a linguistic form, and hence to conceiving of linguistic knowledge as a determinate set of facts and rules, known to all members of the community, and covering the correct employment and interpretation of linguistic forms.

A quite different approach to meaning is to treat it as the product of particular communication situations. This affords the basis for an integrational semantics, where there is no question of pre-arranged programmes at all. It becomes simply pointless to worry about whether, for example, the soldier was still bringing the boomerang when he had thrown it. That is a question which has no communicational relevance whatsoever to the situation as described. It would not even begin to look like a remotely relevant question unless, let us suppose, the soldier had thereupon been reprimanded for failing to do as he was told. And even then it would not be immediately plausible that there was a problem about lexical semantics involved. The barrack-room lawyer would have a hard time at the court martial arguing that the inadequacy of linguistic rules for the verb *bring* had occasioned an unfortunate misunderstanding between the soldier and his sergeant.

To both the empiricist and the anti-empiricist, questioning whether there is a pre-arranged semantic programme at all will sound like a scepticism far more radical than the traditional sceptic's. Indeed, it may sound more like heresy. Surely, they will argue, communication through language would be impossible unless words did have established meanings and all members of the linguistic community operated with roughly the same semantic rules. Put in this plaintive way, the objection seems incontrovertible. None the less, it misses the point at issue. No one supposes that two individuals can somehow achieve instant communication on the basis of words neither has used or heard before. The question is whether it is correct, or useful, or even plausible to represent their past linguistic experience as standing in relation to their present communication situation as the rules of a game to a particular episode of play. That is the analogy on which the traditional sceptic relies to make his point that the language rules are not only hopelessly incomplete, but in principle beyond completable formulation. But there is nothing which obliges us to force this analogy upon language. If language is a game at all, it is a game we mostly make up as we go along. It is a communication game in which there is no referee, and the only rule that cannot be bent says that players shall improvise as best they can.

An integrational linguistics would be concerned with the analysis of this improvisation as a function, simultaneously, of relevant past experience and a current communication situation. It would, however, give priority to the latter for two reasons.

In the first place, the extent of relevant past experience is irrecoverable. Only in the case of very young children is there at present hope of assembling anything like a complete record of evidence which could form the basis for judgments concerning the probable role of past linguistic experience in the communicational articulation of a current situation. In this respect, linguistics is in no better but no worse a position than any study of human behaviour which is presumptively based in some important measure on the individual's accumulation of a lifetime's learning. Doubtless this unsatisfactory evidential situation will improve dramatically within the next quarter of a century. The linguistics of A.D. 2000 should be able to draw upon data storage and analysis facilities which make it possible to monitor linguistic behaviour on a scale which is now quite beyond practical resources. The need to speculate about how linguistic experience is translated into patterns of communicative behaviour will diminish accordingly. But this remains a prospect for the future.

Secondly, what is important from an integrational perspective is not so much the fund of past linguistic experience as the individual's adaptive use of it to meet the communicational requirements of the present. That use is—and can only be—manifest in the communication situation itself. No new technology is required to study it. The evidence is available *in praesentia*. All that is lacking is the readiness to accept it.

On the semantic side, this requires willingness to concede the indeterminacy of what is meant, and on a scale which many may feel goes against the grain of a whole educational tradition. In this they would be right. For the educational tradition in question has been based for centuries on the sacrosanctity of the dictionary. The assumption that we communicate by means of internalised dictionaries is a natural continuation of that tradition, transposed into the terms of Saussurean psychologism. But observing how people set about resolving questions of semantic indeterminacy in practice suggests that in many cases the issue is simply not of a kind where reliance on dictionaries, whether of the internalised or the library variety, would be of much help.

The point may be illustrated by reference to the following (uninvented) case history:

R. ruined her husband's best pair of trousers through inadvertently leaving a hot iron on them. The result was a hole of approximately half an inch in diameter, surrounded by a badly scorched area. R. suggested to her husband, D., that it might be possible to obtain compensation under their fire insurance policy. D. thought this very unlikely, pointing out that no fire had been caused. The wording of the insurance policy itself proved unhelpful. R. recalled that her parents once made a successful fire insurance claim when a coal falling from an open fire burned a hole in a hearth rug. R. and D. decided to make a claim for fire damage. The company's representative called to investigate the circumstances and inspect the damaged trousers. A few weeks later the company paid the claim in full.

This is a case in which the meaning of a particular word, *fire*, is central to the situation, and there is evidently doubt as to whether it covers a particular case. So superficially it appears to be as near to a real-life instance of vagueness, in the linguistic philosopher's sense, as it would be possible to find. But it is not a question of whether the internalised lexicon and semantic rules of the claimants match the hypothetical lexicon and semantic rules underlying their insurance policy. It differs from the boomerang case in that here we are clear about what is at issue as between one description of the facts and a rival description. What is at issue is whether the insurance company pays for the trousers. One reason why hypothetical problems like the boomerang example fail to convince is that they offer no basis for grasping what difference it could possibly make whether the situation is described in one way or the other. Thus the indeterminacy they purport to illustrate is seen to be all too evidently a product of the theoretical vacuum in which the hypothesis is presented.

A semantics which rejects the internalised lexicon model has no reason to waste time on pseudo-problems of this kind. Instead, it will be more concerned to analyse how questions of semantic indeterminacy arise in communicational interaction, and what linguistic techniques are in fact employed by participants to resolve the difficulties involved. Various points about the fire insurance example are typical and instructive in this respect.

First and foremost, there is always a descriptive diagnostic, in the sense that some particular event prompts the question of how something is to be described; that is to say, makes it a discussable issue. Normally, adult human beings do not go around describing their environment for the fun of it. If they did, semantics would be a different enterprise. (This is exactly the point at which the boomerang example loses contact with reality.) Still less do they go around arguing for fun about how it ought to be described. What makes description a discussable issue in any particular case may consequently be expected to determine to an important extent how the participants will use the verbal and non-verbal resources available to them to resolve the question. This is a basic fact about communication which the internalised lexicon model has no way of reflecting. The starting point in the case under consideration is that D.'s trousers have been ruined. If it were simply a matter of describing what happened, the question as to what kind of damage the trousers had suffered would not arise as a discussable issue. For there is no dispute about what happened. The damage was caused by a hot iron. That would be all the description necessary, were it not for the fact that ruining a pair of trousers happens to be a sufficiently serious financial matter for R. and D. to make it worth their while considering how the loss might be recouped. In other words, the question which is going to be the discussable issue does not arise out of the mere domestic facts of the case; for they can be clearly and uncontroversially described without raising any query as to whether fire was involved. That query is introduced into the case in virtue of a quite extraneous but crucial circumstance, namely that R. and D. happen to have a fire insurance policy. They live in a culture in which it is possible to obtain financial compensation for mishaps, under the terms of a legal contract. Without that specific contextualisation, there would be nothing to discuss. The chain which links damage to financial loss, to possible compensation, to contract, and thence to fire would not be constituted. The question whether the damage had been caused by fire would be just as idle a question as whether it had been occasioned by failure to propitiate the gods, or by previous wickedness on the part of D. (which in some cultures might be much more important questions for all concerned, and make the domestic mishap a discussable issue in quite different ways).

The specific contextualisation which supplies the descriptive diagnostic not only determines what is a discussable issue, but also how it makes sense to discuss it.

In Western societies, the law provides countless examples of descriptive diagnostics which are recognisable as falling into this pattern. Individuals and institutions are prosecuted for alleged offences which hinge upon the interpretation of particular expressions in legal acts. Now it is true that in court proceedings of this type, dictionary definitions are not infrequently quoted. What is significant is the reason why. If the dictionary itself put such matters beyond doubt, there would be no need for legal wrangling, and lexicographers would have saved the taxpayer a great deal of money.

The attraction of appeal to dictionary definitions in the courtroom is that they provide a supposedly non-subjective basis for argument about lexical meanings, which would otherwise be lacking. They are accepted as offering unbiassed evidence about certain general forms of consensual agreement. (It may be noted in passing that this is precisely what the definitions supplied by an internalised lexicon could not possibly do; namely, provide non-subjective information about other people's use of vocabulary.) But what has then to be decided is the relevance of that evidence to the local issue before the court.

Very commonly, the courtroom appeal to a dictionary definition arises out of circumstances in which one party contends that something is describable as (an) *E*, but this is (or may be) denied by another party. The appeal to a dictionary definition of *E* then provides a non-circular way to resolve the issue without begging the question of the correct application of the term *E* in this particular instance.

A not untypical recent example in English law is the case of *Hudson v. Marshall*,[1] in which there arose the question of the meaning of the word *souvenir*. What was at issue was whether a child's white T-shirt with a Bugs Bunny motif on it was a souvenir. The justices in the case considered the definition of the word *souvenir* given in the *Shorter Oxford English Dictionary* as 'a remembrance, a memory, a token of remembrance, a keepsake'. Clearly, if they expected the dictionary to supply them with a clear answer to the question of whether Bugs Bunny T-shirts are or are not souvenirs, they must have been disappointed. The question itself sounds bizarre until related to the particular circumstances before the court. These concerned the prosecution of a shop owner in Victoria Parade, Torquay, for selling a Bugs Bunny T-shirt on a Sunday. However, at the time there was in force a local authority order made under section 51 of the Shops Act 1950, providing for Sunday opening of shops for the sale, *inter alia*, of 'souvenirs'. The issue, therefore, was whether, in those circumstances, selling a Bugs Bunny T-shirt was selling a souvenir—which was perfectly legal— or whether it was selling something other than a souvenir. In

---

[1] I am indebted to Andrew Ashworth for drawing my attention to this and the following case. (Hudson v. Marshall [1976] Criminal Law Review 523; Corkery v. Carpenter [1951] 1 King's Bench 102.)

deciding the matter, the question the justices asked themselves was the following: 'Would an ordinary purchaser (usually a parent on holiday) ordinarily buy this article in the Victoria Parade area of this holiday resort as a souvenir?' The relevance of the dictionary definition of *souvenir* was not that it was expected to provide direct information about the *de facto* 'souvenir status' of Bugs Bunny T-shirts, but that it enabled the issue before the court to be re-formulated more generally in terms of intentions. It provided a non-question-begging way of characterising the hypothetical inten-tions of a hypothetical purchaser, so that the question of buying an article of this particular type in these particular circumstances could then be addressed. Whether this was the appropriate use to make of the dictionary definition, however, is itself a further issue. In the appeal hearing against the decision in 1976 in the Queen's Bench divisional court, it was held that the justices had not asked them-selves the right question. The relevant question was held to be: 'Would a shopkeeper in the Victoria Parade area of Torquay, opening his shop on that day, do so in the anticipation that ordinary purchasers would buy articles like this T-shirt as a souvenir of Torquay?' Perhaps surprisingly, the answer to this hypothetical question was held to be 'Yes', and consequently the appeal was dismissed.

The essential points to note are that in both courts the crux of the matter was not whether in general something is describable in a certain way, but whether for the legal purposes embodied in a certain act it is thus describable; and, secondly, the insistence that this has to be determined by reference to whether it is thus describable for the circumstances envisaged; that is to say, with reference to certain kinds of people, acting in a certain way, with certain presumed expectations, intentions, etc.

Analogous considerations apply to cases involving semantic relations between words. In 1950 in the case of *Corkery v. Carpenter* the counsel for the defendant cited the words of the song

> 'It won't be a stylish marriage,
> I can't afford a carriage,
> But you'll look sweet upon the seat
> Of a bicycle made for two'

to show that in popular usage the meanings of the words *bicycle* and *carriage* were incompatible. The relevance of this was that the defendant had been charged under section 12 of the Licensing Act, 1872, which deals with persons drunk while in charge of a carriage on the highway. At the time of the alleged offence, the defendant had been pushing his bicycle along Broad Street, Ilfracombe. The contention for the defence was that in statutes concerning matters relating to the general public words are presumed to be used in their popular meaning, and that in the popular usage of the terms a bicycle is not a carriage. Rejecting this argument, Lord Goddard held that what the word *carriage* meant might vary from one Act of Parliament to another, in some cases being taken to include bicycles and in other cases not. He furthermore cited the judgment of the court in the case of *Taylor v. Goodwin* to the effect that it did not matter whether there were any bicycles in existence at the time when an act was passed, for purposes of determining whether the word *carriage* in the act was to be understood as including bicycles. What governed the application of a term was the purpose of the relevant section of the act, which in this case was clearly the protection of the public and the preservation of public order. A drunken man with a bicycle was no less a threat to the public and to public order than a drunken man in charge of any other vehicle. In this context, therefore, the term *carriage* was to be interpreted as covering any kind of vehicle, including a bicycle.

The kind of descriptive diagnostic which operates in the case of the law is merely one very clear example of a principle which applies to communicational interactions generally. It is not a 'special case', except in that it probes and lays bare to an unusual degree the procedures and the rationale which underlie a determination of 'what is meant'. It comes to terms with the fact that there is no way in which language can provide explicitly and specifically for all conceivable eventualities.

What language can and must do, however, is provide mechanisms for participants to resolve possible communicational uncertainties. The availability of the questions 'What did you say?' and 'What did you mean?' are the ultimate guarantee that we are dealing with language and with human beings, not with computer programmes and machines. But language is amply provided with techniques which make recourse to such questions only a last resort. Moreover, the usefulness of these last-resort questions is itself subject to the same conditions of communicational relevance as all other linguistic exchange. It is no coincidence that the law, which is itself a last resort when ordinary communication between individuals has broken down, should exhibit public and formal versions of the mechanisms which individuals employ privately and informally in pursuing their communicational aims.

The resolution of semantic uncertainties in legal cases is also analogous to their resolution in everyday circumstances in two further important respects. It involves decision rather than discovery; and it is indefinitely revisable. Should it appear to be otherwise, that is merely because the practical utility of logomachy varies inversely with time, effort and tolerance. It is because most human communication is geared to ephemeral practical purposes that so little indeterminacy appears on the surface. As co-operative participants in the communication situations of every day, we intuitively adapt our demands on determinacy so as to avoid the likelihood of getting into difficulties. We do not embark on communicational courses which are likely to end in collision (although we do not always manage to avoid doing so). We respond to the constantly changing exigencies of communication as motorists to the demands of driving in traffic. Verbally and non-verbally, we try to 'give ourselves room', and allow others to give themselves room too. Otherwise we know that we shall get nowhere quickly. That is part of what it is to conduct oneself as a rational speaker-hearer, and hence as a rational human being.

* * *

Rationality is sometimes said to be one of the key concepts in the social sciences. It is a concept which is held to be central to the issue of how we are to understand what is done and what is believed by other individuals, and in other societies than our own. It is certainly true that much discussion has been devoted to this topic by social scientists of varying persuasions, and by philosophers interested in the theoretical problems of the social sciences. Attempts have been made to explain the underlying rationality of various social practices, institutions and systems of belief of an apparently irrational character, especially those of so-called 'primitive' peoples. Distinctions have been drawn between latent and conscious rationality in the ways in which individuals and communities act. Doubts have been cast upon the validity of judging alien cultures by standards of rationality which depend on translating their values and concepts into Western terms.

But these discussions with a focus on or in the social sciences have usually taken for granted that all men, whatever their cultural background, act rationally at least insofar as they act as competent language-users. And taking this much for granted has led to ignoring such questions as why language-using implies or requires rationality on the part of language-users, and exactly how in their language-using the language-users exhibit rationality.

Although language has for centuries in Europe been regarded not merely as a manifestation but rather as *the* manifestation of human rationality, loss of reason has not usually been supposed to entail automatic loss or impairment of language. The lay tradition, if we may call it that, has been that loss of reason may leave the mechanisms of language intact. This assumption is memorably illustrated by the episode of Hamlet's feigned madness in Shakespeare's play. On the very first occasion when the prince's sanity is put to the test in Act II scene ii, he is engaged in reading a book. This is apparently not seen as counterevidence to his supposed insanity. Neither Polonius nor any other character in the play argues that Hamlet cannot be mad because he can still read. Their theory quite patently assumes that madness is perfectly compatible with being able to read and with being able to talk, at least at what we may call the mechanical level. On the other hand, the lay tradition also assumes that insanity will be manifested in certain ways in what the mad person says; and it is precisely for this reason that Polonius seeks to engage the supposedly mad Hamlet in discussion, so that the King and Queen in concealment can hear for themselves the evidence of his madness. This, then, is a pivotal assumption of the test: speech behaviour in ordinary conversation upon casual topics is held to offer a reliable indication of the speaker's capacity to reason.

A typical response to the speech of those presumed to be irrational is, as Trevor Pateman[1] has pointed out, to 'invalidate' it as communication by withholding the reaction it might otherwise be expected to evoke. Thus a doctor in a mental hospital may simply ignore the patient's question 'When am I going to be

---

[1] *Language, Truth and Politics*, Sidmouth, 1975, p. 61 et seq.

released?'; or treat the patient's statement 'My letters are being opened' not as a genuine complaint to be investigated, but as a symptom of fears and anxieties. In this way madness is, to use Foucault's phrase, 'reduced to silence by positivism'. It is as if nothing had been said: or almost. But not quite. For even in these cases, the 'invalidation' procedure is a way of making sense of what is said. For the doctor to treat the patient's statement that his letters are being opened as symptomatic of the patient's anxieties is to presuppose that the patient is using the words 'My letters are being opened' to give an accurate report of unfounded fear.

Similarly, the kind of evidence which is taken to indicate Hamlet's insanity is, curiously, evidence which presupposes that Hamlet has lost none of the rational speaker's capacity to express his thoughts. Thus when Hamlet, addressing Polonius, says 'You are a fishmonger', this prompts immediately in Polonius the interpretation 'He knew me not at first, a' said I was a fishmonger'. It does not occur to Polonius to doubt his own ability to understand what a madman means by what he says. On the contrary, the madman is assumed to be giving linguistically appropriate reports about his own deranged misconceptions, such that rational hearers can accurately identify those misconceptions. The supposition is one of great interest and significance for anyone who is concerned with the analysis of the concept of a language in the Western tradition. The belief is clearly that words can serve not merely as a means of communication between one sane man and another, but equally reliably, and without alteration or adjustment, as a means of communication between the insane and the sane. Yet how, we are tempted to ask, can there possibly be any justification for such an assumption?

Essentially the same objection as this was raised by Gilbert Ryle[1] against Cartesian dualism. It was always an assumption of Cartesian dualism, as Ryle points out, that real people in the real world can and do recognise the difference between rational and irrational utterances. Yet, self-defeatingly, dualism made it impossible in principle for one person to recognise when another person's utterances were rational and when they were irrational. For utterances were held to have immaterial causes located in the mind of the speaker. But since these immaterial causes *were* immaterial and

[1] *The Concept of Mind*, London, 1949.

therefore inaccessible to observation, it might be the case, for all we can tell, that the apparently irrational utterances of idiots or lunatics are actually as rational as those of normal people. Likewise the apparently rational utterances of apparently sane individuals might not really be so. What the story of Hamlet illustrates is that this paradox was not merely a product of Cartesian dualism as an explicit philosophical theory. It had long lain embodied, although unrecognised, in popular beliefs concerning the connexion between language and reason. On this count, if on no other, the concept of a rational speaker is not one to be taken on trust as perspicuous, self-explanatory, or unproblematic.

The first step of clarification it might seem appropriate to take concerns the scope of whatever it is that is purportedly covered by the term *rational*. The first and most obvious danger that emerges is one of verbal vacuity. For if rationality in this context implies no more than that rationality which is on offer, for example, in traditional definitions of the species *homo sapiens*, then describing what speakers accomplish in verbal exchanges as a kind of reasoning is to say nothing at all worth saying. The expression *rational speaker* is demoted to the status of a tautology. Furthermore, it will be a tautology of the worst kind, namely the kind which allows us to persuade ourselves and others that we are saying something new and revealing when in fact we are saying something utterly trivial. In this sense of the term *rational* one might just as well speak of footballers as 'rational sportsmen', and of those who watch them as 'rational supporters'.

Less vacuous interpretations are, however, apparently available. The term *rational*, as we are reminded by Ryle, is often understood in a substantial range of cases as meaning 'capable of reasoning cogently'. But this itself is a characterisation which is by no means free from difficulties. Anyone who is capable of reasoning cogently is also presumably capable of not reasoning cogently. One might well ask: 'What would it be not to reason cogently?' *Cogently* is a word commonly taken to mean more or less the same as *convincingly*. That which is cogent compels assent. One can imagine the case of a sane man trying to convince the inmates of an asylum by rational argument that their confinement in the asylum is in their own best interests; but failing to do so. In one sense, it might seem that he has not reasoned cogently, having failed to secure assent to his proposition. Or one can suppose that Jones attempts to convince Smith in discussion that Smith ought to vote Labour, while Smith attempts to convince Jones that Jones ought to vote Conservative. Does the failure of either to convince the other demonstrate *ipso facto* that the reasoning employed was not cogent?

The alternative to judging cogency by results seems to be to suppose that the phrase *reasoning cogently* is itself quasi-tautological. In other words, reasoning has to be cogent, or it is strictly speaking not reasoning at all. If someone says:

> 'All men are mortal,
> Socrates is a man,
> Therefore Socrates is not mortal'

does that count as reasoning or as raving? Perhaps the most charitable view would be to count it as an attempt at reasoning which has gone wrong. But then strictly speaking it is not reasoning, on roughly the same ground that to sit an examination is not to pass it. If we take this alternative, *cogently* means not 'convincingly' in the practical sense of securing assent from others, but 'convincingly' in the importantly different sense of 'correctly, validly, in accordance with the rules'.

The question then arises: 'In accordance with what rules?' According to Ryle and many other philosophers, the rules would be rules of the kind first formalised by Aristotle. Philosophers who take this view are not, of course, committed to the belief that before Aristotle nobody could reason. On the contrary, what Aristotle did, they claim, was to make explicit certain rules of reasoning that people were already following—and still do follow—without realising it. Unfortunately, on the face of it we cannot tell from the great majority of verbal exchanges whether the participants are acting on those particular occasions as Aristotelian reasoners or not. We can assume they are, or we can assume the contrary. What they actually say is often compatible with either assumption. For in specific communication situations they rarely make their thinking explicit in ways which would allow us to test their reasoning procedures against the Aristotelian rules.

That does not, however, prevent us from hypothetically attributing to them tacit processes of ratiocination which would explain what they say as predictably in accordance with the Aristotelian rules; or at least in accordance with some more or less slipshod version of the Aristotelian rules which might be assumed to be the best that fallible mortals can manage in the hurly-burly of everyday life. Some such interpretation of speakers' rationality often seems to be championed by those theorists who speak of 'practical reasoning' and the ways in which this is evidenced in mastery of a language for the ordinary purposes of communication. In short, there is a temptation to treat the rational speaker as the real-life counterpart of the competent speaker-hearer postulated by modern linguistic theory. A rational speaker is envisaged as a competent speaker-hearer additionally equipped with whatever pragmatic knowledge will enable him to put his linguistic competence to effective use in actual communication situations. He is able in practice to deploy the linguistic resources at his command in ways that make it possible for fellow members of his speech community to understand what he says by utilising their own linguistic competence and pragmatic knowledge.

In outline, this combined explication of speakers' rationality, in which a grasp of the rules of a language plays an essential role in enabling the speaker to formulate the propositions which he needs for his practical reasoning, sounds like an ideal amalgamation of linguistic, sociological and philosophical theorising. Unfortunately, it creates more problems than it solves if the concept of a competent speaker-hearer is tied to a theory of linguistic knowledge based upon the language myth. For that imposes severe restrictions upon what it is that, as native speakers of a language, we are allowed to know. The core of this knowledge, according to the modern orthodox version, is the system of rules generating sentences of a language. But these sentences are far from being the utterances we actually produce or listen to in the speech episodes of everyday life. Sentences are contextless abstractions which unite idealised sounds and idealised meanings in grammatically and semantically well-formed pairs; as distinct from actual utterances, which are the inevitably contextualised speech events produced by live speakers. Sentences are envisaged as formally and semantically invariant items recurrently instantiated in the everchanging flow of discourse. Although not part of discourse, they impart to discourse its recognisably linguistic character.

Such a restrictive theory of linguistic knowledge automatically poses two key questions.

(i) How is it possible to recover determinate linguistic forms from the heterogeneous mass of phonetic signals present in actual speech?

(ii) How is it possible to identify fixed linguistic meanings among the apparently varied and inconsistent verbal usage which speech behaviour in practice presents?

The scientific credibility of modern linguistics hinges essentially on its capacity to answer these two questions. For clearly the public task of describing any of the languages people actually speak is *ab initio* hopeless unless the linguist can plausibly claim to have identified satisfactorily the elements he purports to be describing.

It is significant that in attempting to make this task appear feasible, linguists have relied heavily upon a doctrine of ellipsis which has historical ramifications connecting it unmistakably with the thesis that understanding what someone says may be a matter of 'filling in' certain things which he actually has not said. At first sight this doctrine looks harmless enough. The basic idea is that there is no need for the linguist to postulate sentence-types corresponding to every kind of utterance that speakers are observed to produce, since in many instances the words speakers actually use can be treated as abbreviations for longer utterances which they could produce if required, but cannot be bothered to. Thus, for instance, if Jones asks 'Who does this coat belong to?' and Smith replies 'Mary', then Smith's reply can be treated as short for something like 'Mary is the person to whom this coat belongs'. The word *Mary*, on this view, is not to be treated as a sentence of English. Or, as it is sometimes put, expressions like *Mary*, or *the woman who just left*, and so on, when used in isolation as answers to questions or in similar roles in discourse, instantiate 'incomplete sentences'.[1]

The doctrine of 'incomplete sentences' is sometimes supported by the argument that such expressions cannot count as proper sentences of the language since in any case it would be impossible to assign determinate meanings to them. Thus 'Mary' might mean on one occasion 'Mary is the person to whom this coat belongs', but on another occasion 'Mary is George's wife', and so on *ad infinitum*. There would be literally no fixed or finite set of semantic

---

[1] J. Lyons, *Introduction to Theoretical Linguistics*, Cambridge, 1968, §5.2.3.

interpretations that could be given in isolation to a sentence of the form *Mary*. Hence such a sentence would be, strictly, meaningless, for it turns out to be impossible to say, in abstraction from context, exactly what it means. Therefore it cannot be one of those contextless invariants recognised by linguistic theory as the recurrently instantiated units on which the mechanism of discourse depends. A 'meaningless sentence' or, alternatively, an 'indefinitely meaningful sentence' are both, for these theoretical purposes, equally inadmissible. The theory is committed to affirming the principle of determinacy of sentence-meanings at all costs, because otherwise it becomes explanatorily void.

These are essentially the arguments with which generativists have justified refusing to accept *Yes* as a one-word English sentence, even though 'Yes' is probably the most frequently occurring one-word English utterance. Utterances like 'Yes', it is claimed, 'have an infinite number of possible interpretations and can hence not be described *as such* by a finite linguistic description'.[1]

There is a connexion here with the way in which conversational analysts and other speech act theorists tend to assume that utterances like 'How old are you?' and 'There is a bull in the field' are incomplete in the sense that those precise words do not and cannot fully represent the communicational intention of the speaker, inasmuch as the speaker's intention may have been to warn, to answer, to criticise, to execute a repair, or to perform any one of a number of illocutionary acts which are not explicitly signalled by the intrinsic verbal component of the utterance. Implicitly there is an assumption that some fuller formulation could capture that unstated intentionality, and this assumption occasionally comes to the surface; for example, in Austin's doctrine of explicit performatives, which treats 'I warn you that there is a bull in the field' as the fully-spelled-out version of the utterance 'There is a bull in the field' when issued as a warning. The same basic assumption underlies the transformationalist doctrine of declaratives which postulates an underlying performative verb of stating in the deep structure, which may subsequently be deleted by transformational processes.[2]

---

[1] P. M. Postal, 'Underlying and superficial linguistic structure', reprinted in *Language*, ed. R. C. Oldfield & J. C. Marshall, Harmondsworth, 1968, p. 196.
[2] J. R. Ross, 'On declarative sentences', *Readings in English Transformational Grammar*, ed. R. A. Jacobs & P. S. Rosenbaum, 1970, pp. 222–72.

Insofar as it is committed to assumptions about the radical incompleteness of all or most of what we say, discourse analysis of whatever theoretical hue is in the same leaky boat as the sentence-grammar on which it is tacitly based. Apparently, following the rules of discourse which govern our taking of utterances as warnings, complaints, apologies, etc., is rather like following those annoying directions which end up with '. . . and then you come to Jack's garage, and after that you can't miss it'. Jack's garage is the point beyond which the inquirer is deemed to be able to find the way for himself, and Jack's garage for speech act theorists always turns out to be the linguistic meaning of the words uttered. The linguistic meaning of 'How old are you?', or 'There is a bull in the field' is assumed to be determinate and available to all speakers of English. Discourse analysis simply deals with the directions for the journey between that fixed point and the position where the hearer of any particular utterance of the form in question happens to find himself. But just as directions which take Jack's garage as a point of reference are useless if it turns out that Jack's garage is not there, so procedures for getting from speech episodes to invariant sentences are useless if the invariant sentences turn out to be mere artifacts of linguistic analysis.

On closer inspection, the difficulty which the doctrine of 'incomplete sentences' is invoked to deal with is seen to be one manifestation of a much greater underlying problem. It makes little sense for the linguist to talk of the 'incomplete sentences' of a language unless it is in principle possible to identify which the 'complete' ones are. But if an incomplete sentence counts as incomplete because, in a variety of contexts, it may do duty for a range of more explicit and non-equivalent sentences, then it would seem that we cannot count as representing a complete sentence any expression which requires supplementation from the context to make its interpretation absolutely clear. But now consider in this light the implications of the following example. Jones asks 'Who does this coat belong to?', and Smith replies 'It's mine'. If the answer 'Mary' is legitimately regarded as short for 'Mary is the person to whom this coat belongs', then it is difficult to see why 'It's mine' is not to be regarded as short for, say, 'Smith is the person to whom this coat belongs'. We thus reach a position in which all deictic expressions may be treated as elliptical, as indeed a traditional term like 'pronoun' suggests. A 'pronoun' is so called because it was traditionally analysed in Western grammar as standing for a noun which has been left out. The first person pronoun 'I' stands indifferently for 'John Smith', 'Immanuel Kant', 'Margaret Thatcher' and indefinitely many other proper names. In this way the theory of incomplete sentences joins forces with the theory of deixis, and between them they present linguistic analysis with the problem of elliptical regress. For nowhere, it seems, except in the present particulars of current situations can we find an ultimate anchorage for the identification of what it is we are talking about. Everything we say requires the resolution of some potential deictic ambiguity, some potential uncertainty of reference. And it is relevant to remind ourselves at this point that Aristotelian logic and its modern descendants are essentially wedded to the view that such problems can and must be resolved. For otherwise it would be impossible to identify particular propositions, and without such identification the procedures of syllogistic reasoning collapse.

> 'All men are mortal,
> Socrates is a man,
> Therefore my father is mortal'

will not do as an Aristotelian syllogism because the deictic expression in the last line makes it impossible to identify the proposition in such a way as to guarantee that it follows from the first two. We should need some additional circumstantial evidence about whether or not the person reasoning thus was as a matter of fact the son of Socrates in order to judge whether his inference was valid.

The 'elliptical regress' was anticipated as a problem of descriptive linguistics by Wittgenstein. In the *Philosophical Investigations*,[1] we find some penetrating observations on the topic of 'exactness', in which the problem of saying exactly what one means is shown to be regressive, and in which, moreover, the problem is treated not simply as a problem for the descriptive analyst, but intrinsically as a participant's problem. Suppose, says Wittgenstein, I explain the name *Moses* in the following way: ' "I take 'Moses' to mean the man, if there was such a man, who led the Israelites out of Egypt, whatever he was called then and whatever he may or may not have done

---

[1] §§87–8.

besides."—But similar doubts to those about "Moses" are possible about the words of this explanation (what are you calling "Egypt", whom the "Israelites" etc.?) Nor would these questions come to an end even when we got down to words like "red", "dark", "sweet". —"But then how does an explanation help me to understand . . . ?" '

Those who have understood the importance of the point Wittgenstein is making here have mostly seen it as relating to matters of semantic description. But an exactly analogous problem arises with the elucidation of 'what was said' in the other direction, namely the identification of linguistic form.

When I say the word 'Moses', my vocalisation is, according to modern linguistic orthodoxy, a necessarily inexact way of representing something else. The something else belongs to the language, whereas the phenomena of phonation do not. They are only products of my attempt to signal just which phonemes, lexemes and syntagmata I really mean my hearer to attend to. Thus orthodox linguistics projects a picture of a speaker who is curiously impotent to say exactly what he wants to say in this other respect too. For although he has internalised in some way the phonological forms of the sentences of the language, he can never in practice produce exact vocalic tokens of those phonological forms. The work of rationality is thus required also to bridge the gap between vocalisations and phonological forms. The hearer is expected to infer from the phonetic evidence of what he hears that I meant to say 'Moses'.

To summarise, the enigma of rational speaker-hearers is that although they apparently require some fixed linguistic framework which would enable them to exercise their rationality, the moment we try seriously to identify and inspect that framework, it vanishes before our eyes. The semantic part of the framework vanishes because for any arbitrary utterance X, which utilises some abbreviatory or deictic device of language L, X may represent more than one sentence of language L. Utterances like 'Mary', or 'It's mine' may apparently represent, on different occasions, indefinitely many sentences of English. But then in order to determine which sentence of language L is actually represented by X in any given case, it becomes necessary for the rational speaker-hearer to have available some workable decision procedure for determining the relationship between X and the inventory of sentences of L. This amounts to saying that he already needs to know what the utterance means in order to find out which sentence it represents. But then finding out which sentence it represents is either impossible or superfluous, or both. It is impossible if there is an elliptical regress preventing the establishment of any inventory of non-elliptical sentences. It is superfluous if the whole point of identifying the sentence was to discover a meaning which was necessary to help interpret the utterance. For he no longer needs this if he has already managed to interpret the utterance. He would simply be running round a semantic circle. *Mutatis mutandis*, exactly the same applies to the formal part of the framework. Identification of phonological form is either impossible, or superfluous, or both.

'Give me but one firm spot on which to stand,' said Archimedes, 'and I will move the earth.' The search for some fixed point of linguistic reference outside that continuum of creative activity which itself is language encounters a typically Archimedean predicament. Such a search in the end is vain. The language-bound theorist, like the earth-bound Archimedes, has nowhere else to stand but where he does. He has ultimately no leverage to bring to bear on understanding language other than such leverage as can be exerted from the *terra firma* of his own linguistic experience. An analytic grasp of that experience is his essential task. And a first step towards securing that grasp is to recognise the language myth for what it is.

Bibliography

J. Ambrose-Grillet, *Glossary of Transformational Grammar*, Rowley, Mass., 1978.

Aristotle, *On Interpretation*, tr. H. P. Cook, London, 1938.

J. L. Austin, *How to Do Things with Words*, ed. J. O. Urmson, Oxford, 1962.

F. Bacon, *The Advancement of Learning*, ed. G. W. Kitchen, repr. London, 1973.
Novum Organum, tr. J. Devey (*The Physical and Metaphysical Works of Lord Bacon*), London, 1853.

G. Baker, 'Criteria: a new foundation for semantics', *Ratio*, vol. XVI, 1974.

M. Black, 'Some troubles with Whorfianism', *Language and Philosophy*, ed. S. Hook, New York, 1969.

L. Bloomfield, *Language*, London, 1935.

R. Boudon, *The Logic of Sociological Explanation*, tr. T. Burns, Harmondsworth, 1974.

Y. R. Chao, 'The non-uniqueness of phonemic solutions of phonetic systems', *Bulletin of the Institute of History and Philology, Academia Sinica*, 1934, vol. IV, part 4.

S. Chase, *The Tyranny of Words*, London, 1938.

N. Chomsky, *Syntactic Structures*, The Hague, 1957.
Aspects of the Theory of Syntax, Cambridge, Mass., 1965.
Language and Mind, New York, 1968.
Reflections on Language, New York, 1975.

L. J. Cohen, *The Diversity of Meaning*, 2nd ed., London, 1966.
'Do illocutionary forces exist?', *Symposium on J. L. Austin*, ed. K. T. Fann, London, 1969.

S. R. Curtiss, *Genie: a Linguistic Study of a Modern Day 'Wild Child'*, Los Angeles, 1976.

D. Davidson, 'Thought and talk', *Mind and Language*, ed. S. D. Guttenplan, Oxford, 1975.

G. Evans, 'Can there be vague objects?', *Analysis*, vol. 38, no. 4, 1978.
J. R. Firth, *The Tongues of Men*, London, 1937; repr. 1964.
A. G. N. Flew (ed.), *Essays on Logic and Language*, Oxford, 1951.
K. Freeman, *The Pre-Socratic Philosophers*, 2nd ed., Oxford, 1949.
G. Frege, 'Über Sinn und Bedeutung', *Zeitschrift für Philosophie und philosophische Kritik*, vol. 100, 1892.
Die Grundlagen der Arithmetik, ed. and tr. J. L. Austin, Oxford, 2nd ed., 1953.
Logical Investigations, ed. P. T. Geach, Oxford, 1977.
C. C. Fries, *The Structure of English*, New York, 1952.
V. Fromkin, S. Krashen, S. Curtiss, D. Rigler, and M. Rigler, 'The development of language in Genie: a case of language acquisition beyond the "critical period" ', *Brain and Language*, vol. 1, 1974.
D. B. Fry, 'Speech reception and perception', *New Horizons in Linguistics*, ed. J. Lyons, Harmondsworth, 1970.
H. Garfinkel & H. Sacks, 'On formal structures of practical actions'. In *Theoretical Sociology*, ed. J. C. McKinney & E. A. Tiryakian, New York, 1970.
H. A. Gleason, *An Introduction to Descriptive Linguistics*, rev. ed., New York, 1961.
Grammaire générale et raisonnée, Paris, 1660.
J. Greene, 'Psycholinguistics: competence and performance', *Communication and Understanding*, ed. G. Vesey, Hassocks, 1977.
R. Harris, *The Language-Makers*, London, 1980.
Z. S. Harris, *Methods in Structural Linguistics*, Chicago, 1951.
B. Harrison, *Meaning and Structure*, New York, 1972.
C. G. Hempel, *Fundamentals of Concept Formation in Empirical Science*, Chicago, 1952.
R. Henson, 'What we say', *American Philosophical Quarterly*, vol. 2, 1965. Reprinted in C. Lyas (ed.), *Linguistics and Philosophy*, London, 1971.
C. F. Hockett, 'Two models of grammatical description', *Word*, vol. 10, 1954.
A Course in Modern Linguistics, New York, 1958.
H. Hoijer (ed.), *Language in Culture*, Chicago, 1954.
O. Jespersen, *Language, its Nature, Development and Origin*, London, 1922.
Efficiency in Linguistic Change, Copenhagen, 1941.
M. Joos, 'Description of language design', *Journal of the Acoustical Society of America*, vol. 22, 1950.
J. J. Katz, *The Philosophy of Language*, New York, 1966.
Linguistic Philosophy, London, 1972.

A. Korzybski, *Science and Sanity: an Introduction to Non-Aristotelian Systems and General Semantics*, 3rd ed., Lakeville, Conn., 1948.

G. Lakoff, 'Fuzzy grammar and the performance/competence terminology game', *Papers from the Ninth Regional Meeting, Chicago Linguistic Society*, Chicago, 1973.

H. Lane, *The Wild Boy of Aveyron*, London, 1977.

D. T. Langendoen, *The Study of Syntax*, New York, 1969.

G. W. Leibniz, *Die philosophischen Schriften von Gottfried Wilhelm Leibniz*, ed. C. J. Gerhardt, Berlin, 1875–90.

J. Locke, *An Essay Concerning Human Understanding*, London, 1690.

F. G. Lounsbury, 'Language and culture', *Language and Philosophy*, ed. S. Hook, New York, 1969.

J. Lyons, *Introduction to Theoretical Linguistics*, Cambridge, 1968.

P. F. MacNeilage, 'Speech production', *Proceedings of the Ninth International Congress of Phonetic Sciences*, Copenhagen, 1979.

B. Magee (ed.), *Men of Ideas*, London, 1978.

D. G. Mandelbaum (ed.), *Selected Writings of Edward Sapir*, Berkeley, 1949.

J. S. Mill, *A System of Logic*, London, 1843.

F. M. Müller, *Lectures on the Science of Language*, London, 1861–4.

E. A. Nida, *Morphology*, 2nd ed., Ann Arbor, 1949.

C. K. Ogden & I. A. Richards, *The Meaning of Meaning*, London, 1923.

F. R. Palmer, *Grammar*, London, 1971.

G. H. R. Parkinson, 'The translation theory of understanding', *Communication and Understanding*, ed. G. Vesey, Hassocks, 1977.

T. Pateman, *Language, Truth and Politics*, Sidmouth, 1975.

K. L. Pike, *Language in Relation to a Unified Theory of the Structure of Human Behavior*, Glendale, 1954–60; 2nd rev. ed., The Hague, 1967.

P. M. Postal, 'Underlying and superficial linguistic structure', *Language*, ed. R. C. Oldfield & J. C. Marshall, Harmondsworth, 1968.

W. V. O. Quine, *Word and Object*, Cambridge, Mass., 1960.

A. Radford, 'On the nondiscrete nature of the verb-auxiliary distinction in English', *Nottingham Linguistic Circular*, 5, 1976.

M. J. Reddy, 'The conduit metaphor — a case of frame conflict in our language about language'. In A. Ortony (ed.), *Metaphor and Thought*, Cambridge, 1979.

N. Rees, *Graffiti Lives, O.K.*, London, 1979.

R. H. Robins, *General Linguistics: an Introductory Survey*, London, 1964.

J. R. Ross, 'On declarative sentences', *Readings in English Transformational Grammar*, ed. R. A. Jacobs & P. S. Rosenbaum, Waltham, Mass., 1970.

'The category squish: Endstation Hauptwort', *Papers from the Eighth Regional Meeting, Chicago Linguistic Society*, Chicago, 1972.

'Nouniness', *Three Dimensions of Linguistic Theory*, ed. O. Fujimura, Tokyo, 1973.

B. B. Rundle, *Grammar in Philosophy*, Oxford, 1979.

B. Russell, *The Analysis of Mind*, New York, 1921.

G. Ryle, *The Concept of Mind*, London, 1949.

'Systematically misleading expressions', *Essays on Logic and Language*, ed. A. G. N. Flew, Oxford, 1951.

F. de Saussure, *Cours de linguistique générale*, 2nd ed., Paris, 1922.

H. Sweet, *A New English Grammar*, Oxford, 1892-8.

T. J. Taylor, *Linguistic Theory and Structural Stylistics*, Oxford, 1980.

J. P. Vinay and J. Darbelnet, *Stylistique comparée du français et de l'anglais* Paris, 1969.

F. Waismann, 'Verifiability', *Essays on Logic and Language*, ed. A. G. N. Flew, Oxford, 1951.

J. B. Watson, *Behaviorism*, 2nd ed., London, 1931.

J. R. Watson (ed.), *Browning: 'Men and Women' and other Poems: a Case Book*, London, 1974.

B. L. Whorf, *Language, Thought and Reality*, ed. J. B. Carorll, Cambridge, Mass., 1956.

J. Wilkins, *Essay towards a Real Character and a Philosophical Language*, London, 1668.

N. L. Wilson, *The Concept of Language*, Toronto, 1959.

L. Wittgenstein, *Philosophische Untersuchungen*, tr. G. E. M. Anscombe, 2nd ed., Oxford, 1958.

Tractatus Logico-Philosophicus, tr. D. F. Pears & B. F. McGuinness, 2nd ed., London, 1971.

A. Wootton, *Dilemmas of Discourse*, London, 1975.

Index